Dear Reader:

The book you are about to read is the latest bestseller from the St. Martin's True Crime Library, the imprint the *New York Times* calls "the leader in true crime!" Each month, we offer you a fascinating account of the latest, most sensational crime that has captured the national attention. St. Martin's is the publisher of perennial bestselling true crime author Jack Olsen, whose SALT OF THE EARTH is the true story of one woman's triumph over life-shattering violence; Joseph Wambaugh called it "powerful and absorbing." Fannie Weinstein and Melinda Wilson tell the story of a beautiful honors student who was lured into the dark world of sex for hire in THE COED CALL GIRL MURDER. St. Martin's is also proud to publish two-time Edgar Award-winning author Carlton Stowers, whose TO THE LAST BREATH recounts a two-year-old girl's mysterious death, and the dogged investigation that led loved ones to the most unlikely murderer: her own father. In the book you now hold, BREAKING POINT, *New York Times* bestselling author Suzy Spencer details the astonishing and tragic case of Andrea Yates, and the sad fate of her five children.

St. Martin's True Crime Library gives you the stories *behind* the headlines. Our authors take you right to the scene of the crime and into the minds of the most notorious murderers to show you what really makes them tick. St. Martin's True Crime Library paperbacks are better than the most terrifying thriller, because it's all true! The next time you want a crackling good read, make sure it's got the St. Martin's True Crime Library logo on the spine—you'll be up all night!

Charles E. Spicer, Jr.
Executive Editor, St. Martin's True Crime Library

"a tough thing"

John Cannon, the police spokesperson, stood before a multitude of cameras, his suit stifling in the heat, his thinning hair exposed to the sun. "Shortly before ten o'clock this morning we were called out to this residence from the woman of the home, who said that she needed a police unit to come by her house to check on the children that she was caring for."

Reporters jammed their tape recorders toward Cannon's mouth. He didn't flinch.

"And when the officer found that there were four children at that time on the bed, dead at the scene, a second officer then came by the residence and he did a search of the house, and found a fifth child who was in the bathtub of the residence. The woman at that time was placed and detained and put into custody. She has since been taken away in a patrol vehicle where we will take a formal statement from her. So we have not taken a formal statement as to the why of this. And it's just rather unimaginable."

A reporter asked about the officers' well-being.

"The officers are pretty distraught. The responding officer's got a couple children of his own. These homicide investigators who were here at the house have children of their own. It's rather a disheartening thing to see, and it will be for some time. I mean, it's a tough thing."

BREAKING POINT

SUZY SPENCER

St. Martin's

ACKNOWLEDGMENTS

St. Martin's' big wheel Charlie Spicer and my agent Jane Dystel got together and asked me if I wanted to write this book. I said yes, simply because it would allow me to write about depression and the state of mental health care in the U.S., topics we need to take seriously, but prefer to dismiss. Both cause unnecessary deaths. Both cost our nation in heartache and dollars. Andrea Yates' trial could cost Houston taxpayers $1,500,000, not including prison and medical costs. How much cheaper it would have been—in heartache and dollars—if she'd gotten the mental health care she needed.

I didn't realize, though, that the research for this book would teach me about Texas justice and the Houston version of freedom of the press. While I was writing the book, my friend and fellow true crime writer Vanessa Leggett was jailed for refusing to turn over her research notes on another murder case, which had already been tried and lost by the Harris County District Attorney's Office. As I write my thank yous, one of which is owed to Vanessa, she's still incarcerated. She is the only person serving time for this crime. And she did nothing but try to report it.

Not only is Vanessa paying the price, but so are American taxpayers. Vanessa has sat in federal prison since July 20—a rather expensive "hotel" stay, at taxpayer expense, for a law-abiding teacher and writer for the FBI.

Rusty Yates, who graciously spent hours upon hours with me, will have much more to say about Texas justice and freedom of the press after his wife's trial. My prayers are with him, Andrea, and the Kennedy family.

I also thank my dream editor Anderson Bailey. He is kind and encouraging. And I'm crazy about him.

I have never had so much support from so many people in writing a book. Thanks to Susie Kelly Flatau, who hooked me up with folks in the Clear Lake area and helped me edit the first draft. Additional editorial thanks goes to Diane Fanning and Louise Redd. All three, along with Kathleen K. Greenwood and Kathe Williams, gave me emotional support that was greatly needed.

Don Boyer, Bonnie Cerace, Bill King, and Taffy McDill, all Clear Creek High grads, gave me time and information. Robert and Mary Whitten hooked me up with a source and gave me laughs. Thanks to Phil Patek and the staff at the Microtel in Nassau Bay. They too hooked me up with sources, like Dawn Helman. Thanks to Byron Fike and Becky Morris of Clear Lake Church of Christ. I definitely needed Byron's prayers.

I thank Reilly Capps, Jeremy Tate, Nicholas Zeckets, and Captain Dale Burke for helping me research the Woroniecki family. Thanks to Tracy Alverides and Lou Alverides for talking to me about Rusty Yates as a teen, Lana Dunlap and Judy Bradley for telling me about Andrea's teen years, and Cynthia Clawson and Joyce Matzke for connecting me to folks at Milby High.

Belinda Green helped me with insight into life at the Lazy Days RV park. Terry Arnold was generous with her knowledge of Andrea and the kids.

Thanks to attorneys James R. Clark, James A. Drexler, Kathleen D. Morrison, John Pizzitola, and Kent A. Schaffer. Heartfelt gratitude to Steve Orr and Bonnie Orr. Y'all are great! Thanks to physicians Dr. Karen Bradshaw, Dr. Diana Dell, and Dr. Robert Bayardo and psychologists Dr. Gregory Riede and Dr. Vincent Ruscelli.

Special thanks to Genevieve Hearon and Claire Anderson of Capacity for Justice. And thanks to Vyki Robbins and Mary McIntosh at the Texas Department of Health, Mike

Burns, Jim Coley, Karen de Olivares, Russ Hall, Rita Mills, Mark Stivers, and Curtis Traylor.

Rita Mills hooked me up with Fred King, whose help was immeasurable. And Mr. King hooked me up with Jack Thompson and Janet Warner, who graciously got me a seat in the competency hearing. I owe y'all, big time.

I also thank the *Houston Chronicle*'s Ruth Rendon and Carol Christian. I especially thank Cynthia Hunt of KTRK for providing me time, photos, and laughter. You're a star. I'm indebted, very much, to John Treadgold and Nancy Shafran of KPRC (and who is another Fred King contact).

Thanks to Stephanie Durham for encouragement and Sara Laas for carrying on when I abandoned one project for another. And definitely I must thank my family—Juanita, Siba, Jeane, Townie, and Kathy—for letting me disappear for months on end while I researched and wrote.

But we're back to Charlie and Jane. This book wouldn't exist without y'all. Thank you.

BREAKING POINT

PROLOGUE

The Houston, Texas, police officer eased his turquoise blue squad car up to the middle-class, Spanish-style house at the corner of Beachcomber and Sea Lark. It was June 20, 2001, a hot, sticky morning in the Clear Lake area of Houston, a city that had been built around NASA and the Johnson Space Center, then rudely annexed into the growing metropolis of big oil and big skyscrapers.

The officer climbed out of his vehicle, walked up the concrete driveway, crossed the sidewalk that edged the front flowerbed, then rotated a lever, flipped it, and opened the wrought-iron front gate.

He walked down the sidewalk that traveled about half the length of the house, and rang the bell to a white wooden door. The top half of the door was fitted with nine small windowpanes, but he couldn't see past the white mini-blinds that covered their interior.

A tall, thin woman with long, dark, wet hair and broad shoulders opened the door. The officer walked in, immediately passing a closet on the left that was so full of jumbled craft supplies that the door barely closed. On the right was a small, gated-off living room, packed with four tiny school desks, a nearly wall-sized, dry eraser board, and heaps of home school supplies. Adjoining the converted living room was a dining room used as an office with more desks and a large computer.

The officer moved on, following the woman down a short

entry hallway. In the den, there was a blue sofa jammed against a long wall. To the left of the sofa was a window that looked out onto the driveway. To the right, shoved up next to the sofa, were a TV, video equipment, and stereo equipment.

Just beyond that was a long dining table covered with clutter. A hand-drawn cross was tacked on a wall to the table's left. In the kitchen, the counters were hidden under dirty dishes.

Circling his gaze back into the den, the officer saw a white, brick fireplace with candles on the mantel. To the right of the fireplace was a small, white bookcase and to the left was a long hallway.

A china cabinet and a worn blue love seat that matched the couch were positioned against the wall opposite the sofa. A small chair or two were scattered around the room. The floor was brown tile. Everything seemed dirty.

The policeman turned down the dark hallway, noting that its beige carpet was severely stained. He passed a bathroom on the right and walked into the master bedroom. Partially covering the room's lone window was a sheer window sham decorated with pink flowers. Pink was the woman's favorite color. She'd made the window treatment herself.

He looked down at a mattress on the floor and pulled back a sheet. Beneath it were four dead babies, their clothes wet, their bodies warm, their eyes wide open.

He didn't notice how the home's walls were either off-white or pale blue. Nor did he notice the dead child in the bathtub, in the bathroom he'd passed as he walked into the master bedroom.

It would take a second officer to walk into the old, tile bathroom, with hints of aqua, and see a seven-year-old boy submerged in the tub, his legs spindly like a newborn colt, his skin wrinkling from the water's cold.

CHAPTER 1

"Guarded. People in the Bay Area are guarded," one former resident explained. "That's why nobody talks openly about anyone else's business. They keep their stuff to themselves." She was a woman who grew up in League City, one of the many towns adjoining Clear Lake and comprising what was called the Bay Area—Friendswood, Kemah, Webster, Seabrook, Nassau Bay, even Dickinson.

They were once poor, tiny communities made up of uneducated but smart rice farmers and shrimpers who worked the salt waters of Galveston Bay. The former resident called them "river rats," hardworking men and women with a penchant for alcohol and gambling. They weren't the types who appreciated outsiders.

But in the 1960s, about the time Andrea and Rusty Yates were born, and when Lyndon Baines Johnson was President, outsiders flooded the Bay Area—MIT-educated engineers from Washington, D.C., and Virginia. They were the men of NASA.

Oil and gas land once owned by Humble Oil, which became Exxon, was quickly turned into a space center. Houses sprouted up where oil rigs should have stood—3,000 homes in Clear Lake alone.

Sons and daughters of shrimpers and farmers were going to school with the sons and daughters of rocket scientists and astronauts. On the surface, everyone got along. Beneath the surface, folks were "guarded."

Despite the fact that the frugal engineers were always looking for a bargain, million-dollar homes went up near former gambling restaurants. A Shell Oil access road became busy El Dorado Boulevard. And suddenly, there were 18,000 homes in Clear Lake, not just 3,000.

The Bay Area became a bastion of engineers with flat-tops, slide rules, and pocket protectors. Over the decades, they metamorphosed into family-oriented Republicans who proudly referred to themselves as "geeks." Suddenly, status became important. Women stayed home and cared for the children, while their husbands worked 100-hour weeks at NASA.

They were not the kinds of citizens who brought crime to an area. With the exception of "the killing fields" in League City, there was a murder perhaps every ten years. Bay Area residents were "good, moral people" in a community that thought nothing about giving when there was a flood, a tornado, or a hurricane, said another long-time citizen. They especially came together, she said, when there were children in need.

But she, too, admitted to a guardedness about the community. Again, the finger was pointed at NASA. NASA, by its very nature, by its very work, required and demanded secrecy.

Plus, she said, NASA engineers got so preoccupied with their jobs that they didn't think about anything else. The woman knew; she taught the children of NASA.

John Treadgold steered his dented, white Ford Explorer around downtown Houston. To any speeding motorist, he looked like a typical commuter. But on closer look, something was different about Treadgold's Explorer. The back seat was stashed with equipment. The front passenger seat was loaded with ten radios propped up on a makeshift cabinet so that their dials faced Treadgold's easy reach. Noise ratcheted from their speakers.

Just a week earlier, those speakers had been screaming as the city drowned in twenty-eight inches of floodwaters from Tropical Storm Allison. Treadgold was a KPRC-TV roaming cameraman who had worked fourteen-hour days covering the killer storm, listening to the police, sheriff, and fire reports on his ten radios, rushing to the scene for film footage.

The area John Treadgold currently circled had been transformed from streets into deadly, raging rivers. He, and all the other media workers in the area, desperately yearned for a quiet news week. The day was steaming with heat, humidity, and radio noise that could almost lull an exhausted man to rest.

"Send a supervisor over for these pediatric DOAs."

John Treadgold's body snapped. He shot for the dial and spun up the radio's volume. *Are my ears playing tricks on me?* He hadn't heard any calls about DOAs. But there was a follow-up report tweetering on a back channel, meaning an ambulance driver had called to say he was in service or had "something" important.

Treadgold heard the unit's number, which told him the unit was on the east side of Houston. He phoned his station, the local NBC affiliate, and asked the assignment desk editor to look up the call on the computer. The time was approximately 10 A.M. on Wednesday, June 20, 2001.

"It's a respiratory problem, unconscious," the editor reported. "But later on they put on a note that says 'possible children.' " She gave Treadgold the intersection that marked the call's location.

Treadgold thought about where he was: downtown Houston. He thought about where that intersection was: Clear Lake, twenty to thirty minutes away on the outer edges of Houston, not far from where there had been more major flooding and loss of homes during Tropical Storm Allison. "Well, it's a weird call," he replied. "They said DOA."

His editor called the fire station. "Do you have a DOA?"

"We've looked at our computer, and there's no DOA listed."

"Well, they may have meant *GOA*," Treadgold said, as

he still listened carefully to the ten radios, hoping for an explanation of *gone on arrival*—no one had waited for the ambulance to arrive. "Well, there's nothing else going on. I'm going to go ahead and go down there and see what's happening."

He drove to Clear Lake, arrived at the intersection that had been earmarked by the station's computer check, and saw nothing. He studied the neighborhood—a quiet, comfortable, middle-class community with mostly well-maintained yards. Men jogged down the sidewalks. Neighbors washed flood mud from their driveways.

He reached for the radio, ready to report that there was no story, when he edged around a corner and spotted cop cars and ambulances. He cruised closer and saw a police officer, two paramedics, and a tall, thin man with closely cropped dark hair, wearing a long-sleeved white shirt. John Treadgold knew from the looks on their faces that Wednesday, June 20, 2001, wasn't going to be a slow news day after all.

He drove past the house, around the block, and returned. Two police supervisors and one paramedic supervisor stood outside the house. Treadgold parked his vehicle and got out. Immediately, a police sergeant walked over to him.

"We're not going to make any statements," the sergeant said. "The medical examiner's been called. Homicide's been called. They'll talk to you."

"I heard the call was about children." Treadgold looked into the sergeant's face. It quivered.

"I'll tell you that it's children and there's a multiple amount. And we'd appreciate it if you don't come in the yard." He added that any further information would have to be provided by a Houston Police Department media or homicide spokesperson.

John Treadgold called KPRC. "It's ninety-nine percent confirmed that there's at least two children dead here. There's nobody else here," he continued, and began to set up his camera equipment across the street from the house. As he did, a man and a woman approached him.

"What's the deal?" they asked.

He replied that he wasn't sure.

"That man in the white shirt, his name is Rusty Yates," the woman said. "He just came home from work and went running over to the house."

Treadgold aimed his camera at the house and Yates, still standing outside, his forehead pressed against the brick wall as a gray-haired woman gently rubbed his back.

"Do you know this family?" he asked.

"Yeah, he brought all of his kids over last week for my boy's birthday."

At least one of those kids is not alive anymore, Treadgold thought. "What about his wife?"

Yates tried to peer through a window as a police officer stood blocking the front door.

"She didn't come. She hardly ever comes out. He brings the kids out."

The cameraman nodded as he wondered why Rusty Yates was standing outside. "But does she live there?"

"Oh, yes. She lives there. You see her in the yard, but she hardly ever leaves the yard."

"What's her name?"

The neighbor didn't know.

Teams of homicide investigators drove up and got out of their vehicles.

I don't remember the last time I saw three teams of homicide officers come to a story, Treadgold thought.

"What are all these detectives?"

"I believe somebody is dead in the house," Treadgold answered.

"Oh," replied the neighbor. "I hope it's not one of the kids."

Inside the house, the woman with the long, dark, wet hair sat on her love seat, her hands calmly folded over her lap.

HPD Officer Frank Stumpo looked at her. She looked at him, then looked away.

Rusty Yates moved to the back door. "How could you do this?" he screamed. "I don't understand." He dropped to his knees and peered through a small opening between the window coverings.

The woman sat silently in the love seat. Briefly, she made eye contact with Yates.

"How could you do this?" he yelled. "I don't understand." He yelled it over and over again.

Officer Stumpo closed the window covering tight. "Do you realize what you have done?" he asked the woman.

"Yes, I do," she answered.

Treadgold motioned to a big, blue bus parked behind a wooden fence in the Yates' back yard. "What's the deal with that bus over there?"

"They plan to use that for an RV. The neighbor on the other side is kinda upset about that bus because, you know, Rusty had to extend his driveway for it and now that bus is parked there."

A police officer peered over the fence.

Treadgold swung his camera to focus on the officer.

The cop wiggled the gate. The gate opened, and the officer walked out, followed by the woman with long, dark, stringy hair, and a second officer. The woman wore eyeglasses, gold loop earrings, and handcuffs.

Treadgold zoomed in on her. To him, she looked peaceful as she followed the first officer to the car.

The neighbor lady not-so-calmly ran over to Treadgold. "That's the wife," she said. "Where are they taking her?"

"Well, it looks like she's being hauled in for questioning—" Treadgold moved his camera's focus to a flat bundle of clothing one of the officers carried—"at the very least, since she's got handcuffs on."

"You don't think she did it, do you?"

He thought about the way the police had walked out with

her, neither one touching her, neither one gripping her arms like they usually did with murderers. "Are you sure that's the wife?"

"Oh, yeah."

"Well, she doesn't look like she's crying or anything."

The officer opened the car door for her, and, unsmiling, the woman gazed over the heads of the gathering crowd, then looked down at the police car.

Treadgold checked his watch. He'd been there at least an hour, and not a single other TV film crew had arrived on the scene. *What is the deal?* He phoned the KPRC newsroom. "This is pretty weird. They've just arrested the wife."

The newsroom replied that they'd called the police and hadn't gotten any answers, but a news truck was on its way to do a live broadcast at noon.

Not much later, the station called him. "Have you heard any more?"

All he could update them on was that the officer had placed the flat bundle of clothing into a paper bag. Treadgold asked the station whether they knew the wife was involved.

They didn't, but they said an HPD spokesperson was on his way and would talk to Treadgold. The station was sending a helicopter to do a breaking news insert.

"Well, you know, the other stations can track our helicopter. And right now we're the only ones here."

The NBC affiliate decided not to turn on the chopper's camera until it was directly over the murder scene.

At 11:30 A.M., Wednesday, June 20, 2001, KPRC's live news truck had arrived, and the station broadcast an update stating there was breaking news in the Clear Lake area. Children had been found dead in their home, and details would come at noon.

Fifteen minutes before KPRC's noontime broadcast, John Cannon, a police spokesman, came out of the Spanish-style house and stood before John Treadgold's camera. "When

our responding officer arrived, he was met at the door by
the woman who then was breathing heavily. You could tell
she was disturbed. And at that time, she said to the officer,
'I killed my children.' And the officer said, 'Where are
they?' And she led the officer to the bedroom where there
were four bodies and . . . there was one body in the bathtub."

The officer then went outside and called in the crime,
grief-stricken himself. "And that's the end of everything we
can say right now," Cannon finished.

Treadgold had heard Cannon say that the mother had
drowned the children.

"I just can't believe this," said the neighbor lady, who
eavesdropped. "All those kids were over here. I've even got
videotape of them all jumping around."

Treadgold looked at her. At five minutes to noon, he
phoned the station. "Look, this is really big. There's five
children dead. The police came in and found them all dead
in the bed. The mother's been arrested."

"We're sending everybody we've got down there," his
news producer said.

Rusty Yates was asked into his own house, where the cops
questioned him about his children's clothing. He was inside
for only ten minutes, then he was instructed to go back out.

"News 2 Houston's Phil Archer is the *only* reporter live on
the scene," Treadgold heard as the studio's broadcast filtered
through his earpiece and he focused his camera on reporter
Phil Archer.

"Police were called to this house around ten o'clock this
morning. It was a routine call—a welfare check. What they
found here was anything but routine—five children *dead*
inside. The oldest one just seven years old."

As the tape of Cannon's statement aired over Treadgold's
earpiece, the reality of the crime hit him. He watched his
video of the mother being led out in handcuffs. A quiet,
pleasant neighborhood on a peaceful, summer day—the last

thing he had expected to hear was that a mother had drowned her five children, especially that mother.

He'd seen too many murderers in his twenty-five years as a police beat reporter. The killers' faces were always contorted with anger or laughter. Always, there was extreme emotion. At most, the dispassionate woman John Treadgold had watched looked like an accessory to murder, not a murderer.

"She is on her way now to a homicide division where [police] want to talk to her to take a statement about this," said Archer. The husband, he added, "is inside the house talking to police or, at least, they are trying to talk to him. They are saying he was initially too distraught to be able to sit down and talk to them coherently." The children, he added in closing, were six months to seven years, four boys and one girl.

Patricia Salas, the neighbor, went inside her house and got the videotape of her son's birthday party. Three little boys— now dead—happily swung at and missed a piñata. The news crew copied the tape for future newscasts, as helicopters from the competing stations swarmed in the sky.

Not far away, the police sergeant whose face had quivered with shock as he gave the initial statement stood by. The first responding officer, he said, had immediately checked the children for breathing, then called the paramedics to confirm the DOAs. That officer, said the sergeant, was so shaken up that he was being pulled from the scene and going for counseling.

Treadgold didn't want to think about it anymore. The day had been surreal. He had kids of his own. Kids were muscular and slippery when wet. He just couldn't see how that skinny woman could have grabbed hold of a slippery child and held him under bathtub water long enough to die. He had to block it out of his mind.

"This is such a big homicide case," said the sergeant, "we really cannot make any other comments."

CHAPTER 2

While the first officer on the scene was headed for a meeting with Dr. Gregory Riede, Director of Psychological Services for HPD, Rusty Yates stood outside his home with his mother, as well as a psychologist and a security officer, both of whom were from NASA, Yates' employer.

The grinding roar of hovering helicopters filled the air.

John Cannon, the police spokesperson, stood before a multitude of cameras, his suit stifling in the heat, his thinning hair exposed to the sun. "Shortly before ten o'clock this morning we were called out to this residence from the woman of the home, who said that she needed a police unit to come by her house to check on the children that she was caring for."

Reporters jammed their tape recorders toward Cannon's mouth. He didn't flinch.

"And when the officer found that there were four children at that time on the bed, dead at the scene, a second officer then came by the residence and he did a search of the house, and found a fifth child who was in the bathtub of the residence. The woman at that time was placed and detained and put into custody. She has since been taken away in a patrol vehicle where we will take a formal statement from her. So we have not taken a formal statement as to the why of this. And it's just rather unimaginable."

A reporter asked about the officers' well-being.

"The officers are pretty distraught. The responding officer's got a couple children of his own. These homicide investigators who were here at the house have children of their own. It's rather a disheartening thing to see, and it will be for some time. I mean, it's a tough thing."

Inside, the phone rang and a female voice screamed over the answering machine, "Andrea! Call me! Call me! It can't be you!"

Andrea Yates, though, was in the squad car speeding toward downtown Houston and HPD headquarters, Officer Stumpo at the wheel. His radio blasted the word "bitch" as a radio talk show already discussed Stumpo's passenger.

"Let's just shoot her!" the host railed.

Stumpo glanced in his rear-view mirror and watched his passenger. She stared out the window, her lips trembling. "You're a celebrity," he said.

On Beachcomber, neighbors gathered on the neat sidewalks, their hands grasping at their mouths, shock stopping their lives.

A few blocks down the street, Byron Fike, the pastor of Clear Lake Church of Christ, tried to go on about his workday, despite the fact that yellow police tape could be glimpsed from his church corner. The Yates house was only a two-minute stroll from Fike's office door, down the peaceful sidewalk lined with quiet houses, on the very path he'd designated as his "prayer walk," a walk that gave him time to silently contemplate his ministry and God's will.

During those many prayer walks, he'd never taken special notice of the house with a couple of basketball goals in the driveway and an old, blue bus parked in the back yard. He'd certainly never noticed a mother with long, dark hair and five children, nor realized how the family living in that Spanish-style house with the well-maintained yard would impact his ministry, himself, and his church.

After all, no one at Clear Lake Church of Christ knew

the family with the five dead children. Little did Fike know that the house was pulling his parishioners to its corner.

At 1 P.M., HPD investigators switched on an audiotape recorder, looked into Andrea Yates' spaced-out eyes, and asked, "Who killed your children?"

"I killed my children."

By audiotaping their suspect, rather than videotaping her, jurors would never see Andrea Yates' true affect on the day of the crime.

"Why did you kill your children?"

"Because I'm a bad mother."

Without bothering to ask her why she thought she was a bad mother, the detectives immediately switched to the details of how she had allegedly killed her children.

While his wife was being audiotaped, Rusty Yates stood outside his home, worrying that his eldest son still soaked in the bathtub. He stared at the Medical Examiner's van, which, he'd observed, had taken three hours in arriving.

Six homicide detectives searched inside the home. They flipped on his computer. But it required a password to access.

It remained on with its login prompt onscreen when Rusty Yates was allowed into his home, five hours after he'd arrived at the house. He glared at the lighted computer screen.

By then, rain had started to fall, and the media had gathered inside the garage of Patricia Salas' house, their eyes and cameras focused on the Yates home. Salas had already stood before their cameras explaining why Rusty Yates' wife had not attended the birthday party.

"We asked him how come she didn't come," Salas said into the cameras. "He said she stayed home because she was going through a depression from having babies. That's what he said."

Rusty Yates, by then, was being questioned and audiotaped himself by the police. He told the cops about his wife's medical history, that she'd recently been taken off her antipsychotic medication, that two days earlier, on June 18, he'd taken her to her psychiatrist and he'd told the psychiatrist, "I'm concerned."

Andrea Yates remained at HPD headquarters for about an hour, then she was transferred to the Mykawa Street substation. Cameras surrounded the patrol car in which she'd arrived. Andrea Yates didn't squirm to avoid the camera lens. She simply stared straight ahead.

Newsrooms across the nation and the world broadcast the name of Andrea Pia Yates. She was the wife of Russell E. Yates, a 36-year-old, $80,000 a year NASA engineer who worked at the Johnson Space Center in the super-shuttle program, they reported. She was the 36-year-old mother of five, they said, who suffered postpartum depression and had been on medication for the past two years, since the birth of her youngest boy.

Hairdresser Dawn Helman stared at the TV. She knew Andrea Yates. Yates had been in the salon where Helman worked, just a few blocks and over the railroad tracks from Yates' home. Helman thought back. It'd been a year or a year and a half, but Yates had definitely come into the salon once or twice, with her sons, and gotten her hair cut. Andrea Yates, Helman thought, seemed depressed at the time.

The day had been very busy at HEP Bookstore on Fuqua Road in Houston. Co-owner Terry Arnold hadn't had even had a chance to hear the news. So after she got home that evening, she flipped on the TV and saw the story of the Clear Lake woman who claimed, "I killed my kids."

Arnold immediately switched on her computer and clicked on the online version of the *Houston Chronicle*. She stared at the photo of the stringbean woman with broad shoulders who'd been handcuffed and arrested for the crime. She didn't recognize her.

Then she read the names of the woman's alleged victims. Noah, age seven; John, age five; Paul, age three; Luke, age two; and a daughter, Mary, age six months. *Oh, no.* Her heart sank. She knew the kids. They'd been in her store. She'd held them in her arms and hugged them over and over again. *This has got to be a mistake.* She cried.

"It's just difficult to deal with when you are talking about five little kids who were killed, probably systematically," HPD spokesman John Cannon said into the reporters' cameras and microphones. "You can rest assured it will be carried as a capital case."

Andrea Yates had not even appeared before a judge.

But the media had already checked with Child Protective Services and learned that Yates had been hospitalized for an attempted suicide by overdose, almost two years to the day prior to her children's deaths.

"There was no concern here that the children were in any danger, or that the mother was threatening to them," CPS's Judy Hay told KPRC-TV. "For us to be able to investigate, there has to be some allegation that a child is at risk of being abused or neglected, or that a child already has been. That's not what we saw here."

Terry Arnold reached for the phone to call a friend.

"No, it's not a mistake," she was told. "Those are the right names."

Arnold tossed and turned all night long.

She'd met Rusty Yates before she'd met Andrea and the children. Arnold and her business partner, Joanne Juren, had opened their bookstore in February of 2001.

One day late in March, clean-cut Rusty Yates pulled his blue Suburban up to the store's door, climbed out of his vehicle, stepped up to the sidewalk, and opened the plate-glass door to HEP.

Terry Arnold watched. Not often did a man enter her shop's doors.

"My wife told me about this place," he said. He asked Arnold what kind of store it was—a regular bookstore or a home school bookstore?

She explained that they were a home school bookstore, and toured him around, showing him the different curriculums. There were workbooks and textbooks, toys for teaching, T-shirts for encouragement for both the student and teacher. And most of all, there was a calmness in the store that perfectly matched Arnold's quiet, patient demeanor.

"It's nice. I like it," he said. He wondered if Arnold and Juren were home school parents.

Yes, they were, she told him.

"We have a lot of children. Is there a place where they can play?"

She walked him to the back of the store where there were tiny chairs, a table to match, and a play area. Soon, she learned there were five Yates children. To Arnold, a family of five was no big deal. She had five children of her own; she knew five kids to be an average- to small-sized family by home school standards. What *was* unusual was a father checking out the store before the wife and kids walked in.

"I like it," he said. "I'll tell my wife about it."

Before the clock ticked midnight on June 20, 2001, Andrea Yates had been charged with capital murder for "intentionally and knowingly causing the death of Noah Jacob Yates by drowning, and intentionally and knowingly causing the death of John Samuel Yates by drowning."

The Harris County, Texas, district attorney's office intake report filed that night described Yates as a 5' 7"-tall, brown-eyed, brown-haired, married male weighing 134 pounds. *Male* was later written over with *female*. But she weighed closer to 120 pounds. That was not corrected. The report also described her as not mentally ill.

*   *   *

Rusty Yates' cell phone rang. "Is this happening?" he heard in a thick, Pakistani accent. Yes, Yates replied, immediately recognizing the voice as that of Dr. Mohammad Saeed, Andrea Yates' psychiatrist.

"I asked her if she was having any suicidal thoughts, but not this," the doctor said.

"Right," Yates responded.

Saeed then mentioned that he thought Rusty Yates' mother was *always* at the house with Andrea.

"Well, she wasn't there all day," Rusty answered.

"Is there anything I can do for you?" the doctor asked.

"It's a little late for that now."

Moments later, Yates' cell phone rang again. The caller identified himself as a representative of Magellan.

"Who's Magellan?" he asked.

It was Magellan insurance, which, Yates then learned for the first time, handled the psychiatric care for Blue Cross Blue Shield, Yates' insurance company.

"If there's anything we can do, let us know," the representative said.

Yates simply replied, "Okay," and hung up. *Like they care*, he thought.

Later he contemplated the psychiatrist's words—that he thought someone was *always* with her. It made Rusty Yates wonder if the doctor had known there was the potential for harm.

In the wee hours of the morning of Thursday, June 21, 2001, Andrea Yates stood before a magistrate for her "probable cause for further detention hearing and commitment."

"You have the right to remain silent," she was told.

But she'd already made statements to the police. "I killed my kids."

"You have the right to have an attorney present during any interview with police officers or attorneys representing the State of Texas."

She did not have an attorney.

"You have the right to terminate any such interview at any time."

She did not terminate any interview.

"You are not required to make a statement, and any statement you make may be used against you."

"I killed my children."

Radio talk show hosts were calling for her death in Texas without the constitutional guarantee of a trial.

"If you are indigent and cannot afford counsel, you have the right to request the appointment of counsel, and, if you are charged with a felony, you have the right to an examining trial prior to indictment."

Andrea Yates would not be provided counsel until approximately thirty hours thereafter. She was held without bail.

CHAPTER 3

As Terry Arnold drove to work at the bookstore on Thursday morning, her car radio was tuned to another Houston talk show. "*Anyone* who had *five* kids," she heard, "would *have* to go crazy and kill them. Five kids, how *awful*."

Frustration and annoyance rushed through the body of the mother of five. She believed the radio announcer was blaming the children. Terry Arnold knew better than that. Those children had sat sweetly in her lap. *The didn't do anything to deserve this.*

Arnold was so offended that she grabbed the phone and called her friend Ruth Rendon, a reporter for the *Houston Chronicle*. "Aieh!" Arnold ranted. "This makes me really mad!"

"Oh, my God," Rendon replied. "No one knows her. Can I ask you some questions?"

A few weeks after Rusty Yates had inspected Arnold's bookstore, Andrea Yates and her five children drove up in their big, blue Suburban. Over the next month, Yates and her children visited HEP between four and six times. Each time, 7-year-old Noah climbed out of their vehicle and coaxed his three younger brothers into line, then all four boys walked toward the store holding a hand on the huge, blue stroller that carried baby Mary. When they got to the plate-glass door, Noah always reached for its handle and opened it for his mother and baby sister. *It's like a little entourage bearing in the baby*, Arnold thought with a grin. *It's so cute.*

Noah was obviously the gentleman, leader of the pack. He made Terry Arnold grin. When Noah Yates smiled, his mouth took over his whole face and he became all gums. "You couldn't help but fall in love with that."

"Do you need anything? Some help finding some curriculum?" Arnold asked Yates.

Andrea Yates replied no, she knew what she was looking for. She took her boys to the back of the store, settled them down to play, then started looking through the books.

Arnold watched the boys with amazement; they were friendly and so well-behaved.

"Where are the readers?" Yates asked.

"Do you want a particular publisher?"

"No," Yates answered, "just as long as they're Christian."

Soon, whenever the Yates kids arrived at the bookstore, Arnold turned to her partner and said, "I'm not gonna be at the front or answer the phone. I'm gonna go play in the back with the kids."

Terry and the children would get all the toys out and sit on the floor to play, with Luke, the two-year-old, plopping into Terry's lap and hugging her all over as if he were saying, "I'm cute, and you know it, and you adore me, don't you?"

Yes, absolutely, Arnold wanted to say, as she melted. *This one's mine.*

Luke had piercing, light blue eyes and a natural pin curl of hair in the center of his forehead that just begged Arnold to swirl it with her finger.

"Can I rub on your head for good luck?" she said to all the kids.

They giggled and let her rub their heads.

She turned to Noah and teased him about always wearing a purple shirt.

"It's my favorite color," he said.

"Mine, too," she said with a smile. Terry Arnold wanted her seven-year-old to become friends with Noah. Noah was so smart, reading off the titles of books to her.

Andrea Yates looked at some of the classes the bookstore offered, and talked about signing up Noah. But he was too young for them. Maybe in a year.

Sometimes, mothers quizzed Arnold about their children's academic weaknesses and health. Andrea Yates never expressed any concern about her children's capabilities.

Once, as Arnold cuddled on Mary, Yates talked about how much she enjoyed the children.

Arnold looked at Yates. "Do you think you'll have more?"

"I would like to, but I don't know if we will," Yates replied, appearing a little upset by her answer. "We'll have to talk about it."

"Well, you have a lovely family," Arnold said, trying to ease the mother. "I have five. And I've very much enjoyed it. I would have liked to have had more, but I couldn't."

Andrea Yates seemed to perk back up.

Yates didn't talk a lot. In fact, "We'll have to talk about it," was the only time she remotely mentioned Rusty Yates to Terry Arnold. But Andrea Yates was always friendly.

"After my fifth one," Arnold teased, "I never could lose my stomach, and here you are—" She gestured to Yates' tall, slender body.

Yates laughed and said, "That's just sorta how I am."

"Oh, well, darn," Arnold replied with a quick grin.

Every time Terry Arnold saw Andrea Yates, Yates was well-groomed with jeans, a T-shirt neatly tucked into her jeans with a belt, funky earrings, and her hair clean and neat in a French braid, never loose.

Not only was Yates well-dressed, but so were her kids.

She usually purchased used items, only a few things at a time, and always paid cash.

Andrea Yates wasn't wimpy, timid, or meek. She was appealing and personable, quiet but confident. She didn't come across as browbeaten. And she had pleasant children who didn't seem to be the least bit afraid of their mother. They didn't show any signs of abuse, something Arnold kept an eye out for, since she worked helping find runaway children. Nor did the Yates children appear to be afraid of being friendly. They talked and played with other kids in the store.

Mary, always beautifully dressed in pretty, little-girl things, slept quietly in her stroller. The boys were sweet with each other and never needed correcting. Not even when Arnold got up, went to the front of the store, and brought back her "bug jar," a jar of rainforest rubber bugs. Noah particularly loved it.

The last time Andrea Yates and her five children walked into the store, with Noah holding the door for them, Arnold, a devout Catholic who wore a St. Christopher's medal around her neck, felt blessed to see them. Another child had just trashed the store, and to see Andrea Yates' beautiful, well-behaved children was like a gift from above.

As the kids left Joanne Juren turned to Andrea and said, "I wish we could give your children a gold star for the best behavior, because y'all *are* our favorite customers."

Andrea Yates beamed as if saying, Oh, thank you, you noticed.

That last visit had been just two weeks before June 20, and not one thing seemed different from all of Andrea Yates' other visits to the store—not her appearance, her condition, her demeanor, nothing.

Just twenty-four hours after Andrea Yates had phoned the police, Elizabeth Quigley rode in her car and prayed, expressing her displeasure to God that she did not have a ministry. Quigley, who owned a flower shop across the street from the Clear Lake Church of Christ, which she frequented, had read *The Prayer of Jabez* and had been praying its prayer for a ministry.

After two months of praying, she was downright ready for an answer. She kept praying as she drove. Then she realized what was on the radio—the story of Andrea Yates and her children. Elizabeth Quigley felt compelled to steer her car over to 942 Beachcomber.

The next thing she knew, she was talking to Rusty Yates and finding housing and cars for his family members, who were flying in for the funeral. Quigley wasn't going to be turned away. This was her ministry that God had provided.

In the simmering morning heat of that June Thursday, Rusty Yates wore a dark polo shirt and jeans when he walked onto his front lawn, stepped across the sidewalk, and edged up to the yellow police tape, so close that his belt buckle nearly grazed the vivid crime-scene line. He clutched a framed photograph of his family—Andrea, Noah, John, Paul, Luke, and himself. Daughter Mary, not yet born, was visible only in Andrea's belly, hidden in the photo by her boys.

With his full lips, blue eyes, close-cropped haircut, and his mother standing over his left shoulder, Rusty Yates resembled the epitome of the perfect American son.

"I left the house for work about five or ten till nine, and uh . . . it takes me ten or fifteen minutes to get to work. I was there just about an hour, less than an hour, I got a call from my wife and she said, 'You need to come home.' And I said, 'What's going on?' And she said, 'You need to come home.' You know, I just hung up. I was afraid of her tone. You know, her tone was very serious.

"I left the building, called my mom here," he turned around and gestured toward his mother, a kindly-looking, casually dressed woman with gray hair, "and she was planning on coming over at ten. You know, that's kind of what we did. My mom has been helping out over the past couple of months—helping Andrea watch the kids during the day.

"And she had been coming over for the better part of the day, you know, like ten to five—something like that. And

I would usually leave about eight or nine and get back about five-thirty to six—something like that."

Rusty's mother, Dora Yates, had been a pretty young thing, one of four sisters growing up in Tennessee with three brothers, a dad who ran a sawmill, and a mom who took care of the kids. Dora became a cheerleader, then a flight attendant. When she was 23 years old, she met 40-year-old Russell Yates, a salesman. He was one of five brothers, the son of a preacher who also worked as a railroad man. His mother stayed home and took care of the kids.

Russell Yates was a gregarious man with a deep voice that roared across a room even when he tried to whisper. Dora loved his voice. She had a "thing" for voices. They married and were soon living in Queens.

On September 6, 1964, Russell Edison Yates was born in Queens, New York.

Not long after Rusty's birth, a second son was born, Randall, whom they called Randy. Dora and Russell weren't sure that New York City was a good place to rear two boys. So when Rusty was four years old, they moved to Tennessee, leaving Rusty with three memories of New York—his dad driving up in a brand-new Plymouth Fury 3, riding on a paddle boat and seeing the Statue of Liberty, and banging his lip on a birdbath at Niagara Falls.

When the family first arrived in Tennessee, they rented a house. When Rusty was five years old, they led him and his brother Randy through a home in Hermitage, Tennessee. It had hardwood floors throughout. Rusty loved those floors. It would be their permanent home.

It was the place where Rusty stood outside and waited for the Nazarene church bus to stop and take him and Randy to church. His father, whom Rusty would later refer to as "a bit of an entrepreneur," didn't go to church in those days. But Rusty flourished with his memory for Bible verses.

He was also active in Cub Scouts, with his dad volunteering as Pack Master for Cub Scout Pack 42. Everyone who spoke at their Cub Scout meetings had to use a microphone, everyone, that was, expect Russell Yates. At 6' 2", Russell Yates, the father, was a man as big as his voice. He was also a simple man who was good with tools, a talent his son would pick up, and whom Rusty would later describe as "not a deep thinker."

Eventually, Dora discovered the Hermitage United Methodist Church. It would become the Yates family church home. Even Rusty's father attended. But the folks in Hermitage didn't see the father's outgoing side.

Rusty Yates swayed back and forth as he stood in his yard and continued speaking about his mother.

"And I called her, and she hadn't left yet and, uh, and then I called my wife again and I said, 'What's wrong, Andrea?' And she said, 'You know I need you to come home.' I said, 'Is anyone hurt?' And she said yes. And I said, 'Who?' And she said, 'The children.' And she said, 'All of them.' And my heart just really sunk, you know.

"I was really hoping that my oldest son—My mom," he glanced at her, "occasionally takes one of my—she was rotating between the children to take one of them home with her—between my older three—and she—and I was thinking my oldest son was with her, but he wasn't. He was here.

"So that's about it. I came home and the police were already here, and that's about it."

"Mr. Yates," a reporter called, "can you tell us what kind of emotions you have right now, toward your wife, about your children?"

Rusty Yates stood silent. "Uh, well," he paused lengthily, with his head bowed, "I don't really like the question, but I will say I am primarily concerned with, right now, just tending to my kids and, you know, making sure they get a good burial, are treated good. And, uh, my wife, I am supportive of her, you know.

"It's hard, because on one hand, I know she killed our children, you know. But on the other, I know that the woman here," he pointed to the family photo, "is not the woman who killed my children, so . . ."

A reporter mentioned that Yates had spoken to the police about postpartum depression and asked him to speak about that.

"You want to know what her history was?" Yates asked. "Did you have any idea it was this serious?"

CHAPTER 4

As the crickets chirped and wound their legs tight, then un-spooled them with a high-pitched reel, Rusty Yates contin-ued his sidewalk press conference.

"No," he answered as to whether he knew his wife's post-partum depression was that serious. "She went through post-partum depression with our fourth child, and it was very serious then. She had attempted suicide then, and they, uh, gave her medication. And she really—it took a while, but she just snapped out of it. She was just like herself again, all of a sudden, you know. And that was a couple of years ago, you know.

"And she was fine from that time up until a few months after she had our fifth child. . . . But her dad passed away about three months or so after she had our baby girl, and, uh, you know, that really just sent her spiraling down. I think she was just primed for that depression, you know, that postpartum depression."

A jet roared overhead.

". . . The environment just triggered it—with her dad dy-ing. And we were all hopeful that she would respond to the same medications that she did the first time. But she never responded that well. She, she got to about maybe, uh, sixty-five percent, you know, and, and, and sort of stayed there. She plateaued."

*   *   *

Judy Bradley sat in her home watching the handsome young father on TV. When he held up the photograph, she studied the picture of the mother with the big smile. "Oh, that's Andrea Kennedy," Bradley said.

Time after time on the television news the night before, she'd watched as a handcuffed Andrea Yates had walked out of the back gate and stepped into the police car. The gaunt young woman with, Bradley thought, a catatonic look in her eyes seemed familiar, but Bradley didn't actually recognize her.

But when she saw the family portrait, with a much livelier Andrea Yates in the picture, she knew the woman was Andrea Kennedy, her student from Milby High in Houston.

Young Andrea wanted to be very successful, and proved that by being in honors courses to prepare for college. Indeed, her friends—in a school made up of whites, blacks, and browns with a few rich, many middle class, and some poor—were the upper level students, as far as their grades were concerned. They were all participants in extracurricular activities. And they all planned on going to college.

"I don't ever recall that she ever dated one particular person."

In fact, Yates' best friend from high school, tall Marlene Burda, her buddy on the swim team and friend in the National Honor Society, considered herself and Andrea to be wallflowers. Andrea signed her yearbook, "the struggling butterfly."

"Have you gotten a chance to speak to her?" a reporter asked Rusty Yates.

"No, I haven't," he responded, as a police officer watched over his shoulder. "I want to today. But I, uh, her family is looking into finding out where she is, and they told me today that visiting hours might only be on Monday, Wednesday, Friday.

"I mean, I'm supportive of her. It's hard, like I said, because I am torn. One side of me blames her because she did it, you know. But the other side of me says she didn't, because that wasn't her. She wasn't in the right frame of mind. And, I guess she had psychotic side effects with her depression that led her to do this. She wasn't—I mean—she loved our kids. Anybody who knew her knew that."

What kind of medicine had she been taking? a reporter called out.

". . . With the first depression, what seemed to work was a combination of Effexor, Wellbutrin, and Haldol. And what she was on as of yesterday was Effexor and Remeron, and that's all."

Rusty Yates didn't explain that Effexor, Wellbutrin, and Remeron were antidepressants and that Haldol was an antipsychotic.

He was asked about his wife's behavior before she took the medications.

"Okay, that's a good question," he approved. ". . . It's just the first time she went through the depression, it took several months for her to really become seriously depressed.

"This time," he said, "it was three weeks. And I, uh, uh," he rocked back and forth, "there were things that she did, you know, becoming withdrawn, more robotic in her behavior, uh, you know, she had some nervous habits that she had, you know, particular to her. And so, you know, I recognized it immediately, and we treated it quickly. But you know what happened was just incomprehensible and, I mean, I just can't—looking back, I struggled with it all last night. I couldn't sleep last night. I was, like, was there anything I could have done? . . . and, you know . . . also, what have I got to do? There's a lot to do."

He paused.

"I've got really two tragedies, like my brother pointed out," Yates glanced over at his brother Randy. ". . . One is my children. The other is my wife. I mean, you know, I want her to recover, and it's going to be very hard for her to work through this."

*   *   *

Andrea Kennedy, born on July 2, 1964, in Houston, Texas, was the fifth child of Andrew and Jutta Karin Koehler Kennedy. She had three older brothers and one older sister. Her father was a former Air Force pilot who'd flown World War II bombing missions over Germany. He'd worked as a Ford engineer, and later as an auto shop teacher at Humble High School, in the northeastern Houston suburb of Humble. Her mother was a German-born high school graduate who'd worked as a manager in retail shops.

Andrea grew up in southeast Houston, across the street from Glenbrook Golf Course, where she and one of her brothers used to pick up stray golf balls and sell them. In Andrea Yates' teen years, hers was a comfortable home with a big magnolia tree in its front yard, situated in a middle class neighborhood that eased into upper-middle-class homes with large lots.

Refinery workers, CPAs, and young attorneys lived in the vicinity, before moving up in their careers and many moving out. Twenty years later, the neighborhood across from Glenbrook Golf Course had fenced yards with "Beware of Dog" signs attached to their gates. Andrea's home, the second from the corner of some rough-looking, beat-up apartments, was a well-kept house with one of those "Beware of Dog" signs pinned to its hurricane fence.

A few blocks down the street, near Interstate 45 and Loop 610, was Milby High, now a large, crumbling, and dilapidated tan brick building undergoing renovation.

Judy Bradley had taught biology and drama at Milby, and had had Yates in her drama class and homeroom, with about twenty-five other students. She met Andrea's mother and father during parents' night at the large school. She'd also watched Andrea's siblings in school, and knew that the entire Kennedy family was goal-oriented; they would set higher standards for themselves, and work to meet those standards. In 1982, Andrea graduated as valedictorian of her class.

Bradley couldn't put the person she now saw on the news—unresponsive, trance-like—with the person she knew from high school. "This is not a person dealing with reality," she'd said when she'd watched Andrea Kennedy on TV.

Bradley knew about mental illness and the mentally ill's inability to deal with reality—a relative of hers was a paranoid schizophrenic. It was an ongoing battle to keep him properly medicated. She thought back to interviews with neighbors she'd seen on the news the night before. No one really knew the Yates family.

Judy Bradley knew that being isolated could be detrimental to a person who didn't have an outlet.

The Andrea Yates she knew from nearly twenty years before had had a solid group of good friends. She was a historian in the National Honor Society. She was captain of her swim team. She was goal-oriented. "And she had good character, good morals," Bradley fondly recalled.

"She would be on the quiet side of the student body in the classroom, but she would participate in class discussions and class activities and certainly was friendly. But she was not the very, very outgoing, glad-handing type of student." Other students talked to her. "But she never would have been a class clown or really disruptive in class."

She had a good sense of humor, which was on the dry side. "And she laughed easily. She seemed to enjoy her relationships with the other students. She definitely was more of a participant rather than a leader."

Her dress was undistinguished—simply like those in her peer group. In fact, the 36-year-old Andrea Yates on TV had the exact same hairstyle as the 17-year-old Andrea at Milby High.

Four years after graduating from high school, and toiling her way through college by checking groceries, Andrea Kennedy earned a nursing degree from the University of Texas Health Science Center in Houston. She then worked as a registered nurse at the city's famed M. D. Anderson Hospital.

* * *

The image of Andrea Yates on TV, walking out the back gate, lingered in Judy Bradley's mind. Her former student, the one with such goals of making good grades, looked like a non-entity to Bradley. It saddened her.

"The Andrea I knew," she added, "could never have done that, in her right mind."

A reporter asked Rusty Yates to describe his children.

"That's a good question," he responded. "I was thinking about that last night. And what I want to do is just write up a little bit on each child, the way I remember them." Tears began to well in his eyes. "You know, my mom, she said yesterday—" he gasped for air as he choked with tears— "she was glad to have known them. She spent some time down here the last couple months and . . . that's the way I feel. Precious, precious kids."

Behind Yates, lying in the grass, was a collection of flowers, teddy bears, stuffed animals, and notes in memory of the children, left by strangers, neighbors, and friends.

Had the family problems started with his wife's suicide attempt? a journalist shouted.

"That's kind of an odd question," Yates commented, then stated that his wife had gotten depressed about three months after the birth of Luke, their fourth son, and about three months after the birth of their fifth child, Mary. "And to say they are related, I mean, the symptoms were the same. She was predisposed to getting this depression, and I think that that is—you know—they are related in that sense."

With the press urging, he continued speaking about his wife's depression.

"They," meaning the media, "said she had been treated for depression for two years," he responded. "Well, she hasn't been treated for depression, not continuously. After the first depression, she recovered fully. I have got some little things she did to the kids, like made these little . . . for Valentine's Day, she made these little hearts. They were like little books, little coupons for—like one was good for a hug and one was good for a game of your choice. That sort of thing. She gave that to all the kids. She just came up with it on her own. She loved those kids."

Had he and his wife worried about having kids? he was asked.

"I would say that after going through this a second time . . . we had talked about not having any more children, you know. I talked to Andrea when she was feeling a little bit better. We had a good talk about it. Both of us really went into our marriage saying, we will have as many kids as came along. That's what we wanted. But, you know, her bouts of depression really put a damper on that. We had agreed to delay that indefinitely."

He was asked to describe his children's likes and interests.

"We did things any other family did, you know, like T-ball. I coach a T-ball team with my oldest two kids. They play. We used to go out here and shoot basketball with my oldest son. I was glad, too. Yesterday, I was thinking, he won the last game of horse we played. So I . . . ," he laughed a bit, ". . . I was happy about that for him because he was real competitive." And Russell Yates smiled.

Tracy Alverides glanced at the television humming in her Florida hotel room and saw at the bottom of the screen the words "Russell Yates." Immediately, she looked at the face on the TV. *That's Rusty.*

But the man she watched had graying around the temples. *Oh, my goodness. Have we all aged that much?* She hadn't seen him in nearly twenty years.

He wiped his brow with his shoulder. "He still has the same gestures," she remarked to her sister, who sat with her. She watched him more closely.

Alverides remembered that short, nervous laugh from high school. She also remembered that same monotone voice, and the way he didn't look people straight in the eye. He never had been relaxed with people until he got to know them well. Lots of folks thought it was shyness. "He hasn't changed at all, except for the graying around the temples," Alverides said. He even dressed the same as he did in high school.

She and her sister turned to each other. "I can't believe this happened to him. Of all people, I don't understand why this happened to him. . . . He was a good guy. He was just a good guy. Everybody loved him. He could be buddies with everybody. He would help you out." He tutored other kids. He helped Tracy change a tire. "He said hello to you in the hall. He always had a smile on his face. I never saw him angry." In Tracy Alverides' memory, Rusty Yates could do it all.

A reporter asked Rusty Yates if they home schooled the children.

"We home schooled them. Primarily Andrea during the day, during the morning time, for a few hours. We had normal curriculums we followed. I thought it was going pretty well. I'm not saying it's not stressful, but it was manageable. It's just, she, she couldn't do it while she was depressed. But ordinarily she enjoyed it. . . . Even the ones who weren't school age, they would participate. . . . And my oldest two knew how to read. Noah and John."

John was only five years old.

Yates was asked about efforts to ease Andrea Yates' depression.

"I have got them on a board inside," he said. "We actually went with the children . . . we brainstormed over that for a while—all our idea. Noah and I went through that, and we tried to come up with some ideas of things we could do to relieve her stress."

"Are you supportive of your wife?"

"I am," Yates answered. "Yesterday was hard for me. I was like, you know, I don't understand this. Why did you do this? But you know, I've got to remember that she wasn't

herself, you know. She was just thinking irrationally. You
know, Andrea, if you see this, I love you."

And when Yates was asked again about his wife's suicide
attempt, he responded, "She is a pretty private person. She
doesn't say much, you know."

He was then queried about the fact that she was facing
a capital murder charge.

"I support her," he responded. "That's all I can say. I
mean, as far as our relationship goes, I try to think ahead,
you know. I don't know how we could ever . . . I don't want
to think about it now. As far as just the short term, I want
to help her through this. I want to show her that I love her,
support her, and, you know, be there for her."

And finally, Rusty Yates was asked about the fact that
his wife could face the death penalty.

"I suppose that's the lawyers' decision. Obviously, I
would say that . . . but I think that she . . . obviously wasn't
herself. I think that will come out, you know. Everyone who
knows her knows she loves the kids. And that she is a kind,
gentle person, and what you see and hear and what you saw
yesterday—you know, that's not her."

Rusty Yates still clutched the family photo.

The first policeman on the scene couldn't get the picture of
those dead babies out of his mind.

HPD head psychologist Dr. Gregory Riede advised officers to create different memories—replace thoughts such as
This is terrible, this could be my child with *this is evidence
. . .* and to give inquiring strangers a short, simple non-
answer—I don't want to talk about the worst day of my life.

But cops were talking and telling more than the abbre-
viated versions to reporters. They told the *Houston Chronicle* that Andrea Yates had given her police statement in a
"zombie-like fashion," confessing to investigators that she'd
drowned 2-year-old Luke first, then 3-year-old Paul, followed by 5-year-old John, carrying each to the master bed-

room and placing their wet bodies on the bed, beneath a sheet.

She then reached for baby Mary, and as she submerged the infant in the tub, 7-year-old Noah walked in and said, "What's wrong with Mary?" He realized what was happening, and ran. Yates said she chased him through the house, then drowned him, alongside his baby sister. She carried Mary to the bedroom, but left Noah in the tub, while she called the police . . . and then her husband.

CHAPTER 5

Joe Ruiz phoned his Milby High School swim coach, Lana Dunlap, a woman with an easy, often self-effacing, sense of humor. He'd phoned her about once a year since the early 1980s, she thought, to see if she was still alive. But this time he phoned and said, "Have you seen it on TV?"

She'd watched the TV, she knew the news—a Clear Lake mother had been accused of drowning her five children. And when she saw that woman on TV, the first words that came to Dunlap's mind were, *She just looks sad, just depressed and sad. It's something that has to happen over a period of time.*

Then Ruiz told her that the woman on the news was his former swim captain, the coach's former swimmer.

At first, Dunlap flat didn't believe Ruiz. The Andrea she knew was the sweetest, nicest kid that any teacher or coach would want to have. "She just doesn't look anything like she did." Andrea Kennedy Yates had truly been one of the standouts on Dunlap's best swim team in nearly thirty years of coaching. They'd won district several times.

Andrea Yates wasn't a beginner swimmer, like some of the others on the swim team, who the coach practically had to teach to swim across the pool. Andrea came in with a bit of talent, then got better and better. She was conscientious about practice, got there on time, swam all the required laps instead of faking them, and she was coachable. She was just a plain nice kid.

"The Andrea of today," Dunlap said, "was not the Andrea of that time period. Twenty years," she said sadly, "I guess, has changed a person."

At Milby, in the early '80s, the boys and girls swam together. And each year they elected two team captains, a boy and a girl. Her senior year, Andrea's teammates elected her the female captain of their swim team. "Being the captain of the team didn't really come with a lot of duties. It was just more or less a prestige type thing . . . ," Dunlap explained. "They elected her captain because evidently they liked her enough and wanted her to be it." When it came to swimming, Andrea Kennedy was popular.

"She was pretty serious most of the time, about the swimming and about her studies. I don't remember her being real outgoing or outspoken. Kinda quiet. But that fit a whole bunch of 'em."

Andrea's typical workouts were approximately two hours of doing lengths on the kickboards, laps using her arms only, laps using her competition freestyle stroke, followed by sprints and relays, each Monday through Friday, every day, after school. Some of the swimmers showed up at 6 A.M. for additional workouts before school started. "She was just involved in all that. She could do it all.

"I think she tried harder than a lot of them did. . . . And she was very interested in it. . . . She was probably in the top three of the girl swimmers through those years. She really worked at it."

"If you told Andrea, 'Okay, we're gonna go, say, twenty laps,' you know, go a half a mile, whatever, Andrea would be the one that I would say would finish it. Whereas somebody else next to her might say, 'Well, I finished mine,' but they might be four laps short. But you could count on Andrea finishing the assignment and ready to go again. She just liked swimming."

The kind-hearted coach noted, "She got along with anybody and everybody. She was very mature for her age compared to a lot who come through there. She seemed to be more focused on what she had to do for her schoolwork, focused on completing her assignment, staying in the swimming pool. She's not one that you had to yell at to quit playing in the water and finish up. . . . I wish I'd had every one of them on there just like that. It'd make coaching a whole lot easier."

Having returned to Nashville, Tracy Alverides was busy defending Rusty Yates to folks who'd never even met the man, but who condemned him for his lack of emotion. "Well, that's Rusty. That's just him. That's how I remember him being . . . at his serious points."

Alverides' memory of Yates began in the junior high years with Hermitage United Methodist Church.

Lou Alverides, Tracy's father, and a man who knew the Yates family from church, thought differently. "Both Dora and her husband were very quiet people." Alverides saw Russell Yates at ballgames, watching Rusty play. Russell Yates simply acknowledged Alverides' presence and moved on.

Lou Averides served on the church's scholarship committee where he, Dora Yates, and others reviewed scholarship applications, then selected who would receive the scholarships. Alverides' conversation with Yates was limited to the scholarship, but he admired what a hard worker she was. She was a teacher at McGavock Comprehensive High School in Donelson, Tennessee, not very far from DuPont High, which Rusty attended.

Tracy Alverides recalled that Dora Yates was sweet, soft-spoken, kind—"just a lovely individual all around."

But it was big Rusty Yates, 6 feet, 2 inches tall by tenth grade, that the 5'4" Alverides recalled most fondly. They graduated from high school together. And they were involved in Methodist Youth Fellowship, a group of young, dedicated church members who met on Sunday nights during the school year, and went on church trips during the summer. They traveled to other churches to sing, stopped at amusement parks on the way back, and spent weekends in devotional.

"He could be so carefree at times, then, at the next minute, he could be very serious, you know, about his religion, whatever. Religion was very important to him then, especially."

But Rusty Yates' religious convictions were not the only thing that impressed Tracy Alverides. In her memory, Rusty Yates was a very good football player and very intelligent. "Extremely intelligent," she added for emphasis.

In Rusty's senior year, he was in advanced placement English, chemistry, and calculus, worked as a library aide, was president of the National Honor Society, served on the student council, lettered in football, participated in the Fellowship of Christian Athletes, was selected as a delegate to Boys' State, voted class favorite, and elected Mr. DuPont. By the time he graduated, he'd also played tennis for two years, received the geometry award (his junior year), and been chosen for *Who's Who Among American High School Students* and the Society of Distinguished American High School Students.

"I think what stuck in our minds was that he played football, but was in all the advanced classes. You either did one or the other. You were either a jock or very intelligent or [one of the] kids that did drugs." But Rusty Yates, Alverides said, "He got along with everyone. He was good to everybody. He respected others, and I think people respected him for that." She added, "I never heard him say anything bad about others. Never."

His laugh was infectious. His sense of humor was dry. In fact, he could say something that wouldn't be funny coming out of anyone else's mouth. "But because he said it, it was funny. . . . And it was just amazing how he could go from being so serious and grounded and doing his thing and the next minute he could be so funny. And I think that's why he got along with everybody. He could fit into any situation, whatever was handed to him."

Despite being both a jock and a geek, no one considered
him to be either, Alverides said. "He never labeled anybody.
. . . and I think that's why he got along with them so well."
But his friends were the intelligent geeks. "Very nice people." That's who he ate lunch with, not the football players.

"I remember at one pep rally, people were chanting his
name . . . because he was just so good." Often, he spoke at
pep rallies. And sometimes, when he spoke in front of
groups or when he was nervous, anxious, or excited, his
hands shook.

Sometimes, he appeared to have trouble looking people
in the eyes, but, again, everyone just thought it was his
shyness. He didn't date much with the exception of Lynn
Heatherly during his senior year. She was a short, petite teen
with brown hair and a big smile who he took to the prom.
And when he did start dating her, Alverides said, "everyone
was surprised, and happy for him."

Rusty's father, Tracy Alverides recalled, was tall and,
with his completely white hair, seemed much older than
everyone else's parents. In fact, she thought Mr. Yates was
retired. "I think his father could be very strict."

Rusty thought of his father as "a bit intimidating" and
"very loud, outgoing, friendly."

On August 11, 1981, Rusty's father, Russell Yates,
dropped dead of a heart attack. It was the anniversary of
Russell's own father's death, a man Rusty Yates never met.
The grandfather had died before Rusty was born. Perhaps
that was why Rusty's father constantly said he was going
to live to be 109 years old . . . to reassure himself and his
family. Instead, August 11 became a day that made Rusty
Yates be extra careful.

At the time of the death, Russell and Rusty looked just
alike, same size, same build, just different hair color. By
then, Rusty Yates had developed a personality that he considered to be like both his mother's and father's, yet different—he was more analytical. Alverides considered him to

be very similar to his mother—very kind and sweet.

"I remember when his father died," Alverides said, ". . . even though it was summer, it got around and a lot of the football players, a lot of kids from school, showed up for the funeral."

At the funeral, Rusty Yates didn't weep much. He listened to how the minister used the words, "It's been said that . . ." about his dad. And he noticed how the minister referred to Russell Yates as Rusty. The father went by Russell or Russ, never Rusty.

Tracy Alverides, at the time, felt Rusty was trying not to cry because of his age, because of his peers. But now she thinks he just holds a lot inside.

His father's death simply made the childhood notion that everyone *eventually* dies very real to Rusty Yates.

"But I think his faith is really what has carried him on through school. I remember early in the mornings before school started, there was a room off the gym. I think it was like an equipment room or whatever, but they let us meet in there for morning prayer. A lot of people who were with the Fellowship of Christian Athletes were in there. And then each morning we would go in for about fifteen minutes before school started, and I remember him being there each time.

"I don't remember him particularly doing a devotion, but he was always there. And I think his faith was very important. I think his faith got him through his father's death."

But after Rusty's father died, Tracy felt that she saw Rusty "buckle down a little bit more in his work. I think—I still remember seeing him somewhat the same, but I think it was—I think he became more focused. I don't know if it was because his father died, or it was his senior year and he wanted to get into college." She recalled that at one time, church members discussed whether Rusty would be able to go to college because of financial concerns resulting from his father's death, but that discussion led to the knowledge that he would be able to use his father's Social Security money for school.

"I think all of our parents from church pretty much helped Dora get through some of the difficult times, and I think that kinda may have let Rusty relax a little and get through the last year of high school. I think his mother was always concerned about making sure that they could do what they wanted to—let them have a childhood.

"I wouldn't say she was protective of the boys. She always had a tight rein on them, but she also let them have their freedom. She did a wonderful job raising the boys. She always had the reins on them, but loose enough to let them do what they wanted to do. They were good, respectful kids, always real respectful to other adults."

In the early '80s, Hermitage, Tennessee, was a conservative town with a sense of innocence and a social life that revolved around church and sports. The entire community turned out for the Friday night football games, even if they didn't have a child on the team. The town even turned out for the away games. Afterwards, everyone gathered at Joe's Pizza or Sir Pizza.

One high school girl did get pregnant, and that was a shock to the town. But the worst that kids did in Hermitage was drink and smoke some pot. Punk rock was entering the airwaves. But mostly the music was U2 and Don Henley. Football heroes still dated cheerleaders, and couples attended the prom but didn't dance. Boys wore khakis, loafers, and button-down-collar shirts, or Izod shirts with Members Only jackets. Rusty Yates, a middle-class boy, wore Izods, jeans, and tennis shoes.

"Obviously, he was very disciplined," Alverides said.

When she heard that Rusty Yates wanted to go into the space program, she thought *No problem*. "He was just so intelligent that it blew my mind."

The spring after his father died, Rusty Yates graduated third in his class and was off to Auburn University on a

Navy ROTC scholarship. He majored in math, and tutored athletes. In June and July of 1983, he served on a Navy destroyer. But a year and a half later, in the winter of 1984, realizing the military life was not the life for him, Yates dropped out of the ROTC and gave up his Navy scholarship.

About the same time, Yates began a search for a religious identity. Contrary to what Tracy Alverides thought, Rusty Yates wasn't content with the faith he saw at Hermitage United Methodist Church. But at Auburn, he met a man who would show him a new way.

In college, perhaps it was in 1984, he heard a "kinda quiet and simple" preacher who proclaimed a message of serving Jesus, not serving the church. Rusty Yates listened. He listened, too, as the "quiet and simple" preacher traded barbs with a "fat cat preacher" standing across the way.

The barbs the "quiet and simple" preacher exchanged were the same ones Rusty would have thrown. He was impressed with the preacher. And his message of serving Jesus, not the church, freed Rusty Yates. He suddenly felt he didn't have to go to church; he was privileged enough, he said, to open the Bible himself. And he did.

He also corresponded with the preacher for the next year or two. At the end of that time, he was talking on the phone to his mother and told her, "I think I'm pretty much beginning to believe this stuff." With those words, "joy came over me." He finished telling his mother what he had to say, and then said it all over again because he was "so joyful." That joy, said Rusty Yates, was the Holy Spirit. "From your innermost being will flow rivers of living water," he quoted from John 7:38.

For the next few years after college, he and the preacher no longer corresponded. Then, after he'd met Andrea Kennedy, Yates corresponded with him about "once a year or so."

The preacher's name was Michael Woroniecki.

CHAPTER 6

On Thursday, June 21, 2001, Rusty Yates went to the Harris County Medical Examiner's Office to identify the bodies of his five children. "Just ask anybody that's seen us, seen us in the store or seen us in the restaurant," he said, his voice choking with tears, "Good family."

By then, two memorial funds had already been set up for him, one through Johnson Space Center, another, which got more publicity, through Elizabeth Quigley and Clear Lake Flowers.

That evening, ABC's *Nightline* featured Andrea Yates and postpartum depression.

Chris Wallace opened the show by simply announcing, "It's every family's worst nightmare." The show then cut to Rusty Yates holding his sidewalk press conference.

Soon, HPD Officer Randall Beatty filled the screen. "I mean, we see a lot of homicides, but you don't see a scene like that. That's the first thing I remember in sixteen years that made me cry."

Beatty continued, "And the, the hardest thing is having to deal with just the, the anguish, the human anguish of, of, you know, a man that just heard that his kids had been killed. You know, because you can imagine how someone would react. It was—it was very, very difficult."

But as Rusty Yates' face flashed on the TV again and he said, "I, you know, hugged and kissed everybody goodbye before—before I went to work that day. And that's how I want to remember them."

And Yates talked about his wife's postpartum depression.

"While we don't know if that's why Mrs. Yates drowned her children," ABC reporter John Donvan said, ". . . it would not be the first time this form of mental illness was linked to extreme violence." He reported that a quick search found a dozen similar cases over ten years' time.

Postpartum depression affects up to 20 percent of women who give birth. According to the American College of Obstetricians and Gynecologists, "Postpartum depression is more likely to happen in women who lack the support of a partner or who have had postpartum depression before, a psychiatric illness, a recent stress, such as losing a loved one, family illness or moving to a new city."

Some mothers suffer a more severe form of postpartum depression—postpartum psychosis, which most experts consider to be "rare." However, the American College of Obstetricians and Gynecologists puts that figure as high as three cases of "severe mental illness" for every 1000 births.

Its symptoms are a refusal to eat, the inability to stop a particular activity, frantic excessive energy, extreme confusion, loss of memory, incoherence, suspiciousness, irrational statements, preoccupation with trivia, and bizarre hallucinations.

The British Columbia Reproductive Mental Health Program out of Canada simply states, "During a psychotic episode, the woman loses touch with reality." She may hear voices when no one is around, or she may be delusional and think that someone is trying to harm her, or that her baby is the devil.

Women who have a previous history or family history of bipolar mood disorder or schizophrenia are at greater risk of suffering postpartum psychosis. Women who've previously experienced postpartum psychosis are 50 percent more likely to experience it again with subsequent pregnancies.

"Onset is quick and severe," write Laurence Kruckman and Susan Smith in *An Introduction to Postpartum Illness*.

Women who suffer postpartum psychosis are at risk for committing suicide, and, in "very rare cases," harming their infant, according to the British Columbia Reproductive Mental Health Program. "This is a psychiatric emergency and the woman needs to be hospitalized immediately," the organization advises. "Because of her confusion the woman may not have the insight to recognize how ill she is, therefore, the decision for hospitalization will be made by her physicians."

In Canada, Britain, and Australia, and approximately twenty-seven other countries throughout the world, murder charges are ruled out for women who kill their children within the first twelve months of giving birth.

Dr. Phillip Resnick, professor of psychiatry at Case Western Reserve University and an expert on infanticide, appeared on the June 21 edition of *Nightline*.

Dr. Resnick said the Clear Lake mother was probably "altruistic—that is, a woman who kills out of love rather than hate." He pointed to Rusty Yates' statement that Andrea Yates loved her children. ". . . In all likelihood she perceived what she was doing was in her children's best interest, either by going to heaven or being relieved of some psychotically attributed symptoms by the mother toward the children."

He then added, "I have no doubt that when all the facts come out, we are likely to hear that she honestly believed that she was doing her children a service rather than a disservice."

The *Nightline* conversation turned to Andrea Yates' defense and, in particular, an insanity defense.

"The higher the publicity, the larger the number of children killed, the less likely she is to succeed," Resnick said. "But even if she doesn't succeed with an insanity defense, it would certainly be a major mitigating factor in how she would be sentenced."

The same date that Dr. Resnick appeared on *Nightline*, Dr. Lauren Marangell, a Baylor College of Medicine professor of psychiatry, and Dr. Lucy Puryear, another Baylor professor of psychiatry, spoke to the *Houston Chronicle* about Andrea Yates.

"Whether it's postpartum depression is not the issue," Marangell said to the *Chronicle*. "We don't know enough to say at this point. Depression is a brain-based disorder that is usually treatable and that doesn't typically lead to homicide. Stressful life events can worsen depression or psychotic disorders, and treatment is essential."

Regarding Yates' prescription drug history, Puryear told the *Chronicle*, "Haldol is prescribed for psychotic patients hearing voices or thinking delusionally." She further explained, "The patient usually functions normally as a result of the medication, but is also subject to reoccurrences when he or she goes off it, so it's important to be sure they're not at risk of hurting themselves or someone else."

All three doctors—Resnick, Marangell, and Puryear— were experts who would become important to Andrea Yates' life.

Seven-thirty in the morning on Friday, June 22, 2001, Andrea Yates, dressed in an orange prison jumpsuit, walked into the 230th District Court of Texas with her arms folded across her waist. She stood motionless before Judge Belinda Hill, her back to reporters, her face to a video camera.

Prosecutor Kaylynn Williford quickly disposed of the facts to Judge Hill—the accused had taken the lives of her five children by drowning.

Hill asked Yates if she understood the charges against her.

"Yes, ma'am," the mother answered.

The court determined that Yates was indigent and appointed her an attorney, Bob Scott. Scott immediately asked the judge to impose a gag order. Judge Hill did not rule on his request.

While Rusty Yates watched his wife on TV, prepared to find her an attorney, and made plans to bury his children, investigators were busy "leaking" information to the press. First to the *Houston Chronicle*, then to *The Dallas Morning News*. Reportedly, police said, Andrea Yates had been thinking about killing her children for months.

Officially, police told reporters that Yates was being held in the Harris County Jail psychiatric unit. "There's someone there watching her to make sure she doesn't harm herself," Harris County Sheriff's spokesman Lieutenant Robert Van Pelt said. She was in isolation, on suicide watch.

In fact, as soon as Andrea Yates was led out of the courtroom, completed a ten-minute meeting with her new attorney, and was taken back to the psychiatric unit, prosecutors Williford and Joseph Owmby mounted their own sidewalk press conference.

Owmby was asked about Scott's request for a gag order.

"Whether the judge issues a gag order or not, the effect is the same," he stated. "I'm not trying the case out here. I'm not going to talk about the case."

Did they plan to pursue additional charges against Yates, they were asked—charges for murdering her other three children?

"We haven't made all the charging decisions yet," Owmby answered. "It is possible that we could prosecute just that case, or charge other cases, or charge different cases." He added, "Usually in a charge of capital murder, all acts like that come into the trial anyway." Owmby said he had prosecuted a dozen capital murder cases.

The prosecutors were asked if they planned to pursue the death penalty.

"Chuck Rosenthal is the district attorney in Harris County, and he'll make that decision," Owmby answered.

And when Owmby was asked about the severity of the

crime, he dramatically responded, "It's not an everyday occurrence anywhere. It's not an everyday occurrence in the world. I've been here fifteen years. I've not seen the cases others have seen, but this is the most horrendous thing that I have ever seen."

At 9:50 A.M., Rusty Yates arrived at his home, after spending the night across the street from Johnson Space Center at the Extended StayAmerica, the same place his mother had stayed during her two months of helping care for the children.

Minutes later, five HPD detectives and one investigator from the district attorney's office arrived at the house on Beachcomber. They spent an hour searching again, and then left. Between their two searches, on the day of the crime and two days after the crime, they had confiscated a paddle from the house. Rusty Yates wasn't happy about that.

In the early afternoon, Byron Fike, the tall, slim, tanned pastor of Clear Lake Church of Christ, walked out his office door. He looked to his right; the TV satellite trucks parked near the Yates house were within view. In fact, they'd made the comfortably wide neighborhood street that edged the church's side impassable.

Fike turned to his left and quickly dodged cars as he crossed El Dorado Boulevard. It was one of Clear Lake's main thoroughfares and the road that separated Clear Lake Church of Christ from Clear Lake Flowers, the store Quigley owned.

At Quigley's request, Fike was walking away from the TV trucks and toward a meeting with Quigley, Rusty Yates, his brother Randy, and Rusty's friend Ted Ro. Quigley was calling herself the Yates family spokesperson, and had told Fike that Yates didn't have a church home, so she'd recommended that he phone Fike and talk with him about the possibility of officiating at the children's funeral.

During the phone conversation, Yates had told Fike that he'd visited many churches looking for a church home, that he really liked the churches, he just didn't like the pastors.

Fike stepped into the store, filled with the fragrance of fresh, cold flowers and scented candles, and met Rusty Yates. Fike quickly realized that Rusty Yates didn't trust him. Fike knew he'd have to earn the grieving father's confidence. Over two hours' time, with a kind and casual demeanor, he emphasized to Yates that he wanted to respect the family's wishes.

Then he walked back across the street and entered through a door that would soon be the focus of TV cameras across the world. "We're probably doing the funeral," he told his staff. But he didn't believe it was a done deal. Apparently, though, the media did. They started phoning the church and asking what was going on.

Quigley had announced to the press that the Yates children's funeral would be held Wednesday, June 27, at 10:30 A.M..

Fike turned to his staff. "Our comment to the media is 'No comment.' I don't trust those guys, and I certainly don't want to be talk—we don't have anything to say to those guys anyway. We don't know anything for sure."

Downtown, Rusty Yates was meeting with his wife's mother, Karin Kennedy, her family, and George Parnham, a local attorney who played Santa Claus every Christmas. Parnham had volunteered to take Andrea Yates' case. Bob Scott, Yates' first attorney, was no longer on the job, despite the fact that his request for a gag order remained in effect.

Parnham had arranged for the family to visit Andrea Yates in the county jail. One by one the family members went in and met with her.

Rusty Yates walked in and looked at his wife. He was stunned. She looked completely different. Whereas she'd stared blankly into space when he last saw her sitting on the love seat in their den, she now looked straight ahead with a stern look on her face.

He tried to talk to her.

She didn't say anything back.

He tried to encourage her.

Finally, she learned forward and said, "You will be greatly rewarded."

What a bizarre thing to say, he thought, but he ignored her comment and kept on talking, trying to encourage her. He turned to Parnham, pointed him out, and said, "This is Mr. Parnham. He's going to be your attorney."

"I don't need an attorney. I'm not going to plead not guilty," she answered.

Rusty Yates was taken aback, again. "Well, you know, you can use Mr. Parnham to help you with paperwork and whatnot."

Andrea Yates ended her visit with her husband by saying, "Have a nice life."

Have a nice life. It ripped him apart.

The whole conversation ripped him apart. *She's a totally different person.* It was weird for him. *She's suffering so.*

Andrea Yates was on Zoloft and Respiradol at the time, two drugs that Rusty Yates knew his wife had been on in the past. Two drugs that he knew hadn't worked for her.

Two hours after they'd arrived, Rusty Yates, the Kennedys, and George Parnham walked out of the jail to face the cameras and microphones again.

"She is doing as well as can be expected, considering the circumstances, which I know you understand are extreme," Parnham said, his white beard snowy in the summer sun.

He said the family was supportive of Andrea Yates but only described their meeting with her as "very personal." He explained, "You can imagine that it was as intense, as private, and as heart-rending as any meeting between two individuals that I have ever witnessed." He also said the family would not be making any more statements until after the funeral.

* * *

Friday evening, after the sun had set and the humidity was only a gloss on the skin rather than a thick, petroleum jelly coating, dozens of friends, neighbors, and strangers gathered in the front yard of 942 Beachcomber for a candlelight vigil in honor of the children.

Four times that many people stood across the street watching, photographing, and taking notes.

Mothers hugged their daughters as they lighted their candles, and Rusty Yates and his family walked out of the house.

The news media crowded forward.

With tears in his eyes, Yates asked them to move back. "I want to have quiet for the kids," he said. He hugged a few people, then thanked everyone for coming. And he asked them to pray for Andrea. "That will help a lot. She's suffering."

The group sang "Amazing Grace," as they stood staring at Rusty Yates and a tree that was surrounded by flowers, balloons, stuffed animals, and notes for the children. The only thing Yates remembered about the evening was bending down and hugging a child.

By then, DuPont High School alumni from all over the nation were emailing their school's Website and posting messages of support for their former Mr. DuPont High.

Traci Turner Johnson and Missy Gregory McNamee asked for prayers for Rusty. Kevin and Sandy Jackson provided addresses and phone numbers for donations going toward the children's funeral expenses. And for days on, Rusty Yates' classmates wrote, all supporting their friend from high school.

Saturday morning, Byron Fike's home phone rang incessantly with reporters telling *him* that he was officiating at the Yates children's funeral. Fike didn't want to talk to the media. He decided to talk to the Lord instead.

God made two things clear to him. First, Rusty Yates

was his top priority—he was his ministry. Fike thought Yates was a man of faith, a man who believed in the Lord Jesus Christ, but also a man who had no church family and no one to minister to him. And somehow, Fike understood, he had been invited in, and that was going to be his role— minister to Rusty Yates. "God made that very clear to me."

The second thing God made clear to Fike was, "I'll let you know when to talk, and I'll let you know what to say. And it's not now."

"You know, I just can't tell you a whole lot," he said to the calling reporters.

Still, the media kept calling . . . and started swarming the grounds of the church. It was the plague of the media locusts.

Fike and his staff knew they had to do something. They instructed the media not to set foot in the church itself and to allow its members to worship on Sunday morning.

Miles away, the phone in HEP Bookstore kept ringing; Terry Arnold picked up the cordless phone for the umpteenth time. Caller after caller said they were close friends with Andrea Yates. Caller after caller refused to give their names. But they seemed to know private things about Yates.

They thanked Arnold for speaking up for Andrea in the newspaper. They wanted to do it themselves, they said, but they were too angry to talk. They were grateful someone was painting a picture of her as something other than a monster, because Andrea Yates was "very, very kind, loving, and sweet and nice and talented and smart and funny." Andrea Yates, they said, was all the right things.

Arnold thought back to Rusty Yates' visit to the store. *If I wanted to go to a store, my husband wouldn't go check it out first.*

She argued with herself. *Well, maybe he was just in the area, and he just wanted to pop by.* She tried not to read too much into it.

*   *   *

George Parnham, Andrea Yates' new attorney, was busy
researching his client and meeting with the press. "I've ac-
cumulated evidence in the last twenty-four hours that
strongly suggests that the mental status of my client will be
the issue, which means entering a not guilty plea by reason
of insanity," he told the *Houston Chronicle*.

CHAPTER 7

" 'I was a stranger, and you invited me in. . . . I was sick, and you looked after me. I was in prison, and you came to visit me.' " Byron Fike stood before his congregation and read from his preaching Bible with soaring voice.

He had arrived at his church early Sunday morning, June 24, 2001, to pray and figure out what he was going to say to his members. When he had walked into the sanctuary for its 10:30 A.M. worship service, Rusty Yates and two of his uncles sat in the pews. Fike had invited the congregation to open their Bibles to Matthew, Chapter 25.

" 'I tell you the truth, whatever you did for one of the least of these brothers of mine, you did for me. . . . Whatever you did *not* do for one of the least of these, you did not do for me. Then they will go away for eternal punishment, but the righteous to eternal life.' "

Fike turned to the parable of the Good Samaritan—a beaten and battered man found on the side of the road, ignored by the righteous, and comforted and aided by a despised Samaritan. He reminded his church that that parable began with the question, "Who is my neighbor?"

"Well, Russell and Andrea Yates are our neighbors," Fike told his congregation. "We are going to treat them as though Jesus Christ Himself were in our midst, because that's what Jesus told us to do. They've got a problem, and we can help them. And we're gonna do it."

As church ended and the worshippers began to meander

out the doors, they were met by a film crew hoping for one shot of Rusty Yates, the churchless Christian, leaving the house of God.

Fike stopped Yates and his uncles. "Why don't you stay for the visitor lunch?" It was a potluck lunch the church had every Sunday, provided by one of the women's Sunday school classes. Yates and his uncles accepted.

His big, blue-eyed, and handsome uncles talked about how they were coming together as a family. "Until this happened a couple of days ago . . ."

Rusty Yates stared at a table packed with children. He admitted that he couldn't sit at the table with the kids, watching them eat and goof off. Still, he rarely took his eyes off the children.

"We were going to have lots of kids," he said, "but I don't think we'll have any more children now."

After lunch, Fike met again with Yates to discuss the funeral. The service, they decided, would be limited to friends and family, because it was important to Rusty Yates that those attending the funeral would be people who knew his children. And finally, the funeral deal between Yates and Fike was finalized—Clear Lake Church of Christ was officially holding the services for Noah, John, Paul, Luke, and Mary Yates. It was then that Fike *knew* it was time to make a statement to the media.

Fike sat down at his computer, typed out the statement he'd made to his congregation, then called in his office manager.

"Okay," he said, "it's three-fifteen. Call the news media. Tell them I'll meet them at four o'clock outside the office, and I'll do a press conference."

Two local TV affiliates and *The Dallas Morning News* made it.

Fike read his statement. "We are going to serve [the Yates family] for no other reason than that they have a great need, and we can do some things to help them. Our Lord Jesus has helped each of us when we were in desperate need of Him. As His servants, we are going to allow His love to flow through us to help the Yateses." He continued, "In keeping with Jesus' teachings, we are going to serve them as if they were Jesus Christ Himself in our midst."

He announced that the Yates children's funeral would be held at the church and a visitation would also be held at the church on Tuesday, June 26, from six to eight in the evening. "There will be no cameras, video equipment, or any kind of recording device allowed at the visitation or funeral."

He spoke with the Dallas reporter, a young woman who'd been reared Catholic and had attended Fike's service that day, her first Protestant service. She asked Fike if he was going to be counseling Rusty Yates.

"Well, I don't do formal counseling," he answered. "What I do is help people know the Lord. I give spiritual direction, spiritual guidance."

When her article came out, Fike grinned—the reporter had written that he did "spirited" counseling. He later told a Colorado congregation, "We weren't real sure what that was, but we knew it was exciting."

Downtown, Andrea Yates' family visited and prayed with her.

"I think the devil's in me," she said. "How long do you think the devil's been in me?"

Monday morning, George Parnham was on CBS's *Early Show*, ABC's *Good Morning America*, and speaking with print reporters, already defending his client. "My observation is that she is still in a very deep psychosis," he said at CBS. "We are having her treated and examined by very professional mental health experts who care deeply for their patients."

To ABC, he said, "She is obviously very heavily medicated. I anticipate that eventually the medication she is on will kick in and there will be some ability to have a rational conversation with her. That moment in time has not arrived yet."

He told Reuters, "She's flat-lined, for want of a better phrase. Basically what my visitations consist of are unilateral conversations and observation." Psychosis, he added, was the only explanation for the crime. "That screams out as a logical reaction when observers see that a mother has taken the lives of five children and the mother by all objective evidence was a loving mother until she ventured into this black hole of acute psychosis."

He added at ABC, "We are in the process of gathering as much information as we can concerning her medical history." And he confirmed, "I do know that she has been under psychiatric care for some time . . ."

On Monday, Byron Fike knew it was "going to be wild from then on." Despite the fact that it was his usual day off, he occasionally phoned his office. It was crazy—all three church lines ringing incessantly. The media wanted him because most had missed his news conference, which was the way he had wanted it. By his own admission, Fike was scared that the media were going to twist his words and make them into something he hadn't said or meant.

The ministry to Rusty Yates, though, didn't daunt him— God was providing what he needed for that. Early Tuesday morning, Fike returned to his office and spent time in prayer, preparing for media interviews. And one verse out of Matthew 10 kept popping into his head as he prayed: "But when they arrest you, do not worry about what to say or how to say it. At that time you will be given what to say, for it will not be you speaking, but the spirit of your father speaking through you."

Byron Fike knew that Matthew 10 referred to words Jesus had spoken to His disciples, telling them they would be arrested and put on trial.

By then, Andrea Yates had spent nearly one week in the Harris County Jail.

"Lord," Fike prayed, with Jesus' words on his mind, "would You just give me the same promise? Would You make that true in my case, because I really don't want to go out there and speak based on me. I really want to portray You to the news media."

He got up, put a sign on his door that read "DND"—Do Not Disturb—and sat down to write the Yates children's funeral service. He yearned to write words that Rusty needed to hear. Fike wanted to give mourners permission to question God. Already, he and Yates had named the funeral service "From Tragedy to Triumph"—that was what they wanted to communicate to the people who came to grieve.

Andrea Yates was hearing the words of Satan, emanating from her cell's cinderblock walls.

Tuesday afternoon, Byron Fike did a couple of radio interviews and sat down again with Rusty Yates and prayed. Yates wanted to deliver his children's eulogies himself. He remembered how the minister eulogizing his father hadn't known the man. Rusty didn't want that happening to his own children. That's why he had to do his kids' eulogies.

At 2 P.M., the children's caskets were delivered to the church, in preparation for that evening's visitation. After praying with Fike, Rusty Yates, for the first time, spent time with his deceased children.

At 2:46 P.M., George Parnham, and his new partner on the case, attorney Wendell Odom, stood before Judge Belinda Hill, a former prosecutor. Next to the defense lawyers were the district attorneys, Joe Owmby and Kaylynn Williford.

The *Houston Chronicle* had reported that "prosecutors had not yet decided whether to pursue the death penalty against Yates, but legal experts say they could have difficulty doing this if her husband opposes it, as he had done so far."

While Andrea Yates remained in her psychiatric jail cell, the opposing attorneys stood before the judge for the entering of her ruling on the gag order requested by Yates' court-appointed lawyer, a gag order Parnham and Odom opposed. But they already knew the answer. They'd been before Judge Hill earlier in the morning and had been told her ruling; the press had reported it, too.

The judge issued the gag order saying, "This court has a duty to preserve the defendant's right to a fair trial by an impartial jury and, if possible, to ensure that potential jurors will be not prejudiced by pre-trial publicity."

Her gag order specifically emphasized the "counsel's willingness to give interviews" as the problem. But she included in her gag order not only the attorneys, but their staffs, law enforcement officials, and witnesses.

By then, Houstonians and Americans were grabbing up copies of *Newsweek*. A portrait of the Yates family was on its cover with the headline, " 'I Killed My Children.' What Made Andrea Yates Snap?"

In the story, Officer Frank Stumpo, the cop who'd driven Andrea Yates to HPD headquarters, was quoted as saying he'd offered Rusty Yates a glass of water as the grieving father had stood outside 942 Beachcomber on Wednesday, June 20. "Rusty replied that a glass of water would be nice, but that he doubted anyone would find a clean glass in the house. Stumpo looked around anyway, and couldn't find one—until Andrea calmly pointed him to the china cabinet."

George Parnham had told the *Houston Chronicle*, "I find it curious that the police would leak such statements to the media, particularly prior to even the children's funeral." He added, "This was obviously done to affect the credible development in the public's eye and taint a fair adjudication of a possible insanity defense."

But with Judge Hill's gag order, George Parnham and a grieving Rusty Yates were prevented from rebutting the police leaks. Andrea Yates, the police said, had head lice and was treated for sores on her head. Andrea Yates, her husband wanted to say, did not have head lice. Noah Yates, he wanted to say, was not the type of boy who would have disobeyed his mother and forced her to chase him through the house.

Subpoenas were issued for Andrea Yates' medical records from Devereux Texas Treatment Network and Dr. Mohammad Saeed, ordering Saeed and Devereux Custodian of Records Beverly Bedard to turn over those records to attorney John V. O'Sullivan, and additionally ordering the two to appear before the 230th District Court on Tuesday, July 3, 2001.

Afternoon melted into evening, rain began to pour, and family, friends, and co-workers slowly began arriving at the Clear Lake Church of Christ, passing through a gauntlet of volunteers asking the visitors who they were and why they were there. They simply wanted to protect Rusty Yates and his children.

Byron Fike stood near Yates, ready to assist the young NASA engineer. But as he watched Yates, Fike noticed that Rusty was ministering to the visitors, not vice versa. Believing that Yates didn't need him, Fike walked to the far back of the long building, where his church was sheltering the media from the storm.

"That's just part of what I do," he told reporters. "I really try to help them find God in their grief."

He was asked what he was going to say at the funeral.

His message, he said, was going to be hope in the resurrection of Jesus.

Quietly, a reporter asked Fike if she could go into the sanctuary—where the family, visitors, and caskets were.

"Why do you want to go in there?" he asked, protectively.

"I just want to pray."

"I'll escort you in there. But you can't talk to the family."

The reporter sat in the back of the sanctuary and prayed, then asked Fike if she could see the children. The minister walked her down to the front of the church and to the open caskets. Tears welled in her eyes. Fike walked her out.

Unknown to Fike, standing in the foyer of the church, unwilling to go in and look at the children, was another reporter, Ruth Rendon, accompanying her friend, bookstore owner Terry Arnold.

Arnold moved up the aisle to get one last gaze at her favorite little customers. John, Paul, Luke, and Mary all seemed at peace, as though they were sweetly sleeping. Noah didn't. He was more discolored than his siblings and looked anxious in the face.

Arnold pictured him frantically racing through the house for his life. She wondered if the anxious look she saw was the same look of anxiety he'd worn on the morning of June 20. She thought of how he always looked happy in her store. He appeared so different now. It really bothered her.

She shook her head trying to get his anxious, discolored face out of her brain. But it wouldn't leave. And the caskets were just so little. She tried not to think about it. But the sadness washed over her like a stain.

She saw Byron Fike's distraught wife and tried to comfort her.

Liz Fike confessed that the whole event had been odd for them—they'd thought Rusty Yates would need a lot of help from them. Instead, he had spent his time comforting them and explaining things to them. They—the Fikes— were impressed by Yates' deep faith and spirituality, she told Arnold. "He's a rock."

Arnold walked over to Rusty Yates. "I'm sorry for your loss," she said to the young father. "We really enjoyed seeing Andrea and the children in the store. If you need anything . . ."

"Thank you," he answered, and said that Andrea enjoyed going to the store, too. He briefly looked Arnold in the eyes and said, "When was the last time that she was in?"

"It was about two weeks ago, before this happened."

"That's interesting." And he walked away.

* * *

Terry Arnold moved over to a NASA engineer she knew. "How well did you know him?" Arnold said, glancing at Rusty Yates.

"Not well," the engineer answered. Later he told her, "Nobody knows him very well. He stays to himself."

Arnold looked around the church. No one but church members wearing volunteer stickers seemed to be at the visitation. *Did they not have any friends?* she wondered. *You would think there'd be masses of people here. Didn't anybody care about these people, these kids?* It left her silent with sadness.

But Dianne Clements of Justice for All, a victim's rights and pro–death penalty group, was not silent. "Rather than being outraged and up in arms, her family and neighbors are going on and on about how lovely she is. How lovely is a woman who murders her five children and chased the seven-year-old and dragged him back?" she ranted to the press.

Rusty Yates couldn't respond. While at the church for his five dead children's visitation, he'd been served with the gag order.

CHAPTER 8

The coastal Texas morning seared hot, humid, and hazy with pollution. It was the kind of June 26 where sweat rings develop on crisp, white shirts by simply standing in one place for too long. Volunteers from the Clear Lake Church of Christ eased from one end of their black-topped parking lot to the other as if simply trying to stay in motion, to stir up a breeze and stay fresh . . . or to keep grief a few safe steps behind. They were there to direct funeral traffic.

Already, five black hearses were parked close to the sanctuary. Press photographers in jeans and sneakers watched them, tried to ignore them, stared at them, tried to act as though this were just another gig . . . not the story of five tiny, white coffins filled with children drowned by their depressed mother's hands. The photographers maneuvered their heavy equipment from one location to another, searching for the best shot.

Women dressed in black, and with heads down, strolled into the church. Tan-legged cops in shorts nervously strolled outside. A white-T-shirt–clad man wheeled up in a small pickup truck. He stepped out of his vehicle, put on a crisp, white shirt, and tucked it into khaki pants. "Are you a family member?" he was quickly asked. "Yes."

Fat drops of water wept from trees protecting the neighboring back yards from the asphalt lot. The yards were filled with swing sets that sat silent. The parking lot was edged with television satellite trucks that hummed incessantly, their noise broken only by the occasional bark of a dog.

Across the street, a woman carried out her garbage. A few blocks away, children played basketball. Life went on ... for many. At the Yates house, flowers, balloons, toys, sympathy cards, and pamphlets about depression surrounded the tree that had become a shrine to the dead children. A TV crew knocked on a neighbor's door and asked for one more interview.

A few blocks away, back at the church, the cops in shorts slowly gave way to cops in long, black pants ... or cops dressed in khaki slacks and white shirts and big, white cowboy hats. Anchormen and women primped while mourners walked past tan brick pillars tied with black bows, then moved down a church corridor past posters filled with Yates family snapshots. There was one photo of Andrea with her children, one of Rusty sleeping with a baby, and the rest were pictures of the kids, laughing, playing, smiling, being alive.

An usher scurried over to a woman carrying an infant. "There's a nursery," he emphasized. She smiled, in her dowdy, small-print flowered dress with a big white collar, and politely answered, "I'll need that when I nurse." She then walked into the sanctuary with her thin, gray-skinned husband and baby. Their older son had played with the Yates children in the home school T-ball league.

They sat down. She held her quiet child close to her bosom, and they stared at five small, white coffins, their casket lids flipped open wide like five long, exhausted yawns.

A cop walked by and his keys jangled noisily against hymns softly piped over the speaker system.

Angels, flowers, and ribbons with each child's name adorned the caskets, which were arranged in a semi-circle, almost as if they were risers for a children's choir about to perform. And promptly at 10 A.M.—seven days and ten minutes after Andrea Yates phoned 911—an *a capella* choir rose from the back pews of the church and began singing,

"Great is Thy Faithfulness" and "I Know Whom I Believed."

Ten minutes later, Rusty Yates slipped through a side door and viewed his children's bodies—so tiny that not even a nose peeked out from their white coffins. Before, during, and after the funeral, women of the Clear Lake Church of Christ gathered in a side room for a prayer vigil, praying for the family of Rusty Yates and the families of Clear Lake.

"My Jesus I Love Thee" and "Near to the Heart of God" the choir continued to sing.

Byron Fike stood and prayed. "Father, we approach Your throne today with great needs. Father, we need Your strength. We need Your insight. We need Your help."

He looked at the congregation. "The word 'tragedy' is an understatement for why we are here today . . . And when tragedy strikes, we turn to God and we ask, 'Why, God? Why did You let this happen?' . . .

"As terrible as today is, and it is terrible, it is not the end," he said softly. "There is a day coming," and his voice began to rise, "when every wrong will be made right. There is a day coming when the dead will arise. . . . And when Jesus returns, it will once again be 'very good.'

"But today, today, is not good. . . . But we hold on to hope—the last chapter has not yet been written . . .

"As Rusty and I talked about what we wanted to do in this service, we wanted to simply begin by addressing the horribleness of what has happened. And Rusty now is going to talk to you about his children. This is something very dear to his heart . . ."

Yates, slim and handsome in a dark suit and white shirt, stood before the congregation and softly began to speak. "This's gotta be the hardest thing I've ever had to do." He stopped to clear his voice, then continued. "I can't tell you everything there is to know about them, but I can give you just a little glimpse of who they were."

Yates looked heavenward, to a big screen that stretched above the caskets. A photograph of a grinning Noah appeared, his index finger outstretched and holding a bug, and Rusty Yates smiled.

"I'll just start with Noah and tell you a little bit about him. And I really, I was thinking about how I should present this, because we're at a funeral, we're mourning. But I was telling my relatives some stories over the dinner table the other night, and that's kind of how I'd like to be able to tell you these stories, you know. So if I say anything, you know, a funny story, don't feel too awkward about laughing . . . I'm just going to . . . spend a few minutes on each child . . .

"Noah, he's our first-born child . . ." Rusty looked into Noah's flower-adorned casket. The seven-year-old dead child wore a multi-colored sweater decorated with an emblem of a truck. "He's smart and very independent." He loved to play alone, do crafts, and draw, particularly rainbows. "He's probably drawn over a hundred rainbow pictures."

Noah could take a trip to Wendy's, dig out the free toy, play with it for ten minutes, then start taking it apart . . . only to put it back together again, all by himself. Yates reflected the pride of a father perceiving his child following in his engineer's footsteps.

The seven-year-old had a book that played music, but he didn't like the quality of the speaker. So he took out the speaker, got another talking book, took out its speaker and installed it in the first book . . . by using a hot-glue gun for a soldering gun. The hot-glue gun, Rusty smiled, was all Noah's idea.

He spoke of how Noah loved to watch *Who Wants to Be a Millionaire?* and *Scooby-Doo*. One evening, he said, when it was way past Noah's bedtime, Noah wanted to watch the movie *Air Bud*. Yates said no. Noah begged, and finally bargained—if he could answer a question about the U.S. Presidents, he could stay up and watch the video.

"And I thought to myself . . . I'll just pick the absolute hardest question . . . and he'll get it wrong and have to go to bed." He asked Noah when President James Garfield was

born. "And just before I could hardly get the sentence out
of my mouth, he said . . . '1831.' He had a big smile on his
face." Noah had learned the date by studying a placemat on
the table with information about the Presidents.

"This picture here, that's him. He was a very gentle boy."
Noah loved to collect bugs, everything from bumblebees to
frogs. His father spoke of a trip they'd taken to Florida, with
a bug jar containing a caterpillar in their vehicle. That photo,
Yates said, was Noah with *the* caterpillar. And as they
drove, Yates heard "my wife and Noah and everybody" yelling, "It's coming out! It's coming out!" The caterpillar
hatched into a butterfly that they soon set free.

Yates stared into Noah's casket. "That's kind of the way
I feel about Noah. It's time to set him free." He touched his
child's coffin. "I love you," he softly spoke.

The father crossed over to John's casket, looked in, and
then reached toward him. John, who wore an orange-and-
black sweater, was a "rough-and-tumble kind of guy" who
loved to roughhouse, play T-ball in a home school league,
and had a contagious smile with a gap between his teeth.
Whereas Noah had a rattle that he loved to caress, John
threw his rattle across the room. John, he said, made friends
easily and loved to have his brothers around. "Can Noah
go? Can Paul go?" He patted John's coffin. "I love you,
John."

Four blue balloons, and one pink one, flew behind Paul's
coffin. Yates gazed into Paul's casket, looked as though he
were touching him, and wept, "Paul, he was just the . . .
Paul, you know, perfect, precious Paul."

Three-year-old Paul was the only boy in the bunch who
loved to hug, Yates said, and because of that, all the other
children wanted to be with him and share his bunkbed.

"He was also the best behaved of the children . . . you
just ask him to do something once and he just did it from
then on. It's like, my wife asked him to close the bathroom

door when they left, 'cause we had a little safety lock on there, and no one did it except Paul."

Yates once asked Noah who was the best behaved and Noah answered Paul, followed by himself.

"The cutest thing that I remember about Paul is this." The father held up a tiny, worn T-shirt and showed it to the congregation. Imprinted on its front was a moose with outstretched, hugging legs. "Bull Moose," said Yates, was Paul's nickname. Paul had picked up the name after he'd read a story about a caboose that chose to live in a tree. Then they found the moose T-shirt at a garage sale. And thereafter, they had to wash it every day for Paul to wear—it was Paul's favorite.

He smoothed his hand over Paul's coffin. "I love you, Bull Moose."

He stepped back over to Noah, looked at him, then moved to Luke. Luke was the kind of guy to take what he wanted, Yates recalled. "I remember sitting in the hallway when he couldn't even walk, and he tried to get by me. . . . He was going to get by whether he'd push me or poke me in the eye, whatever he needed to do . . ." And because of that, Rusty Yates called his son Luke, "Bulldozer."

He was also the child who had trouble with boundaries and couldn't sit still. Yates recalled taking all five children to a T-ball game, when Andrea was in the hospital, and instructing Paul and Luke to sit in the bleachers, while he coached Noah and John, and a woman watched Mary, who was crying. For an hour and fifteen minutes, Paul quietly sat in the hot sun. "Every time I'd look over there," Yates smiled, "Paul was just perfectly still. . . . Luke . . . he had his hand on the bleachers and that's the last he saw of the bleachers."

Each morning, Luke got his bowl, his spoon, and his cereal, climbed up in his chair, and waited for someone to come pour his milk for him. "He'd do everything he could himself."

He truly thought he was ten feet tall and could make the

tallest basket in basketball, despite the fact that he was only
two years old. One night, he reached up to the bright, full
moon, believing he could touch it.

Luke had penetrating eyes, Rusty said. The father talked
about his own trouble making eye contact with people, but
he could get lost as he gazed into Luke's eyes, making him
forget the very words he needed to speak.

He gazed at and touched his dead children, then looked
up at the mourners as a slide of Mary flashed on the screen.
"Andrea asked me about kids. . . . We agreed to, you know,
just to have how many ever came along. And she said to
me, 'Do you want boys or girls?' And I said, 'Well, I want
to get a basketball team, then we'll talk about girls.'

". . . When Andrea was carrying Mary, I thought, 'Man,
it's another boy,' because I just pretty much thought that
was all we would ever have. . . . And when Mary came out,
I was like, 'Wow!' you know. I was just stunned."

Six-month-old Mary rested in a pink sleeper with roses
embroidered on the front. Pink roses draped over her casket.
"I didn't know what to do. . . . I hadn't been around girls
very much," he said. "But with this tragedy, I'm just thank-
ful that I had a little girl, you know, and spent time with
her. She was so sweet."

Mary had an open-mouth grin and would lean forward
to kiss her daddy. Yates looked down at the note cards he
held in his hand. He seemed to search in his mind for a
story he could tell about his only daughter.

Slowly, he told of going grocery shopping with the children while Andrea was in the hospital. The rule was that
each child had to have a hand on the cart. So as Mary rode
in the cart, with two boys on either side, each with a hand
on it, Yates recalled, "It reminded me of those scenes where,
you know, the men are carrying, like, a princess . . . It
looked like Mary was a little princess." The memory
brought a smile to his face.

"They were really happy kids." He told stories of games
he played with the children. He talked of how he spent every

spare minute he had with them. "It wasn't like they were just generic children that happened to be mine. I mean, they were my friends."

He looked up at the screen, waited for a slide of Mary to go off, and a verse from Matthew to fill it.

"I'm going to say goodbye to the children." Yates reached for a stack of baby blankets. Breaking down, he prepared to place a blanket in each child's coffin. Noah had given his "blankie" to Mary, Yates explained. "But I remember it being his, so you can take it back, Noah."

The father's sobs echoed through the church, driving some mourners from the church in tear-stained rushes. "I'll miss you so much. I love you. Goodbye." Words choked in his throat. "Thanks for everything we did together." He cried more. "Bye-bye, Noah. You're in good hands, now."

He moved to Luke and pulled out "Dim-Dim," Luke's favorite blanket. "Rest in peace, Luke. Rest in peace." Again, the father's words choked and were indiscernible, but the anguish was clear. "I love you. I hope to see you again."

Yates turned to Mary, as more big tears flooded his heart. He paused lengthily and sniffled continually trying to compose himself. The congregation tried the same.

"This is Mary's little blankie," he said, holding it up for the mourners to see. It was a loosely crocheted baby blanket. "She was so cute, because she loved this blankie. Her little toes used to slip through it."

He was silent for a moment.

"Goodbye, my little princess. I'm sorry we didn't get to know each other better. Sorry I didn't see you grow up. I love you. Rest in peace, my little girl." More tears and sniffles emanated from the father, followed by a deep sigh. The casket was closed.

"Paul never seemed to have his own blanket." In fact, despite the fact that he wasn't attached to one, there always seemed to be blankets floating around, one of which would land in his bed. "You're such a good boy. You're the best," he wept. And his voice squeaked as he repeated, "You're the best." He sobbed, "I hope to see you again.

"Precious John," he choked. "You had the biggest smile. I love you. I'll miss you," he wept. "See you in heaven." And Rusty Yates cried. He would not let go of the little children who had already left.

"I just enjoyed them immensely," he said.

He took moments to compose himself.

"I want to share something with y'all. . . . This is a time that you really, you know, you lose faith in God. And it's a time where . . . how could God let this happen?" He spoke of when his father died when he was a teen. "I didn't blame God, I just thought, I didn't understand, you know, at the time the Spirit comforted me. I didn't have any scripture to go on, or anything like that. I just knew that in some strange way it was for the best. I didn't really understand why."

Still sniffing back tears, Yates pointed to Matthew 10:29. "It makes it . . . clear the love God has for everybody. I mean, think about that. It says Jesus said that, 'Are not two sparrows sold for a cent? And yet not one of them will fall to the ground apart from your Father.' Think about that, a little bird, you know. And look at us compared to birds, you know. . . . It says the very hairs on your head are all numbered. You know, I work with numbers and that's hard to imagine, right?" He continued, "And He says, don't fear."

His words were fast, his sniffles persistent. "And that's the perfect thing. I look at these children, and I know that God cares for each one of these kids. And as parents, you know, you train 'em and teach 'em, and live with them, and you do all you can, and it takes some comfort in knowing that they're in His hands."

But Rusty Yates posed the question everyone asked. "How can this be? How can this be? But this verse says, hey, it's okay not to understand." He explained, "My thoughts are not your thoughts. My ways are not your ways"—we, as humans, worry about little things on Earth that are not important to God.

And Rusty Yates rapidly mumbled on. "If we follow Him . . . if we love Him . . ." But soon the young man broke down again, his voice squeaking. "This is hard for me to read." He read Job 1:21—"The Lord gives, and the Lord takes away." "I read it the other day and started crying." He wept more. And, he said, "If the Lord giveth and the Lord taketh away, that's exactly what He's done. He gave me all of these children and now He's taken them away."

He turned to his audience, and said, "Blessed be the name of the Lord. Trust in Him. Thank you."

And as the service closed, the choir sang the words, "How I love you, child. How I love you . . ."

Mourners walked out the door to their vehicles, some exiting to the Catholic church where those not going to the graveside service had been told to park. Those going to the cemetery climbed into their trucks and cars, parked headlight to taillight, as church members had expected a standing room only crowd.

But there had been space enough for more mourners and cars alike. Only a few NASA co-workers had shown for the funeral. Many of the NASA women had boycotted it.

CHAPTER 9

Car and truck engines were turned on, and air conditioners were revved to high in an attempt to keep the sticky Houston air at bay. Reporters who'd sneaked into the funeral service—a few had been invited—sat in their cars busily scribbling their stories. Carbon monoxide fumes choked the sky, already gray with smog.

The funeral procession finally began its measured drive down El Dorado Boulevard, passing emaciated pine trees trying to thrive in the median. Shopping housewives stuffing groceries into their cars stopped and looked up, their faces lined with sorrow. Workers grabbing a fast burger at McDonald's, or doing a quickie oil change at the lube store, also stopped, moved toward the street, and watched.

Helicopters hovered in the haze. Motorcycle cops raced up and blocked passing motorists trying to go about their normal lives. A few drivers glowered and tried to flit out into the procession. The cops glared back, forcing the drivers into their places. Most, though, sat patiently, respectfully. Road crews silenced their machinery, took off their hardhats, and stared, their lips a straight line of pain.

And still, the helicopters buzzed overhead. The processional eased left onto Interstate 45, completely stopping traffic that normally sped toward Galveston. Not a single car tried to dart forward. Just an exit or two down, the funeral cars left the freeway, then turned right and into the Forest Park East Cemetery in Webster, Texas. At the entrance, motorcycle officers stood by their bikes, their helmets over their hearts, and tears in their eyes.

The family and friends gathered beneath an awning, the heat and humidity as thick as the clouds that were beginning to form above. Yards away, photographers stood beneath their own awning, quietly stretching for pictures of Rusty Yates touching his children's caskets.

Byron Fike stood beside the children and said, "If we only have hope in this life, we are to be pitied above all men." It was from I Corinthians 15.

He read Psalm 23. "The Lord is my shepherd . . ."

And the people sang, "Jesus loves the little children, all the little children of the world . . ."

Slowly they left, easing back into their air-conditioned cars, leaving a few photographers and funeral workers behind. The photographers aimed their cameras at the white caskets and flowers as backhoes began to dig the children's graves. One photographer shook her head. Reporters, she said, walked out of the viewing of the babies' bodies on Tuesday night, their faces white.

A funeral worker in a dark suit stopped, and also shook his head. He'd been in this business his whole life, he said, and this was the first time he couldn't handle it—he'd had to walk out of the funeral when Rusty Yates had started placing the children's blankets in their coffins.

Later that day, the Kennedy family visited Andrea Yates in the county jail. She stared into the eyes of her brother, Andrew, who lived just minutes from the Yates house, and her sister, Michele Freeman, who lived in Georgia. When they looked back into her eyes, she seemed, Michele said, "like she's a million miles away."

Finally, Andrea asked if there had been a funeral.

When they responded yes, she just nodded.

Freeman didn't think her sister understood what she'd

done. "She was crying for help, but she couldn't speak. We miss our sister very much," she later said.

Patrick Kennedy, Andrea's brother who lived in California, explained, "There was just a blackness in her eyes. I don't know if she was there or in her heart, but from what I saw in her eyes and the response I got from her is that she is just not there." He spoke of her suicide attempt after her fourth child. "That same person was back again, the darkness, no response . . ."

TV reporters stood near the Yates home for their 10 P.M. newscasts discussing the rumor, which was false, that Andrea Yates was pregnant with their sixth child. Still lying on the ground behind the reporters were flowers, balloons, toys, candles, and poems in memory of the children, and pamphlets and brochures on depression and postpartum depression in memory of their deaths.

"Rusty Yates is going to see his children again, and that's the triumph of the situation, in spite of the tragedy," Byron Fike later spoke. "God knows how to turn tragedy into triumph. He did it through His own son, who died on the cross and rose on the third day. And He's gonna do it for each of us, too."

That night, after the 10 P.M. newscasts were off the air and their cameras and lights were finally switched off, Rusty Yates walked into the humid night, stood on his driveway, dribbled his basketball, and shot basket after basket. His neighbors peeked behind closed curtains and watched.

Newsweek asked Brian Kennedy, the brother who considered himself closest to Andrea, about his family's opinion of Rusty Yates. "I'd like to say some things, but the truth will eventually come out," he answered.

Tracy Alverides read Brian Kennedy's statement; she also read Officer Frank Stumpo's comment that Rusty Yates "doubted anyone would find a clean glass in the house." It was a comment that made her stop, just as it had many women in the Clear Lake area. *If you can find a clean glass in the house.* She simply couldn't see her friend from high school and church being sarcastic like that. *Did Rusty change over the years? What happened? After all, people can change*, she thought. But she couldn't see him changing that way. She focused on the fact that Brian Kennedy didn't explain what he meant.

Thursday, June 28, 2001, TV viewers across America woke to Andrew Kennedy and Michele Freeman.

"My sister was a very good mother, and I'm kind of confused," Andrew Kennedy said on CBS's *Early Show*. "I knew something was wrong, but, you know, I tried to talk to her and ask her, 'Is everything OK?' and she'd say, 'Fine.' But . . . I could tell by looking at her that it wasn't OK."

Michele Freeman admitted that depression ran in the family—she and two of her three brothers were on antidepressants. "I just want everybody to know that it's time for us to start observing people with signs of depression. My co-workers . . . noticed the change in me, and they supported me."

In her slow Southern accent, she continued, "If you see signs of depression . . . ask and promote . . . any kind of support you can."

At MSNBC, Andrew and Michele clasped hands as they spoke, both looking as though they needed the support. Michele was pale and appeared still in shock. "She was the perfect mother," she said of Andrea. "As a sister, I often admired and looked up to her as a mother of four myself."

She went on, "It was kind of a joke around here. We'd say, 'When are you going to stop having kids?' " She added, "We all were concerned about her being pregnant again, because we wanted to see her get better after . . . she had tried to commit suicide." And she said, "She was trying to be a good wife."

Their sister, they'd learned, had been suffering much

longer than they knew—she'd been treated for depression
back in the days when she worked as a nurse. In the last
months, though, they'd noticed her becoming more and
more reclusive.

"She had those blank looks on her face, and she had a
look in her eyes that looked like she was," Andrew Kennedy's voice choked with weeping, "looking for help or
something." He explained further, "We could tell by looking
at her that she wasn't doing fine. She'd lost weight. She
hadn't laughed in at least a year. Not once."

And each child she had, Andrew said, placed more pressure on her.

"We are looking into other factors," Michele noted.

They'd call the Yates home, trying to check on their sister, but often their calls went unreturned. "We're trying to
find out all that went on," Andrew said. He wasn't sure how
much support Rusty Yates gave Andrea.

"There are many factors to this situation," Michele
pointed out. "The medical field, yes, I agree, did not ag-
gressively treat my sister."

By that afternoon, the media blitz was all but over for Byron
Fike. He was the featured guest on a radio interview with
folks from the Reverend Billy Graham's organization. For
Fike, it wasn't the funeral that was tough; it was dealing
with the media . . . and the angry public.

His church was inundated with rageful emails. Those
emails were from people who had no hope through Jesus
Christ, the pastor believed.

To him, serving the Yates family was no more, and no
less, important than serving any other family; it just got
more press because, in his words, the world deemed it was
very important. "What God wants," he later preached, "is
people who are faithful, not people who are out to make
headlines."

But the headlines didn't stop. No matter how desperately
the Kennedy family wanted to quietly mourn, the media

were constantly banging on their doors and ringing their phones. There were at least twenty interview requests a day. At Andrea's mother's house, a note was tacked on the door, politely pleading with reporters to let them grieve.

But Andrew Kennedy spoke to *The Dallas Morning News*. "You could tell things weren't right. She stopped eating. She got real skinny for at least the last six months. . . . She got so that her milk dried up, and she couldn't breastfeed Mary."

A friend became so concerned, he said, that she began keeping a diary of Yates' decline. "She begged Rusty . . . 'You need to get her more help.' " So, Rusty Yates put his wife in Devereux Treatment Network, for the second time.

That friend, who was not identified in *The Dallas Morning News*, was Debbie Holmes—"Andrea! Andrea! Call me! Call me! It can't be you!" They'd been nurses together at M. D. Anderson.

Andrew Kennedy also told the *News* that for several years Andrea and Rusty had been involved with an out-of-state religious group, which the couple supported with financial contributions. Six months before the children's deaths, Andrea had asked that proselytizing information be sent to her family. The information was sent, and it condemned her faith of origin, Catholicism.

"To me, it was kind of a cult religion," Kennedy said. "They believed in God, but they made statements that, like, 'Catholics were going to hell.' It had some stuff from the Bible. . . . But there was something about it all that just wasn't right." It caused conflict between the families.

Kennedy closed, "I would like for Andrea to get the help she needs. I think with God's help and people helping out, she'll get better." And he added, "I don't think it would do society good, or my family or Andrea any good, to execute her."

At Hair Innovations salon, the salon Andrea Yates had visited, Dawn Helman's customers were gossiping. The kids all had Biblical names, one client pointed out. Noah, from the Bible, he said, survived the greatest flood of all time. Noah Yates, he correlated, was killed after a great flood in Houston. Noah Yates, he stated, was the last and hardest to kill.

An attorney client of Helman's said she knew the Yateses and they were "weird." All Rusty Yates wanted to do, she said, was reproduce. And the kids weren't allowed out of the house.

Another customer said she worked with Yates, and she wondered if the murders were planned by Rusty Yates planting ideas in his wife's head.

Many women at NASA didn't like Yates, mothers gossiped a few blocks away. They said he made offensive comments to them—why aren't you home, you should be home where you belong.

Some of those women were in counseling, trying to learn how to deal with and speak to Yates upon his return to work. "If I have to say to him, 'I have to go home to take care of my kids,' how do I . . ."

A few more blocks away, at a more upscale hair salon on Bay Area Boulevard, hairdressers and customers were busy rattling on about Yates, as well. Once around April, a second time around May, the NASA engineer had walked into the salon and gotten his hair cut, without an appointment.

"Are you married?" the hairdresser had asked him.

"Yes," Yates replied.

And that was all he said . . . in the salon, where crosses decorated its walls and where a small TV constantly hummed with cartoons.

Rusty Yates didn't get his hair cut professionally, a supporter of Andrea Yates vehemently retorted. He *made* Andrea cut his hair, and her hands shook when she did, because she was so scared she was going to mess up, he said. Karin Kennedy, Andrea's mother, had told him that.

CHAPTER 10

Terry Arnold talked with people who were involved in the same T-ball team as the Yates kids. They knew Rusty Yates had shown up at a few games without his wife, but they didn't know she was in the hospital. If they'd known, they said, they would have tried to help.

She checked with the Sagemont Baptist Church home school support group, of which Andrea Yates was supposedly a member. Yates and her children had attended only a couple of field trips. No one had talked to her more than, "Hi, nice to see you. Have a good time."

In fact, they had such little conversation with Andrea that no one could remember how she had gotten involved in the group. She just appeared to have shown up one day and seemed "just like anyone else."

Arnold debated in her mind whether to contribute to the memorial fund that Elizabeth Quigley had set up to help cover funeral expenses. But she wanted to know what happened to any excess dollars that might be raised beyond the funeral expenses. She called Sterling Bank, the keepers of the fund, and asked. All excess dollars defaulted to Rusty Yates, she was told.

The knowledge that the fund defaulted to Yates bothered Arnold. She'd set up funds before. And prior to their creation, it was established that any excess dollars went to a designated and named charity.

*   *   *

Monday, July 2, 2001, was Andrea Yates' thirty-seventh birthday. Normally, when her birthday rolled around, she started kidding her husband about being married to an older woman. There was no joking in 2001.

The following day, Dr. Mohammad Saeed, Andrea Yates' former psychiatrist, and Beverly Bedard, custodian of records at Devereux Texas Treatment Network, her former psychiatric residence, appeared before Judge Belinda Hill. Yates' Devereux medical records were turned over to prosecutors and defense attorneys.

Additional subpoenas for medical records were issued to Karen Conway, custodian of records for Memorial Hermann Prevention & Recovery Center in Houston, and, again, to Dr. Saeed, ordering Saeed and Conway to deliver admission forms, nurses' notes, physicians' orders, progress notes, psychiatric reports, psychological testing medication reports and logs, discharge summaries, and more to George Parnham. The two were additionally ordered to appear before Judge Hill on July 24, 2001.

That same afternoon, Yates' attorneys, Parnham and Odom, filed a motion in the 230th District Court of Harris County, Texas, requesting a competency hearing for their client. The defendant, they said, presently had "neither sufficient ability to consult with counsel with a reasonable degree of understanding, nor a rational or factual understanding of the proceedings against her . . ."

Mental health experts agreed, the lawyers said.

In an attached affidavit, Odom wrote, ". . . Counselors have made numerous visits to Harris County Jail in order to consult with [Mrs. Yates] regarding the charges pending against her. Although Mrs. Yates, on many occasions, acknowledges my presence and can answer questions regarding routine matters, I have found her to be unable to consult with me . . ."

He added that Parnham and Yates' first attorney, Bob

Scott, had also been unable to consult with Yates "with a reasonable degree of rational or factual understanding . . ." and that mental and medical health science professionals "have expressed their belief that Mrs. Yates is incompetent to stand trial."

She had been "previously diagnosed as having a mental disease and defect diagnosed as a severe form of depression as well as postpartum depression with psychosis," he stated. ". . . Mrs. Yates is presently in a psychotic state and . . . would not be competent, presently, to stand trial."

He closed, ". . . With her history of mental illness and the bizarre nature of the offense with which she is charged, [the Defendant] has already raised the issue of incompetency for purposes of a hearing."

Three days later, in Laguna Niguel, California, a woman charged with trying to drown her twin babies pleaded guilty to child endangerment and was given five years probation.

"This is not a child abuse case. This is a postpartum depression case," Superior Court Judge Pamela Iles said at the sentencing. "We want to walk you through this nightmare you've been through."

As the defendant, Paula Thompson, stood before the judge, she carried in her purse the *Newsweek* with Andrea Yates' photo on the cover.

"I pray for her every night," Thompson said. "I know how she felt. It's an illness."

Thompson was sent to the University of California, Los Angeles, Neuropsychiatric Institute and Hospital for evaluation.

The same day Thompson was sentenced, Judge Belinda Hill of the 230th District Court of Harris County, Texas, ordered Andrea Yates to undergo a psychiatric exam to establish her competency to stand trial for capital murder.

"This isn't murder. It's the poor result of a psychotic state," said a man who was closely familiar with Houston's criminal justice systems. "Andrea is a sick puppy . . ." and then she killed her kids. "The system broke down," he ranted on. "That woman is nuts. I don't think she was sane on the day she did this. I don't care what the cops say."

The man suggested checking into D.A. Chuck Rosenthal.

Rosenthal and Yates attorney Parnham had faced off in a Houston courtroom in 1992. Rosenthal, then an assistant D.A., was prosecuting Calvin Bell, who shot and wounded two HPD officers at a local elementary school. Parnham successfully defended Bell on a not guilty by reason of insanity plea.

"Chuck plays to win," the man said, and he "hides" police reports.

Two and a half weeks after the Yates children were drowned, the defense still had not seen the statement Andrea Yates had given police on June 20, 2001.

The following week, the *Houston Chronicle* and Yates' attorneys Parnham and Odom filed briefs in the 14th Court of Appeals in Houston, Texas, trying to fight Judge Hill's gag order on the Yates case. The *Chronicle* attorneys argued that the gag order was unconstitutional, unnecessary, and could be replaced by less restrictive means of ensuring a fair trial.

Parnham and Odom declared that the order infringed on their client's rights. As Yates' attorneys, they wrote, they had "not only a right but, in fact, a duty to counteract what they perceive as false information concerning their client."

Whereas prosecutors Joe Owmby and Kaylynn Williford were neutral about the gag order on June 26, 2001, suddenly they had Scott Durfee, general counsel for the Harris County District Attorney's Office, fighting *for* the gag order. Durfee claimed that the *Houston Chronicle* had no standing in the case, had not appealed first to the trial judge, and that the gag order was justifiable.

Two days later, the Harris County Medical Examiner's Office released the autopsy reports of the five Yates children.

Each child suffered multiple bruises to the front of the hips from being held face down and repeatedly hitting a hard, flat surface, presumably the bottom of the tub. Additional bruising on the outsides of the arms and legs indicated that they were held down at their hips, backs, and the backs of their legs, as their arms and legs flailed for survival.

Seven-year-old Noah, the son who fought his mother, according to the police "leak," had the most prominent bruises of all the children on his hip bones, particularly his right hip bone.

There was also a bruise on his inside right knee, two bruises on his right leg, one on the back of his right leg, a bruise on the outside of his left knee, bruises on the front and inside left leg, outside left leg, and back of his left thigh toward his knee. The contusions on the back of his legs might have been from being pressed down at the back of his right leg and left thigh.

More contusions appeared on the back of Noah's left arm and shoulder, as if they had struck the tub. His left forearm and right elbow were bruised. There were bruises on the inside of his right arm, as if he had been grabbed hard.

Both of his hands showed a slight wrinkling from the water.

A green-yellow, one-week-old, two-inch–by–three-quarter-inch bruise marred his forehead. There was also a small scrape on the left side of the bridge of his nose.

He wore shorts and a T-shirt over multi-colored briefs, all of which were wet.

There was a fresh, purple-red bruise, 0.6 centimeters by 0.6 centimeters on the left side of five-year-old John's forehead. On his right upper leg, just below his knee, was a one-half-inch–by–three-eighths-of-an-inch contusion, another contusion on the right knee, and another on the right lower leg.

There was a yellow-tan-brown bruise on the upper right leg, its color indicating that it was an older injury, and a second older contusion on his left leg. At the funeral, Rusty Yates had described John as a "rough-and-tumble kind of guy."

Fresh, purple-red contusions and a scrape marred his left knee and leg, again from striking a flat, hard surface. There was also bruising on the inside of his left leg.

On the back of his left upper arm, near his left elbow, and on his right forearm close to his elbow, there were more contusions, presumably from his arms banging the inside the tub.

His hands had a "washer-woman effect," possibly from being in the water longer or from being wrapped in a wet sheet. He wore a long-sleeved pajama outfit that zipped up and was soaking wet. The five-year-old child also wore pull-up diapers decorated with Mickey Mouse and Pluto designs.

An HPD detective attending the autopsy collected a hair found between John's pajamas and diaper. Another hair was found in John's hand.

Three-year-old Paul had a small wound within a contusion on the inside of his lower right lip. It looked as though his mouth struck the tub knocking his lip into his teeth.

There were bruises on the front of his left hip, again indicating that he was drowned face down. There were more contusions inside the left knee, leg, and close to the ankle, and on the front of the left leg. On the right leg there were bruises just below the knee and closer to the knee.

A three-eighths-of-an-inch contusion stained his left forearm toward the elbow.

His left hand was wrinkled from the water, but his right hand wasn't.

"Perfect, precious Paul" wore white pajamas with black trim and fire engine designs over white briefs, with red-and-blue trim and green, red, and blue designs, not diapers like five-year-old John.

Like John, two-year-old Luke had a bruise on the left side of his forehead—near the hairline, close to where Terry

Arnold liked to swirl his natural pin curl. There were faint bruises on the right side of his chest between his armpit and breast and more bruises on his right knee, leg, and thigh and left knee and leg.

But on tiny Luke, the child his father described as one who could never sit still, there was a strikingly large five- to eight-day-old bruise, four and one quarter inches by seven-eighths of an inch, on his left thigh extending toward the left hip.

His right elbow had an older, scabbed over scrape and two fresh, small bruises. There were more new bruises on his right arm, right wrist, and left arm.

His small right foot was wrinkled from the wet, gray sock he wore. His left foot was not wrinkled because there was no sock. He also wore wet, heavy, soiled diapers covered by red shorts with a multi-colored T-shirt decorated with fire engines.

Six-month-old Mary suffered the fewest injuries. She had a contusion on the right side of her forehead, near her eyebrow, and a contusion on the upper portion of her right ear.

She was dressed in a one-piece, purple Carter outfit over a white, disposable diaper, all of which were wet.

Each child had a frothy, blood-tinged fluid coming from the nose and mouth, which was typical of death by drowning, and a result of water in their lungs. Contrary to popular lore, water in the lungs does not cause drowning. In fact, water blocked the children's airways, which caused their asphyxiation and drowning.

Rusty Yates told police and reporters that he had left the house around 8:50 in the morning on June 20. Each flailing child had to be held under water at least one to two minutes before losing consciousness, then held down for another four to eight minutes before actually succumbing to death by drowning. Six-month-old Mary would have taken even longer to die, because babies have less need of oxygen.

Andrea Yates phoned police at 9:52 A.M., almost one hour after her husband said he had left for work. In sixty minutes, Andrea Yates had allegedly grabbed five children, chased one of them down, according to police "leaks," and held them each under water for ten minutes or more.

About three weeks after the deaths of his children, Rusty Yates told Clear Lake Church of Christ members that he'd just moved back into the house after staying at his mother's apartment, and he was having a really hard time sleeping. With a distant look in his eyes, he said it'd been a really bad week. "Wednesday, I found out things I just didn't want to know." He didn't elaborate.

July 16, 2001, a few twigs and bagged leaves were left next to the curb of the Yates home. A neat row of dead potted florist plants edged the front flowerbed. The blue Suburban was parked in the driveway with space enough in front to shoot baskets. A brightly colored child's basketball goal still stood in place, next to the regulation height basketball hoop.

Houston Chief of Police C. O. "Brad" Bradford had issued a memo to every HPD employee warning them not to leak one word about the Andrea Yates case to any reporter, or anyone, for that matter—not spouses, relatives, friends, no one.

But officers were still leaking damning information. Baby Mary was in her bassinet on the floor next to the tub while each child was drowned. The children were laid shoulder to shoulder on the bed, their eyes open.

Weeks earlier, Dora Yates, Andrea's mother-in-law, had discovered Andrea filling the tub with water and had asked her why she was doing it. "Oh, we might run out of water. I just thought I'd fill it up," Andrea had answered to Dora, according to the investigator on the scene who knowingly spilled the information.

By then, Dr. Mohammad Saeed's office at 3723 Fatta Drive in Dickinson, Texas, had been vacated. When Andrea Yates had been his patient, her husband Rusty had driven

her to the office that was located off Interstate 45, not far
from their children's gravesites.

More women phoned Terry Arnold at HEP Bookstore, again
thanking her for speaking up, and also telling her that they
suffered postpartum depression and were "going to do something brave about it." Unlike Andrea Yates, these were not
women with large families, nor were they women who home
schooled their children.

On July 20, 2001, George Parnham and Wendell Odom filed
a motion in the 230th District Court requesting the grand
jury transcript of "any medical witness who testified" in the
case against Andrea Yates. The attorneys wrote, "The mental state of the Defendant, Andrea Pia Yates, is a paramount
issue that will be developed in both pretrial matters as well
as during the course of the trial on the merits itself.

"If there has been testimony presented to a grand jury
relative to any aspect of the mental stability of Andrea Pia
Yates at or about the time of the commission of the acts
made the basis of this allegation, this information could be
relevant to the defense of Mrs. Yates.

"The need for preserving the confidentiality of the Grand
Jury testimony is outweighed by the Defendant's need for
disclosure."

The grand jury had yet to render its decision regarding
Yates.

"This is a big case," said the man familiar with the inside
workings of the Houston criminal justice systems. "Chuck
Rosenthal is thinking, 'I've gotta look good. What's going
to make me look good?'

"I would not be surprised," he added, "if Rosenthal seeks
the death penalty against Andrea."

                        *   *   *

On Tuesday, July 24, 2001, Judge Belinda Hill ordered a third psychological examination of Andrea Pia Yates. It was due August 6, 2001, two days before her scheduled arraignment.

CHAPTER 11

At the Harris County Clerk's Office, Clear Lake branch, located just blocks from the Yates home, folks gossiped. One man raged about the evil Andrea Yates who coldly murdered her children.

A woman lowered her head and whispered, "I understand." She, too, she said, had suffered postpartum depression, had had bad thoughts about her children, and had heard voices and seen visions. She was doing okay, now, she said, because she was on medication.

Andrea Yates, she said, wasn't taking her medication. The woman who'd hosted the birthday party the weekend before the deaths was a friend of hers. And Rusty Yates had told the people at the party, she said, that Andrea wasn't taking her medicine. He'd also told them they wanted to have another child.

The partygoers thought that sounded a little weird, considering his wife wasn't with him because, according to him, she was depressed from having a baby.

Andrea Yates was the talk from therapist to therapist, therapist to client, and therapist to friend. No one could stop analyzing her. Women therapists in particular demanded that the focus switch from postpartum depression, to a look at the system—the family system, the church system, the marriage system, the justice system. "It is a system of oppression," stated one Clear Lake professor of psychology, who was also a mother.

Unless the therapists were psychologists for the prosecution, they seemed to be sympathetic to Andrea Yates.

"Clearly, she was psychotic," said Dr. Vincent Ruscelli, a psychologist in the Clear Lake Area. "She had a psychotic component to her depression. It would be diagnosed technically as a major depressive disorder. Recurrent because it's happened more than once. Obviously severe. With psychotic features and with postpartum onset . . ."

Ruscelli continued, "Usually, when they diagnose . . . postpartum depression, that's just kind of designating the onset of the depression. It has all the classic nature depressive characteristics, you know, the fatigue and a sense of worthlessness, and the emptiness, the sadness, suicidal ideation, thoughts of dying. Not fear of dying. And I think clearly she had to be hallucinating, perhaps delusional in her view of herself."

He began speaking about his own grandchild and how much energy he expended watching the three-year-old. "It doesn't matter how tired you are. You've gotta keep up. And I marvel at mothers who can take care of more than one child. And here's a woman who was overwhelmingly depressed. . . . And to think of her trying to manage five children, and home school the children, I just can't believe she could do it, even if she weren't depressed."

Andrea Yates wasn't simply watching five children. She was watching five children, three of whom were in diapers, including five-year-old John.

"That may be that she was discounting her ability as a parent because she wasn't even able to toilet-train her child," the psychologist said. "How couldn't she question her ability, being that depressed? Just trying to keep up, I'm sure she felt awful as a parent, because it sounds like she had very high standards for herself."

He mentioned a plaque he'd seen in the Yates house,

photographed in media reports. The plaque, he said, read "Blessed are the children."

"And the dad's focus was apparently, you take care of the children and forget about yourself. She may have been that type of individual anyway, a caretaker, a nurturing person, pleasing everybody else, and forgetting about herself in the process. I think that's a good way to end up depressed."

"I don't think [Rusty's] a sociopath. I think he's a denier. I read somewhere that he would get his kids to play little games to try to cheer her up. Well, you're not gonna cheer somebody up who's overwhelmed with depression..." You're particularly not going to cheer up with games someone who has the responsibility of caring for five small children. "Where would she rest? Where would she have any time for relaxation? Time for herself to go exercise or take a walk with friends or have lunch with friends? She was just totally isolated."

And echoing the sentiments of many female therapists, he noted, "She was going to conform to what his wishes were, and that's to keep those kids out of harm's way.... She had to subordinate her own needs for those of her husband's. Please everybody else and forget about yourself."

"I haven't heard great things about Devereux," he commented, despite the fact that it had a national reputation. "I've had some people go through there on substance abuse issues. I didn't feel they got good care." The evaluations were superficial, he said, and after the patients received the "superficial" evaluations, they were placed on medication.

"I blame that on managed care, personally. It used to be in the old days... you had to do very thorough evaluations—psychological testing, battery of tests, very thorough evaluations." He mentioned social histories on both sides of the family, questionnaires regarding behavior that parents and even teachers filled out, all of which took eight to ten hours to administer, interpret, and write up as a report at a cost perhaps of $130 an hour. "So it's very expensive."

The insurance companies, he said, no longer did that, and no longer paid for that. All they allowed, he said, was a two-session test as an evaluation. "Our tests are not so good that we can just give one or two of them and then make a diagnostic, because they all have a kind of low validity."

On July 30, 2001, the Harris County grand jury indicted Andrea Yates for "intentionally and knowingly" causing "the death of Noah Jacob Yates by drowning the complainant with a deadly weapon, namely water, and intentionally and knowingly" causing "the death of John Samuel Yates by drowning the complainant with a deadly weapon, namely water."

Additionally, she was indicted for "intentionally and knowingly" causing "the death of Mary [Deborah] Yates, hereinafter called the Complainant, an individual under six years of age, by drowning the complainant with a deadly weapon, namely water."

The charge on both indictments was capital murder. And, both indictments made Andrea Yates eligible for the death penalty—the first because she allegedly murdered more than one person, the second because she allegedly murdered someone younger than six years old.

Yates was not charged with the murders of John Samuel and Luke David because, according to prosecutors, their deaths would be brought out during the trial, anyway. According to other attorneys, she was not charged with those deaths in case prosecutors didn't win a conviction against her—it gave them fallback charges.

That same day, George Parnham and Wendell Odom filed a "notice of intent to offer evidence of the insanity defense." The notice stated that the attorneys had "received opinions from two psychiatrists who state that at the time of the offense the Defendant, Andrea Yates, was 'mentally insane' as that term has been defined in Section 8.01 of the *Texas Penal Code.*"

*   *   *

"She's clearly insane," psychologist Dr. Vince Ruscelli emphasized again, despite not being a witness for the defense. "You can't have that kind of history and all of a sudden—bam—you kill five kids. She's a nurse, and most nurses are pretty nurturing kinds of people, caretakers. And you don't just suddenly drown five kids. Something went wrong."

CHAPTER 12

About two weeks after the deaths of Noah, John, Paul, Luke, and Mary Yates, a NASA co-worker of Rusty Yates' sent out an email asking if anyone had any spare bedroom furniture. The email explained that Yates needed it to fix up an extra bedroom.

Some NASA employees and their spouses found the email offensive, as though Yates were calling in the interior decorators to fix up his bachelor pad. In fact, one NASA wife spoke of seeing Yates and two men lunching together less than a month after the deaths, laughing and talking "with no more gravity than if his wife had burned his dinner."

But most NASA workers kept their discomfort to themselves. The engineer who felt that Russell Yates was "probably half the problem" or "had a lot to do with what happened" didn't want to get caught expressing those sentiments to the worker who "had sympathy for him." The only thing they had in common was their mutual shock over the children's deaths.

So after a day or two of disbelief, the situation with Rusty Yates was rarely mentioned at NASA. Some feared they'd lose their jobs if they spoke. Others feared they'd be called to testify. They even consulted attorneys who advised, "Keep your mouth shut."

*　　*　　*

Thursday, August 2, 2001, the Fourteenth Court of Appeals denied the *Houston Chronicle*'s request to throw out the gag order in the case against Andrea Yates. In their opinion, written by Justice Charles W. Seymore, the court referred to the crime as "an undeniably tragic episode" that resulted in a "maelstrom of media attention."

The court stated that Judge Hill "initially was not inclined to grant a gag order." Instead, she "admonished counsel for both sides that she intended to try the case in court and not in the press. However, the parties evidently did not heed the warning . . .."

Seymore wrote that the *Houston Chronicle* had been present during the gag order hearing and had asked to be heard. "Judge Hill noted, however, that the Houston Chronicle was not a party to the criminal proceedings or to the gag order, and declined to entertain its objections at that particular time, stating she would visit with counsel after the hearing."

The Court of Appeals ultimately decided that Hill's gag order did not infringe upon the media's First Amendment rights of freedom of the press. Indeed, Seymore cited a Virginia case as proof: "The Court described that right, however, as only a right to sit, listen, watch and report. The press has no right to information about a trial superior to that of the general public." And, in citing a case against Warner Communications, Seymore additionally wrote, "In short, the media's right to gather information during a criminal trial is no more than a right to attend the trial and report on their observations."

Rusty Yates walked into the Clear Lake Church of Christ sanctuary with his mother, Dora. He wore a white, short-sleeved shirt and a telephone on his belt. He sat toward the front, in what had already become his usual spot.

Kids, wild, loud, and rowdy, ran up and down the aisles. Their parents, casually but well-dressed, went on about their business. The church was as full of worshippers as it had been on the day of the Yates children's funeral.

An announcement was made, asking members to pray for and minister to a family that had suffered death from another murder. They lived in the community of Friendswood, where Rusty and Andrea Yates had once lived.

In the church bulletin was a typed request to "continue to remember" in thought and prayer "Russell Yates."

Yates swayed nervously as he stood for the music. His hair appeared a bit grayer.

Ephesians, chapter five was read aloud—"Husbands, love your wives."

The Lord's Supper was offered. On that Sunday, August 5, 2001, the church with the tan brick walls and pine cathedral ceilings seemed a bit brighter than it had on June 27. Light shined through its stained-glass windows.

Byron Fike spoke of Psalms 90—"Make us glad according to the days Thou hast afflicted us, and the years we have seen evil. Let Thy work appear to Thy servants, and Thy glory unto their children." He read Numbers 27:12—"And the Lord said unto Moses, Get thee up into this mount Abarim, and see the land which I have given unto the children of Israel."

It was impossible to avoid the presence of children.

And the choir closed the service singing, "How I love you, child. I love you. How I love you, child . . ."—the same, last song they'd sung at the children's funeral.

Rusty Yates left the sanctuary with his mother, his head slightly bowed. He exited through the same door he'd entered on the day of the funeral.

They moved into the hazy, gray sunlight of summer and strolled toward his home, looking relaxed with each other. Suddenly, a hefty woman, perhaps his mother's age, sprinted in her heels for them and called out. Yates and his mother stopped, turned, and walked back to meet the woman. They chatted, they laughed, then headed toward home again. But one more time, a woman dashed up to them, this time in a car. Again, she looked to be about his mother's age. They chatted, they laughed, and the Yateses walked on home.

The day before Andrea Yates was scheduled to be arraigned in the 230th District Court of Harris County, a former co-worker of Rusty Yates sat down in a comfortable home, not too far from the Clear Lake Church of Christ and the Yates house. The co-worker, like so many in the Bay Area, didn't want anyone to know his name as he spoke about the now-childless father.

As another NASA employee, who lived even closer to Yates, had said, "It seems like a conflict of interest" to discuss Rusty Yates.

So, as teens filtered in and out of the house, the former co-worker promised to say only nice things. He first met Rusty Yates when the young Auburn student arrived at Johnson Space Center to work in the NASA cooperative program. The students who were selected for the program were bright, often a 3.5 grade point average or above, energetic, and loved to learn.

The norm for co-op students was to work three alternating school terms or semesters at NASA. The students were assigned a task, the man explained, "such as write a program, build a something, analyze a something, such as a part of the shuttle." At the end of the semester, the students went before their manager and gave a report, which resulted in a grade.

Most of the co-ops, as the man called them, who wanted a job with NASA were offered a job, unless there was a funding issue. Obviously, Rusty Yates accepted his offer and went to work full-time as a junior engineer, spending his early years in the space shuttle star-tracker area. "He seemingly did okay," the man reported. "He wasn't the brightest star."

But Rusty Yates was a man to himself, even then. If his supervisor asked him to do a task, he went off and did it. "He didn't complain. He wasn't a whiner."

The man had worked with Rusty, off and on for five or six years, including the time Rusty Yates married Andrea Kennedy. But the man never met the pretty brunette with the big smile. "I didn't know he had five kids until the tragedy."

The last time the man saw Rusty Yates socially was in mid-April 2001 at the recently opened Krispy Kreme doughnuts, not far from either of their homes. The man was there with his daughter, exiting as Yates entered.

"Hey, what are you doing here?" Yates said, amiably.

"Well, my daughter got free doughnuts for her report card," he answered, as Krispy Kreme rewarded students with a doughnut for every A they earned.

"Oh," Rusty replied, with a polite smile, "my wife is home schooling my oldest, and so he doesn't get a report card like the school district gives out." Then Yates added, "Maybe she should start giving report cards or something, so he could get free doughnuts."

The man didn't know that Andrea Yates was in and out of Devereux Texas Treatment Network. . . .

"He was a pretty quiet guy, to himself, you know." He then spoke of seeing Yates on TV and noted, "That pretty much portrays his demeanor at work. He's not one of these, you know, high-energy types. He was smart and knew what he was doing."

Yates could be funny, with a dry sense of humor, and he did his share of cutting up with the guys in the lab. "He liked to have a good time, laugh at the jokes. If something crazy happened in the lab that was funny, he would laugh." But no one can seemingly ever remember a funny thing Rusty Yates said. "He wasn't like the class clown. He wasn't anything like that. But when the situation would arise, he would laugh just like everyone else. Nothing bizarre. Nothing strange, back then."

On occasion, there'd be a quick, "Are you going to Tennessee?" Both men were from the Country Music State. And there'd be a, "Well, I'm going at Christmas," or Thanksgiving, or "My mom came here."

But Yates never really talked about his family . . . or anything personal, including his religion. Perhaps, the man said, they talked about sports. But there also wasn't time to socialize; the engineers had a schedule to meet and a job to do. Eventually, though, the men's jobs went in different directions, sending Rusty Yates to another building. "So I sort of lost track of him."

Sorrow, he said, was the reaction at NASA. They "feel bad for the guy. Here he lost all of his kids, and in essence his wife at the same time." It was the worst possible scenario, he said. "It's just been strange that people that knew him when he was in our building . . . they haven't been willing to say much about it."

But that, the man admitted, is the way NASA and even his neighborhood were. "We know everybody to a level, but we're not in their business every day. Some are more social than others, but at work, we're all there to do a job." There just isn't much social interaction, he explained. "We just don't do that. Everybody comes to work, does their job, and goes their various directions on nights and weekends."

Rusty Yates, the man stated, "was not any more of a loner than anyone else. He was not as boisterous as some of the others." There were some who were more social, but there were an equal number who were less social. "In his early years, I'd put Rusty in the middle. He wasn't a social butterfly, and he wasn't the 'close the door and don't bother me' type either. He was just an average guy."

He was Mr. DuPont High to Mr. Average Guy, who landed on the cover of *Newsweek* when his wife claimed, "I killed my children."

CHAPTER 13

Like seemingly every summer day in Houston, Texas, August 8, 2001, was hot, humid, with a chance of rain and a certainty of a hazy sky of smog. Around 8:25 A.M., Rusty Yates and his mother, Dora, parked in one of the cheaper lots in downtown Houston, blocks away from the courthouse, and began strolling to Andrea Yates' arraignment.

Rusty appeared comfortable in the morning humidity. He wore a white shirt with long sleeves, a blue tie, black slacks, and black shoes with flat, rubber soles that were silent with his steps. His mother, too, was in black pants, with a coordinating tan-and-black, short-sleeved top. She was easy with her son.

They walked toward the new criminal justice building, which should have housed Andrea's proceedings, but was closed due to the June flood damage, then turned at its corner toward the makeshift courthouse, still a couple of blocks away. Days earlier, it had been evacuated due to a gas main break. Houston justice seemed to get all the wrong kinds of breaks in that hot summer of 2001.

The mobile phone hooked on Rusty's waistband rang. He answered it and told the caller to just turn on the TV and look on any channel because "it" would be on them all. Rusty carried a folder, the color of the sky, if it hadn't been shrouded in smog.

"Mr. Yates, if you want to avoid the media, they're just right up there," said a stranger.

He turned and looked at her, but only a sidelong glance. "That's okay," he replied. He was "used to it" was understood whether the words were actually spoken or just silently conveyed. He added that he couldn't say anything to the press anyway because he was under the gag order. His mother turned and, with a slight grin on her face, said, "So am I."

Rusty asked the stranger if she knew where the makeshift courthouse was. "They told us 301 San Jacinto," he said.

A few steps more and there was the raging herd of media cameras, marking 301 San Jacinto, and charging Rusty and his mother. They calmly walked through the stampede as if he were a medicine man who could soothe the running cameras with his magic. And Rusty and his mother did walk safely into the building, while other passersby got elbowed and shoved. Rusty turned at the door and gave the cameras one more look, a grin. One couldn't quite tell if it was a slight smile or a slight grimace of trepidation.

Inside, the courthouse was as chaotic as it was on the outside—too many people trying to get to too many judges and too few rooms. Judges were forced to share courtrooms, due to the flood damage. So while red-and-white temporary signs posted in the hallways said that Judge Belinda Hill of the 230th District Court was assigned to a small courtroom on one floor, her Andrea Yates case was assigned to a larger courtroom on another floor.

That courtroom's gallery was filled with thirty or forty journalists, one pool video camera, and one pool still camera. Rusty and Dora Yates sat alone in the center front row. Rusty rested his arm on the back of the wooden pew, just behind his mother's shoulders, then turned and stared at the media. He exchanged quiet words with a reporter or two sitting behind him, while everyone else in the room stared at a side door, waiting for his wife's entrance.

A court employee walked in, placed a temporary, stick-on sign that said "Judge Belinda Hill" on the front of the judge's bench, then walked away. George Parnham and

Wendell Odom moved over to Yates and briefly conferred with him.

The room turned with one smooth motion—Andrea Yates was led into the courtroom. Her shoulders slumped, she walked with the trouncing gait of an athlete.

She wore an orange Harris County Jail jumpsuit and gold, wire-rimmed eyeglasses. Her hair was still stringy, but not as dirty-looking as it had been weeks before. The bald spots on her head—from pulling out her own hair—were not prominent, perhaps only because her hair was brushed over them.

She was so much thinner than weeks earlier that her jaw-bones were more visible. Her shoulders were hunched so that her shoulder blades stuck out like small keels on a boat. She was skin stretched over bones.

Parnham, just a bit taller than his client, lightly and caringly placed his hand on her back, and guided Andrea Yates to sit down. In the dim, fluorescent lighting emitted from a low ceiling, Yates looked almost green. Judge Hill looked like she was sitting on the other side of a pond, shrouded in a fluorescent fog. With her head tilted slightly to the right, Yates stared toward the judge blankly, her jaw muscle movements visible as she subconsciously ground her teeth. The time was 9:10 A.M..

Andrea Yates and her attorneys stood. Rusty leaned forward in his pew. Prosecutor Joe Owmby, also standing, read the indictment: "In the name and by authority of the State of Texas, the duly organized Grand Jury of Harris County, Texas, presents in the District Court of Harris County, Texas, that in Harris County, Texas, Andrea Pia Yates, hereafter styled the Defendant, heretofore on or about June 20, 2001, did then and there unlawfully, intentionally and knowingly cause the death of Mary Yates, hereinafter called the Complainant, an individual under six years of age, by drowning the complainant with a deadly weapon, namely water."

Without a photograph of Mary flashed on a screen, as

Rusty Yates had done at the children's funeral, the reading of the murder indictment seemed a barrage of technical, unfeeling vocabulary, not the emotion-charged crime that had the third-largest county in the nation saddened, angry, confused, and at odds.

But everyone in the room knew there was ultimate power behind the words—Andrea Yates was eligible to die by having her veins pierced with a lethal injection.

"Your Honor, Mrs. Yates pleads not guilty by reason of insanity," Parnham said for Andrea, who stood quietly and motionless.

Owmby read the second indictment: "In the name and by authority of the State of Texas, the duly organized Grand Jury of Harris County, Texas, presents in the District Court of Harris County, Texas, that in Harris County, Texas, Andrea Pia Yates, hereafter styled the Defendant, heretofore on or about June 20, 2001, did then and there unlawfully, during the same criminal transaction, intentionally and knowingly cause the death of Noah Jacob Yates by drowning the complainant with a deadly weapon, namely water, and intentionally and knowingly cause the death of John Samuel Yates by drowning the complainant with a deadly weapon, namely water."

The phrase "during the same criminal transaction" once again made Andrea Yates eligible for the death penalty.

"Your Honor, Mrs. Yates pleads not guilty by reason of insanity," said Parnham, again speaking for a mute Yates.

With that, Wendell Odom, second chair for the defense and the attorney who was focusing on Yates' medical defense, began arguing his client's mental competency—the ability to understand and help her attorneys with her defense.

A psychological exam performed by Dr. Steven Rubenzer, a psychologist for the Harris County Mental Health/Mental Retardation Authority, and turned in to Judge Hill the day before the arraignment, found that Andrea Yates met a "legal level" of competency.

But the defense wanted the jury, not Dr. Rubenzer, to make the competency determination, Odom stated. There was a question in his and Parnham's minds that there actually *was* a level of competency. "Dr. Rubenzer concluded she met a *threshold* standard for legal competency." The defense had had two experts of their own—psychiatrists—go over the material, and they both found Yates incompetent to stand trial.

Judge Hill granted the defense's motion.

"The State is ready to proceed on the competency hearing," said prosecutor Owmby.

The defense was also ready, Odom replied, with the exception of doing some discovery—they needed access to Yates' psychological records from the Harris County Jail as well as additional information from Dr. Rubenzer.

Judge Hill informed the defense that they must put those requests in writing.

Owmby countered that the prosecution didn't have the records to provide.

Odom, seeming as though he were urgently trying to get information to the press to counterattack the earlier police leaks for the prosecution, stated that the defense also wanted access to any grand jury material that was relevant to the competency hearing.

Judge Hill told him he'd have to be more exact.

"Of course, I don't know what all went on in the grand jury," Odom replied. "Perhaps the testimony of the treating physician," and he mentioned the name of Dr. Mohammad Saeed.

Owmby admitted that Saeed did testify before the grand jury, and the media mongers leaned forward, hoping for a slip of information.

Like Odom, Parnham seemed to desperately want to slip the press their side of the story. He told the judge there had been press reports that "a mental health expert familiar with Mrs. Yates" had testified before the grand jury that there was no evidence of psychosis when the expert treated her.

That report was attributed to a prosecutor, Parnham noted calmly but forcefully. And Dr. Rubenzer did indeed say that Mrs. Yates was suffering a severe mental illness, he added, and was only "marginally" competent to stand trial.

"Dr. Rubenzer does clearly say she is competent and does say she suffers from a serious mental disease, not a severe mental disease," Owmby argued back.

Judge Hill granted the order to turn Dr. Saeed's grand jury testimony over to the defense. In fact, she specifically wrote on the order, in her own hand, "As to the testimony of Dr. Mohammed [sic] Saeed grand jury testimony," so that no other grand jury evidence would be released to the defense.

The leaks were not coming from the prosecution, Owmby pressed on, but from the defense and Dr. Rubenzer *did* say that Yates was competent to stand trial.

"I have a tape of a reporter announcing to the nation that Mrs. Yates was not psychotic at the time Dr. Saeed released her from his care," Parnham shot back. That report, he said, was attributed to the State.

Dr. Rubenzer's report said she was "marginally competent," Odom added.

"This isn't a competency hearing," Judge Hill interrupted. And she made it clear that she wasn't going to hold the competency hearing on that day, without a jury, for all the press to hear. But, she stated, since there was so much conflicting information, the matter of competency must be presented to a jury.

Dora Yates leaned closer to listen.

The prosecution said they wanted to examine Andrea Yates.

The defense said they wanted to know the nature and the scope of the exam before they responded.

The judge said the competency hearing would be set within two weeks.

At 9:32 A.M., twenty-two minutes after it had started, the arraignment was over. Andrea Yates was led out of the courtroom without ever glancing once at her husband.

Rusty and Dora Yates sat for a few moments, then stood. Dora's black purse hung over her right wrist. A tiny gold watch dug into her left wrist. Finally, she and her son walked out of the courtroom . . . as prosecutors and defense attorneys gathered at the judge's bench and conferred, then gathered at the prosecution's table and conferred some more . . . until a tattooed bailiff with a hearing aid waved the gag order in reporters' faces and forced them from the room. "Haven't you read this?" he said, still waving the paper. "It says you must leave the courtroom immediately."

Indeed, the day before, Judge Belinda Hill had issued an order instructing all "spectators and media representatives" to "immediately leave courtroom number 7-7 and all cameras shall be removed as soon as possible," after the proceedings were concluded. The judge's order also demanded that the pool video camera *not* record any sound—nothing the judge or attorneys said.

It further stated, "Media personnel outside the courtroom shall not create distractions and shall avoid restricting movement of persons passing through the halls and/or doors to the courtroom."

Any person who violated the order was subject to contempt and expulsion from the courtroom. And "all persons employed by a media organization" were "presumed to have notice" of the order, whether they had seen it or not.

Reporters filled the hallway, frantically punched numbers into their cell phones, and called in their stories. "She didn't look at him once," a reporter yelled into her phone.

But back in the courtroom, prosecutors had already turned over to the District Court Clerk the State's motion to order Andrea Yates to submit to a mental health exam . . . to be designated by the State, just as they had requested moments earlier. The motion also stated that if Yates refused to submit to such an examination, the defense's psychological exam should be excluded.

Seven floors down, a lone trumpet player stood on the

courthouse street corner and played into the air, his sounds muffled by the constant hum of TV trucks. Cameras ignored him as they stared at the courthouse doors. Rusty and his mother exited, each with slight grins on their faces. "I didn't come prepared to talk today," he said. "We're under a gag order still."

An AP reporter asked him about a white envelope he had handed Andrea's attorneys. "He doesn't work for free," Rusty answered, and he and his mother walked the blocks back to their vehicle.

The cameras stayed and waited for the attorneys. When they walked out of the building, the camera crews and reporters bumped the trumpet player from his corner, and into silence. Like Rusty Yates, the attorneys begged off. "Oh, I can't comment on that," said Parnham. "I'm gonna keep walking," said Owmby.

But late that afternoon, just in time to make the evening newscasts, Judge Belinda Hill briefly loosened the gag order for the prosecution only. Harris County District Attorney Chuck Rosenthal notified the press that the State "will seek death as a penalty" against Andrea Yates.

"District Attorney Rosenthal said that he believes that the citizens of Harris County ought to be able to consider the full range of punishment in this case, including the death penalty," said the notice to the press.

"The decision was made a long time ago," Rosenthal told reporters. "It seems fairly appropriate to break the spell and let people know what's going on."

The defense was not allowed a response.

Other attorneys did respond, explaining that the D.A. was simply trying to get a "death-qualified jury" because jurors willing to sentence one to death were more likely to find a defendant guilty. Jurors opposed to the death penalty were more likely to find a defendant not guilty by reason of insanity.

The community also responded to the announcement. In

seven hours' time, Houston TV station KPRC logged thirty-four responses to its survey question—Should Andrea Yates get the death penalty? Almost 60 percent of that night's respondents said emphatically yes—"She should be led straight to the gurney." "Postpartum depression or not, Andrea Yates is still a murderer." ". . . She should have someone drowned [sic] her like her kids. . . ." "I think of those little kids looking up at her with those scared little eyes while she held them underwater, and my heart just breaks into a thousand pieces."

The coroner's report had indicated the children were drowned face down, not in a position to stare back with "scared little eyes."

A few Houstonians said that death was too good for Yates—instead, let her sit in a cell and stare at photos of her children for the rest of her life. "Yes, I feel sorry for her!" wrote "Rosa." "But what about those kids! Why did she have all those kids? If she knew she was depressed. Did her husband make her?"

On August 9, 2001, Joseph S. Owmby, assistant district attorney for Harris County, Texas, officially submitted to the district clerk's office the "Notice of the State's intent to seek death as a penalty."

The notice said, "Comes now the State of Texas, . . . in open Court hereby notices this Honorable Court and Defendant that the State will seek death as a penalty . . ."

George Parnham went before Judge Hill, trying once again to get the gag order at least modified so that Rusty Yates could respond. She only allowed the attorneys to announce the formation of a defense fund.

So on Thursday, the day after Andrea Yates' arraignment, Parnham, Odom, Rusty Yates and his mother, Andrea's mother, and Andrea's brother Andrew, gathered with a few members of the press in a small room to announce the establishment of a fund for Andrea's defense.

"For those who wish to contribute, a defense fund has

been established at Horizon Capital Bank, for the purpose
of offsetting expenses in the mental health defense of Andrea Pia Yates, charged with capital murder. The State of
Texas has made it known that it will seek penalty of death,"
Wendell Odom read.

"The account is styled: 'Andrea Pia Yates Defense Fund,'
Horizon Capital Bank, One City Centre, 1021 Main Street,
Houston, Texas 77002, attention bank tellers.

"Any contributions received that exceed expenditures
necessary for the defense of Andrea Pia Yates will be designated for use in the areas of women's mental health issues,
particularly postpartum depression and psychosis. The actual
recipient or recipients of these funds will be announced in
the future."

But the reporters wanted to know how Rusty Yates felt
about the possibility of his wife being put to death. He'd
love to answer that question, he said, as he slowly rocked
back and forth, but he couldn't because of the gag order.

Parnham interrupted. "The gag order prohibits all of us
from discussing the feelings relative to the wife and mother
being charged," he said slowly, as he thought and weighed
his words with many "ums" and "ahs" interspersed.

Attorneys throughout the city could understand his hes-
itancy. "She's one tough, mean judge," one Houston criminal attorney said of Belinda Hill. "There is no slack in her
courtroom. Without batting an eye, she would hold someone
in contempt and throw them in jail."

Andrea's mother and brother never said a word.

On a Houston radio show, though, a host did. He offered
to be Andrea Yates' executioner.

CHAPTER 14

On August 13, Karin Kennedy broke her silence and gave an interview to Jim Cummins of NBC. "It's a terrible feeling when your daughter is in pain like that and you can't hold her and hug her," said Kennedy, her white hair a serene powder puff around her exhausted face. "This is what really hurts me. Because I can't touch her. We touch through the glass, you know, and it's heartbreaking."

With her head often bowed slightly, her eyeglasses slowly slipping down her nose, Kennedy told NBC that she and her son Andrew visited Andrea up to three times a week.

"She's getting better," said Mrs. Yates. "She's facing up to things." Andrea asked about the children, she noted. "Where they were. And if they had their own casket. We told her yes. And then she cried out, 'Why did I do this, why did I do this?' "

The day after Mrs. Kennedy appeared on NBC news, George Parnham, Wendell Odom, and Joe Owmby gathered with Judge Hill to set the date for Andrea Yates' competency hearing.

Parnham told the judge he'd spent several hours with Yates on the previous Friday, the same day the district clerk had filed the defense's motion requesting a competency hearing *prior* to the disclosure of the "raw data" utilized by

Dr. Steven J. Rubenzer, psychologist for the state, in his "competency evaluation."

"The medication that Mrs. Yates is now being administered is having a dramatic impact on her progression," Parnham said. "We still have a question as to whether or not she rises to the level as envisioned by the code, the level of competency."

"If Mrs. Yates is incompetent," Judge Hill responded, "and it's determined by a jury she's incompetent, then we need to get her somewhere where she can be treated, so we can move on down the road, wherever that road is going to take us. My thinking is the sooner the better."

The competency hearing was set for Monday, August 27, 2001, then pushed back one day to August 28.

The day after it was set, the defense filed a motion for discovery—"any and all records, recordation, notes, memorandum, or any other item that was used by Dr. Steven J. Rubenzer in his competency evaluation."

After church on Sunday, August 19, the Clear Lake Church of Christ Sunday-school ladies providing the potluck lunch begged visitors to eat. "Stay," they insisted, as they surrounded the guests, almost like the Red Sea had parted and was about to close up again. "We're the best cooks of all the classes," they added with teasing grins. There was no denying the ladies . . . and their kindnesses as they ushered the guests into line, like fish forced to flow with the water.

Standing near the front of the line was Rusty Yates. He politely waited for a female guest to go ahead of him. "You go first," she said. He gentlemanly urged her to go first. And they went back and forth until she said, "No, you go first. In my family, the men are always served first."

Rusty Yates' face shined. "Oh, really?" he said, then stepped into the serving line and began heaping his plate full. As he stood in line, as he got his drink, as he sat down and ate, the Sunday-school ladies came up to him, smiled, and asked about his mother. She was back in Tennessee, he

answered, and, no, she wouldn't be back in time for the
class they were so excited about and thought she would
enjoy.

"When will she be back?" they asked.

"In about a month," he said.

Rusty Yates had an easy grin, a pleasant demeanor, and
impressive charm as he told stories to the ladies who surrounded him, women who were decades younger than the
Sunday-school cooks who mothered him so caringly.

A co-ed asked him what he did. He answered that he was
project manager at NASA, but he was really better at soft-
ware development. He talked about his love and knack for
math—sitting in geometry class in Hermitage, Tennessee,
his sophomore year, bored to death because he could look
at the blackboard and figure everything out before it was
explained. "It was just obvious," he said, and added that he
couldn't figure out why the other students couldn't see that,
too.

He repeatedly mentioned, "The teacher hated me." That
is, he said, she hated him until he went off to a middle
Tennessee math competition and took third prize. Then, she
loved him, and let him and another student—who was a
senior—sit separately from the rest of the class and do advanced problems.

The college student said she was a psychology major who
was home from College Station, the locale of Texas A&M.

With that, Rusty joked about having helped a friend
move to the College Station area the weekend before—pulling a U-Haul trailer behind his "truck" at 70 mph. The U-
Haul was not supposed to be towed faster than 45 mph, and
it was flipping and flying in all directions. He grinned.

To the women who seemed of childbearing age, he talked
about taking a trip to the Grand Canyon in April after Luke
was born, "before Andrea got sick." They were traveling in
their forty-foot bus, which weighed 33,000 pounds, he said,
and arrived at the East Rim of the Canyon just as he saw
dark clouds blowing in. He thought it was a thunderstorm,

so he ushered everyone out of the bus for pictures before the rain came.

Then he discovered it wasn't rain, he laughed; it was snow. He had to maneuver the forty-foot bus around the Canyon's edge and down its winding, narrow roads, all during a snowstorm. They finally arrived safely at an RV park in Flagstaff, only for him to make a turn too wide and get the 33,000-pound bus stuck on a rock. It took him two hours, he said, still laughing, to break the bus free.

Rusty Yates smiled at the memories of his family and talked about the Website he'd created, yateskids.org, which had their photos on it. He couldn't share any more information about, or photos of, the children with the media, though, because it might hurt his plans for the future, he explained. He insinuated that he might write a book; he'd already talked to an author, whose name he couldn't exactly remember. But the Kennedy family, he said, had paid Andrea's attorneys $30,000, he had paid them $10,000, and before it was all over he expected to have to pay them $100,000. So he had to consider that in his decisions for the future, he said.

Rusty Yates often spoke with his head slightly bowed, but his eyes lifted to watch the persons he was speaking to. If you only knew Andrea, he said, you'd love her. On occasion, his blue eyes looked watery, as if he were about to cry, and he jumped up to get more food, scooping up three desserts, then inhaling them, before pronouncing with a shake of the head, "I can't eat brownies. I just don't have the sweet tooth my mother has."

When it was pointed out that he'd just eaten three desserts, including a brownie, he jumped up and got a sandwich and explained that he had to eat bread with his sweets.

"How do you cope?" he was asked.

Sometimes, he said, his hands trembling, he was just numb, going through work "like a robot." The silence in the house, after once being filled with the noises of seven people, now empty except for one, got to him. He had to immediately turn on the TV when he walked through the door; he really missed the hugs and the kisses the kids gave him every evening when he came home.

"Let's change the subject," he announced. When Rusty Yates told a story with a bit of laughter and joy, he could look straight in the eyes of his listeners. His upper eyelashes were long and full. His lower lashes were short and stubby, as if begging for mascara. His blue eyes were a bit bloodshot. Always, between the stories of fun and laughter and good memories, Rusty Yates kept slipping back to conversation about Andrea and her illness.

"If Andrea weren't on trial," he said, "who would be?" He asked the question over and over again without response from his listeners. Then finally, frustrated, he answered his own question—the doctors, the medical community, the insurance companies. The combination, he said, prevented patients from getting the full care they need. Instead, they were given the care the insurance companies approved—in Andrea's case, a ten-day stay, he said.

Rusty Yates recalled that in 1999 at Spring Shadows Glen Hospital, Andrea had had a great doctor and great care. There, they put her on Effexor, Wellbutrin, and Haldol. His head lowered and he seemed to shake it in sadness as he mentioned that when Andrea sank into her most recent depression, he was still tired from the first depression. So when she was first admitted to Devereux in March of 2001, he only asked, "Is the doctor any good?"

"They're all good," he was told.

Rusty Yates never knew that Dr. Mohammad Saeed had gotten his medical degree in Pakistan, had done his residency at the University of Texas Medical Branch in Galveston, and was a member of neither the Texas Medical Association nor the American Medical Association (although these memberships are not required of licensed physicians).

They're all good.

But on that hot day in August, sitting in the Clear Lake Church of Christ, Yates wished he'd asked more about Dr. Saeed. He explained that he'd begged the Devereux doctors to put Andrea on the same medications she'd been on at Spring Shadows Glen, the medications that he said had worked. The Devereux doctors wouldn't do it. Haldol was an old drug, he was told. They put her on Respiradol.

In May, Andrea Yates was readmitted to Devereux for another ten-day stay. According to what Rusty Yates told his Sunday luncheon companions, at that time, Andrea was on 450 mg of Effexor, among other medications, and was, in his opinion, severely overmedicated.

On the last night of her second stay at Devereux, he said, he and Andrea attended a two-hour group therapy session. Andrea introduced herself as "Andrea Depression," he said, and then didn't speak another word. He watched the other patients. He listened to them as they talked. *Andrea is the sickest person in here*, he said he had thought.

So, when he arrived at Devereux at six o'clock the following evening, he was stunned to find her standing with her packed bags. He asked the staff what was going on. They said Andrea was being released. According to Rusty Yates, the nurses lowered their heads as if in shame and embarrassment, and turned to walk away without saying a word, knowing that Andrea was too sick to be released. They couldn't do anything else, Rusty understood, because the ten-day insurance stay had run out.

So he took his wife home.

She seemed to him, he said, to be 60–65 percent herself, although, he admitted, he's not a professional who could measure that.

On Monday, June 18, he said, he took Andrea to the doctor and told him that she wasn't doing well. According to Rusty, the doctor wrote in his notes that she was doing well. Rusty protested and asked the doctor if her antidepressant could be changed.

"Well, since it's not working anyway . . . ," Rusty quoted
the doctor. The psychiatrist said he would reduce the Effexor from 450 milligrams to 300 milligrams. Rusty protested and quoted his own extensive research on the
antidepressant. He said he'd read that it shouldn't be reduced by more than 75 milligrams every three or four days,
not 150 milligrams in one day.

It's okay, he said that the doctor had answered.

That Monday night, Rusty Yates went to the pharmacy,
got the new prescriptions filled, came home, and gave them
to Andrea. "And Wednesday morning, the kids were dead,"
he said.

On July 16, 2001, nearly one month after the murders, Rusty
Yates said he received a phone call from the Harris County
Jail doctor. She said she was going to put Andrea on the
medications she was on in 1999—Haldol, Wellbutrin, and
Effexor.

"She didn't know the significance of what she was saying," said Rusty. He seemed to shake his head again. If
they'd put her on Haldol when he'd first asked, he said, "My
kids would be alive, Andrea would be in recovery, and we
wouldn't be famous."

CHAPTER 15

Like seemingly every city in America in 2001, there was a Starbucks on corner after corner in the Clear Lake area, some almost within walking distance of Andrea and Rusty Yates' home. At one of the three Starbucks on Bay Area Boulevard, the next major street just southeast of the Yateses, a woman rushed in, glanced from side-to-side, ordered a latte, and sat down. She had known the Yateses since before they were married. She wanted to talk.

Her husband had played tennis with Rusty Yates on Saturday nights after the kids had been put to bed. "They were always talking about taking things apart or putting things together. It was just a man thing for them."

Her speech had been rapid, then it slowed. "I think he"— her husband—"had been surprised at it all, but I don't know if it's out of loyalty to Rusty that he doesn't want to get involved in it, because I think everybody was focusing on where was Rusty in all of this and why did they continue with five kids, which, you know, was always real peculiar to us."

According to the woman, Rusty and Andrea Yates weren't the affectionate type. They didn't touch when talking to each other. They didn't call each other "honey" or "sweetie," just "Rusty" and "Andrea." But the first thing the couple said upon meeting the woman and her husband was that they wanted to have six children. That was when Rusty and Andrea were engaged. "And it's hard to recall all of this, you know, because you never thought it was going to be significant stuff."

Over the din of coffee being ground and lattes being steamed, the woman couldn't recall if Rusty *and* Andrea *both* had wanted six children, or if Rusty had wanted the six children. "I feel strongly that at the time it was more Rusty who wanted a large family. And she is the type of person . . . that went along. She was this submissive wife. From the minute I met her, you know, submissive, meek, and mild. The nicest person you'll ever meet."

"She was the most devoted, dedicated mother I had ever seen. She was one of these people that you envied, because you saw her just give her all to her family, you know? I mean, she wasn't selfish at all."

She admitted, though, that she didn't know Rusty Yates all that well. They didn't have *that* many conversations. "He was not real friendly or outgoing. Not with females, any-way."

She said Rusty "could not have married somebody just like him, because then he could not have been domineer-ing." He needed, she said, someone who was submissive. "Somebody who would buy into his future plans. Andrea was that sweet, easy-going person. . . . I think he probably saw this was a mild, meek person. . . . I think that attracted him to her—because I think he had these beliefs and values way before he even married her. He wouldn't have married a strong—I mean he wouldn't have married a Katie Couric. He wouldn't have married somebody like that. He wanted somebody he could control. And I don't say that in a neg-ative way.

"But I say it in a way that he had his future planned out for him." He wanted a wife who stayed home and took care of the kids.

To the woman sitting in Starbucks, it was also confusing. "He was, he *was*, the dedicated, the devoted father, always there. All those things that you want in a husband, you know, that helped you. I *know* he helped her with those kids. I *know* he was a good provider. . . . And I think it was good that he saw that Andrea could not work and raise the kids. But then there's that thin line where . . . he didn't want *anybody* babysitting the kids. He didn't want *anybody*, because he didn't want any secular thoughts put in their heads. . . . That's got to be domineering—no free time for herself. . . . I never saw her *do* anything *on her own.*"

"But then you wonder, here's an educated guy, right, that cannot see that this is going to take a toll on this woman because he goes to work and has some kind of interaction with adults." That fact hurt the woman who admired Andrea Yates for being the other half of that perfect couple, a woman who totally devoted herself to family.

"And she would have been a person who wouldn't have stood up [to Rusty]. . . . I don't know if she felt like this was Prince Charming who swept her off her feet . . ." The woman couldn't continue.

She knew Andrea and Rusty met at an apartment complex they both lived in in Houston. But that's all she knew. "They were real private about things like that." In fact, when the woman read news accounts that Andrea and Rusty had lived together for a year before they married, she was shocked.

At the time, Andrea was working in the oncology department at M. D. Anderson. "And she loved her work," said the woman. Andrea talked about the goings on at the Medical Center. She and the woman talked about the stresses in nursing due to the problems with managed health care, and how the nursing shortage adversely affected them. "But you can tell a nurse—they're caretakers. And you could tell she had those qualities in her. She was a little caretaker. And . . . I'm sure she was a very good nurse."

In fact, after Andrea Yates had stopped working, and not long after Noah had been born, the woman said to Yates, "Andrea, you ought to think about going to work *per diem.*"

She explained to Andrea that that was part-time work, which could help keep her nursing skills up.

The woman saw a spark in Andrea's eyes, and Andrea asked how much it paid.

"Twenty-three dollars an hour." She explained that that's what she'd done when her children were born—stayed home with them so that they weren't reared in day care centers, but worked two or three days a week to keep her nursing skills honed.

Andrea, bright-eyed and excited, replied, "Oh, well, that's interesting."

But that was the last of that conversation. Going back to work, keeping up her nursing skills was never spoken of again. "I don't know if she discussed it with Rusty . . ." And the woman's voice trailed off.

She only recalled that Andrea Yates worked right up until Noah was born. "I never saw any depression in her at all." In fact, after the children were born, Andrea Yates often dug in the flowerbeds while the children played in the yard. She sometimes walked the children down to the mailbox and back. But they never walked any farther unless Rusty was with them. Indeed, Andrea and the children often waited in the yard for Rusty to come home from work.

Then, in the evenings, they put their children in their strollers and walked through their neighborhood.

"He was just real attentive in that way, but . . . I'm just bothered by the other part . . ."—that after Andrea "had her first breakdown, why they still continued to have Mary. *Why* he didn't come to his senses, or *why* he continued to think she needed to home school, *if*, you know, she had a mental breakdown."

The woman, who has been a psychiatric nurse for ten years and was intimate with Devereux's daily routine, then pointed out that in group therapy sessions, a patient introduced himself by giving his name and illness. So when Andrea Yates, on her last night of inpatient care at Devereux, introduced herself as "Andrea depression," she was not saying that Depression was her last name, as Rusty Yates had previously implied. She was simply stating her illness.

"That's what they teach them over there . . . to introduce yourself to all the new people who come in and you tell them why you're there."

When the children died, the woman hadn't planned on going to the funeral. "But then I got up at 4:30, and it's like the Lord was telling me, you need to go to put closure on it." As a woman and mother, she had too many thoughts and questions of Rusty Yates. "I needed to go hear what he had to say . . . so I wouldn't picture him as a bad guy."

And despite the fact that they'd had little conversation during their years of friendship, the woman felt there was a connection between Andrea and herself—mother and nurse. And as a psychiatric nurse, the woman felt she needed to stand up for Andrea Yates and say what she felt—there were never any signs of depression or psychosis.

"The Andrea I knew was not capable of this or never showed signs of it." Her own daughter, said the woman, loved Andrea. "Andrea was always so sweet to her. And this was the Andrea I knew. I don't think I ever heard her raise her voice."

She added, "And I've had days like that, when you just want to scream, and nobody hears you and your husband goes off to work, you stay at home, and then he comes home and you should be bright-eyed and bushy-tailed, ready for another eight hours with him."

The woman went silent. She leaned forward. "I remember, uh—" For the first time, she sputtered in her speech. Eventually, she uttered, "I've been haunted with this, and I don't know where it's going to go. Um. We had a conversation with Rusty when we first met, and I haven't said anything. I haven't told anybody this at all. Not anybody because I don't want to . . . you know, accuse him."

And the conversation wandered as the woman backed away from her potential accusation.

"A woman who drowns, you know, that takes those kids away from their father like that, I think subconsciously . . . she's trying to get back at the husband one way or the other. And that stayed with me. And then I thought, the Andrea I knew would never have done this to her kids. And the Andrea I knew worshipped Rusty—and put him on a pedestal. But then, what happened that she became psychotic?" The psychiatric nurse had discussed this with a psychiatrist.

". . . So was this a way," she began to stammer, as if she didn't want to speak her next words, "for her to stand up for herself after all this time," she paused, "by taking his kids away from him," she stopped again, "because subconsciously, maybe she felt like she never had a say-so in it, or she just went along with his plans for the future. I guess that's what I wanted to find out."

She added, "We'd better look at the whole picture. Not just a woman who has a hormonal imbalance. Let's look at the whole picture. The environment. Did she have a support system? . . . It's very important to have a support system. The medications can do this. Psychiatrists can do that. But when they leave your facility, and they go into the real world, they don't have their doctor there to see them. They don't have the nurses there 24/7. They are in the real world, and they have to have a support system—a caring husband, a caring brother or sister, or parents . . . that can help them graduate to the normal lifestyle that they had before this happened."

And she closed, "I don't know if I'll ever see her again. I don't know if I'll ever get to talk to her again. But . . . if it's going to help Andrea and help women, and this is what I told my husband, I'm willing to say something, because I do feel like women are still, you know, taken lightly. And we're made different than men, and I don't think men see that yet."

On August 21, Judge Belinda Hill postponed the Andrea Yates competency hearing to September 12.

That same day, she sentenced 15-year-old Prentise Waire to sixty years in prison for raping and murdering his two-year-old niece. Waire, who was borderline mentally retarded and a known addict who had been sexually abused by a deceased older brother and whose mother was dead, pled guilty to the charges. Despite the fact that adults had been in the house at the time of the crime, his victim had died because of neglect by those adults, Waire could not remember the events of the evening because he had been high on paint thinner. Three educators had found Waire to be loving and nurturing, and two of those educators had felt the youth was taking the blame for someone else.

"I need help, miss," Waire begged of Judge Hill. "You can't do me like, miss. Why? Can't I get another chance, Miss Belinda Hill?"

Waire's attorney claimed that Lester Sherman, the dead older brother who had raped Waire, was the perpetrator of the murder.

"I ain't even touched my little niece," the 15-year-old exclaimed. He then stared at his family sitting in the courtroom and said, "This is what I get? I get sixty years for nothing?"

The prosecutor on the case was Kaylynn Williford, the same young, blonde prosecutor assigned to Andrea Yates' case.

The day before, August 20, two subpoenas were issued to M.D. Anderson Hospital, one to Tiffany Williams for Andrea Yates' employment records, another to Dr. Georgia Thomas, custodian of employee health records, for any and all medical records relating to Andrea Yates. During Yates' employment at M.D. Anderson she had been counseled about depression. She was, after all, faced each day with cancer patients, not all of whom survived.

Also on August 20, the *Houston Chronicle* reported that the Red Cross had treated more than 13,000 Houston-area residents for mental health issues, and Mental Health and Mental Retardation Authority of Harris County had treated another 6,000, all since Tropical Storm Allison had devastated the area and killed twenty-two persons in June, the same month Andrea Yates claimed, "I killed my children."

CHAPTER 16

In the summer of 1989, 24-year-old Rusty Yates grabbed his radio and towel and walked down to his apartment pool in southeast Houston. He carefully laid out his towel, tuned his radio, then stretched out and stared at a fascinating young woman in a bikini. *Gosh, she's great-looking.* Long and lean, with an incredible, taut body, she floated in the water, looking as though she were sleeping, her arms fully extended, her toes just barely gripping the pool's edge. He didn't think he had a chance with her. Not him—he was a geek, he thought.

But he tried anyway. He said a few words to her. She didn't pick up on the conversation. He let it pass.

A few weeks later, on his twenty-fifth birthday, his buddies from NASA took him out for a celebratory night of free beer and big tequila shooters. Yates' friends were buying, so he did the heavy drinking. The following day, he woke up sick, ready to throw up for maybe only the fifth time in his life.

He thought about how horrible he felt; he thought about how he only made stupid decisions when he was drinking. Rusty Yates made a decision the day after his twenty-fifth birthday to only have an occasional beer.

As the sticky days of September crept into the cool nights of November, Yates sat in his upstairs apartment one evening talking on the telephone. His conversation, though, was interrupted by a knock at the door. Without bothering to hang up, he swung open the door. He dropped the phone. A beautiful, well-dressed young woman with long, dark hair stood before him.

She was the same woman he'd seen floating in the pool.

She explained that she lived downstairs, and the night before, her car had been bumped in the parking lot. She wondered if he might know anything about it.

He didn't.

They talked a few moments, and she left.

Yates picked the phone up and told his friend on the other end that the most stunning woman had just knocked on his door. "I'm gonna have to find out who she is."

She was Andrea Pia Kennedy.

She and Rusty started dating.

A year later, she confessed to Rusty that she'd purposely planned that November knock on his door. A girl who had few close friends, she'd been out to dinner by herself, felt a little lonely, and knocked on his door just to meet him.

He would never have known it. Andrea, he believed, could be hard to read. He'd ask her if she wanted something, like, say, something to drink.

She'd reply, "You don't have to do that."

But in Rusty Yates' mind, that wasn't what he'd asked her. He'd asked her a simple yes-or-no question—do you want something to drink, yes or no? He soon learned that that was a Kennedy family trait, and particularly an Andrea Kennedy trait. She didn't want to be a burden to anyone. And that made it difficult, in fact, downright work, to give to her, Rusty believed.

They dated from that November 1989, until they moved in and shared an apartment together in 1992. Some of her friends thought that Rusty and prudish Andrea didn't have sex while they lived together.

That summer, Andrea received a note sent from Barcelona, Spain—mailed to her at the apartment she shared with Rusty. It thanked her for some cookies and contained a newspaper photo of the traveling evangelist Michael Woroniecki. His arms stretched as he steadied a giant banner over his head. The banner read, "All that matters is that you are a sinner headed to hell."

She received a second letter thanking her for sending money to Woroniecki. That letter told her to "seek Jesus." Only Jesus, it said, could give her life and fill her emptiness. Jesus, it said, was one who could identify with her every struggle.

Both notes were written by Leslie Woroniecki, the evangelist's wife, as he and his family preached their faith at the Barcelona summer Olympics.

Just a few days before Christmas of that same year, Rusty, simply and traditionally, proposed to Andrea. According to Rusty, Andrea seemed "surprised and happy." She said yes.

On March 30, 1993, Rusty Yates closed on his own house in Friendswood, Texas. At $90,200, it was the smallest and least expensive house in the upper-middle-class neighborhood of large, brick homes, but it was brand-new and roomy enough for two, with the potential for more. He moved into it on his own.

Then, on April 17, 1993, Russell Edison Yates, Jr., and Andrea Pia Kennedy became man and wife in front of 100 friends and family members in a small chapel at Clear Lake Park. The Reverend Ronald L. Collins officiated. He was a non-denominational pastor who had been selected simply by pulling his name out of the phone book. Rusty Yates had specifically wanted a non-denominational pastor.

Collins' church affiliation was Church of New Life and The Good Life Church, both officed out of his home in Pasadena, Texas. The pastor also did business as Independent American News Service, American Image Publications, Independent Auto Sales, Independent Aviation, and numerous other companies. "Independent" was in many of those company names, and many of his company names involved aviation services.

After Collins performed the wedding ceremony, the guests walked from the chapel to an adjoining room for the reception. Later Rusty and Andrea left for a honeymoon in Cancun, Mexico.

He'd given her a set of Samsonite luggage for her wedding present. Andrea had given him a set of golf clubs.

By June after their April wedding, Andrea Yates was pregnant. She worked until Noah Jacob Yates was born on February 26, 1994. She had him by natural childbirth. And from then on, Noah was her job. She breast-fed him, read to him constantly, and taught him to walk. The lines of responsibility were clearly delineated. Andrea took care of the baby. Rusty provided the living.

He set up an accordion file for each of them, tabbed with their expenditures—groceries for Andrea, tools for Rusty, clothing for Andrea, car repair for Rusty. Stuffed into each pocket was the budgeted cash for the month. If Andrea needed groceries, she reached for her accordion file, flipped over to the grocery tab, and dipped in and got the needed dollars. It was a cash-only basis at the Yates house, where Rusty referred to the accordion file as "the bank."

By the spring of 1995, just slightly a year after Noah was born, Andrea was pregnant again. The following August, Rusty Yates hit a hole in one on the golf course. He was halfway to accomplishing his golfing dreams—a hole in one and a low handicap.

On December 15, 1995, John Samuel Yates was born. With two babies, Andrea was becoming a little overwhelmed. Rusty sold his wedding present golf clubs because he no longer had time to golf. He was needed at home. He helped with Noah, while Andrea breast-fed John. Still, the division of labor was clear. Andrea cooked the meals and bathed the children. Rusty made the living and helped when he was home. Each evening, they'd load the children in a buggy and walk in the neighborhood.

According to Rusty, Andrea Yates was not the type of

woman who would ever come right out and say to him, I need to work again. She was, after all, hard to read. And she was the type who would take on everything. If she had the car packed full of packages and groceries, she'd figure out a way to carry them all in at once, rather than make two trips. She loved to do things fast, which was contrary to Rusty.

He liked to plan his projects, concentrate on one thing at a time, and concentrate on it hard. She liked to pound out her crafts, a trait Noah embraced. By the time he was two, Noah started drawing, whipping out picture after picture. But despite all the crafts Andrea indulged in, she wasn't a person who could concentrate very long on one task, according to Rusty. Indeed, that's why she whipped out so many crafts—she liked to do several things at once.

Each Wednesday afternoon, Andrea took the kids over to her mother's house for lunch and a visit. "Mummie's house," she called it. While there, she took walks with her father, who ailed from Alzheimer's.

For years, Rusty Yates had wanted to travel in a bus or trailer and not have a permanent home or a permanent job. In 1996, he learned that NASA planned to send him to Clearwater, Florida, to work for Honeywell. He felt like that'd be his opportunity to check out life on the road.

About the same time, Andrea wrote Rachel Woroniecki, Michael Woroniecki's wife, who had apparently changed her name to better reflect a woman of God. In her letter, Andrea expressed loneliness. Indeed, she wrote that it was hard to be alone so much. She asked for advice on books the boys might like. And she talked about a possible move out of their Friendswood home.

Rusty Yates called a realtor to put his house on the market and made plans to buy a travel trailer. He told the realtor that he'd really just like to rent the place in case it didn't work out for them to live on the go.

"How much do you want to rent it for?" the realtor asked.

"A thousand a month."

The realtor, Brandy Lee, and her husband, Cary Lee, rented the house themselves.

Rusty Yates had his wife sell all their possessions, their wedding gifts, most of their furniture, everything but his tools and workout equipment, which went into a ten-foot–by–ten-foot storage facility.

Rusty, Andrea, Noah, and John then moved into a Jayco 376FB travel trailer with upgrades, which included fancy cabinets and a fancy stereo.

Rachel Woroniecki answered Andrea's letter, talked about the darkness of the world and the importance of Andrea seeing her loneliness in relation to salvation. When compared, she implied, loneliness was not significant. Woroniecki directed Andrea to Titus 2, a New Testament chapter about the role of young women—love their husbands, their children, be sensible, pure, workers at home, kind, and subject to their own husbands so that the word of God would not be dishonored.

She said that Jesus "knows how wicked you are, how weak & vulnerable" but God "is able to sympathize with your weaknesses . . . Even the loneliness works to draw you to seek and find security in Him."

When Russell and Andrea Yates pulled their new travel trailer into the Lazy Days RV Campground in Hitchcock, Texas, on October 12, 1996, they were a proud and happy family. They had a new blue Suburban, the new thirty-eight-foot Jayco travel trailer, two beautiful and smiling baby boys, a life full of fresh dreams, and not a penny of debt. The fact that their home and trailer were paid for in full was something that Rusty Yates bragged about to the trailer park's manager, Belinda Green.

Green was a woman with an easy and comforting smile, long blond hair, and four children whose ages ranged over a twenty-year time span. She was someone who knew a lot about trailers, trailer park life, and life in general. Rusty Yates, who knew nothing about trailers, took to her almost as if she were a second mom, constantly running to her for advice.

"Well, most people have a truck or Suburban that they use for towing their trailers, and then they get a small, second car for doing their everyday running around," she told him.

Rusty Yates bought a small, second car that he drove to and from the tiny, RV-oriented community of Hitchcock, past the Gulf Greyhound race track, down Interstate 45, and to Johnson Space Center.

He returned to Green for more counsel. In fact, he showed up at her doorstep so often that when she looked up and saw him walking in, she joked, "Oh no, here comes Rusty, again."

But Rusty, Andrea, Noah, and John Yates were at Lazy Days only long enough to pay their $240-a-month rent once before they moved to Florida, where Rusty had work to do for NASA.

When the Yates family pulled into the Holiday Campground in Seminole, Florida, Andrea Yates was pregnant with their third child. But in November, her stomach cramped fiercely. Rusty had to rush her to the hospital in St. Petersburg. Andrea miscarried.

The following January, Andrea stood with a video camera in the tiny, crowded bathroom of their travel trailer while Noah stood at the sink, mimicking his dad shaving. Andrea helped Noah scoot his mirror into the proper place while she taped his reflection, complimented him, and laughed.

In May, she focused the video camera on Rusty and Noah as Noah rode his first two-wheel bicycle down the lanes of the Florida RV park. Soon, Rusty let the child go on his own, while John toddled after his big brother.

"There's our boys," Andrea said, full of pride and glee.

*　　*　　*

June 17, 1997, six months after the Yateses had left Texas, Green watched the Yates travel trailer pull back in to Lazy Days. This time, when Andrea stepped out of the thirty-eight-foot trailer, she was six months pregnant.

Green gave the couple the best spot in the RV park, a place next to the bathhouse where there was lush, green grass for the boys to play in. There was a fenced-in, minuscule pond across the drive that attracted the bugs Noah loved.

In the evenings, Rusty put the boys in a little wagon and pulled them and a load of garbage up to the Dumpster. Other evenings, he, Andrea, and the boys went for bike rides or strolled up to the manager's office to get their mail and visit. Never were the husband and wife the least bit affectionate with each other . . . or the children.

In the daytime, when Rusty was at work, Andrea pulled the kids in the wagon when she did laundry, and jumped in the small, community pool with the boys when they swam. The boys ran up and down the ramp to the manager's office, screaming and laughing.

Noah constantly picked flowers and brought them to his mother and Green. He got so excited talking to Green, wanting to know the names of each and every flower, that the words couldn't spill fast enough out of his mouth. And with Noah talking at such high speed, John couldn't talk fast enough to squeeze in what he wanted to say.

Since Noah loved butterflies and Green's children could hatch butterflies, Andrea asked Green about her butterfly plants. Green shared some of the plants with the young mother, who set them out near her trailer. But the flowers never grew.

Noah constantly drew pictures of flowers and butterflies and presented them to the beloved trailer park manager. For a long time, she kept them as keepsake treasures. And he continued bringing her flowers he picked—the tiniest and sweetest of flowers.

*   *   *

"There go the best young parents I've ever seen," Green used to say.

In those days, Rusty Yates was a friendly young man. He confided that, after he graduated from high school, his mother drove him to college. But just before they got to Auburn, his mother stopped at a convenience store and bought him some Vienna sausage and crackers. They drove on to the college, and when she dropped him out at his dorm's doorstep, with his Vienna sausage and crackers in his hand, his mother said, "You're on your own now."

Rusty Yates said nothing more, but his face indicated to Green that he wanted to. And she wondered why he was telling her that story.

Andrea Yates, Green thought, was too perfect a mother. After Paul Abraham was born on September 13, 1997, Andrea would hand Paul to Green as though he were the most precious gift and an honor to hold.

Immediately after Paul was born, Andrea started jogging to get the weight off. Rusty jogged, too, more often than Andrea.

Whereas Andrea was patient but firm with the boys, Rusty, Green observed, was quick to correct them.

Meanwhile, hundreds of miles away, Michael Woroniecki was shouting on the Indiana University Campus, "Quit listening to Mommy and Daddy and grow up." Woroniecki, with his wife and six children, stepped onto the campus on October 20, 1997, to preach his faith. "I feel like I need a sledgehammer to get you to listen," the *Indiana Daily Student* reported him as saying. "Just look at the New Testament and see that the way out is not in Christianity and not in the church."

Woroniecki's six children handed out pamphlets and proclaimed their faith, too. That disturbed the Indiana students. They didn't see that the sober Woroniecki children had a life. Daughter Ruth told the students that she and her siblings had no friends but each other. The children were home schooled. And not one member of the family had a job.

The students wanted to know where the Woronieckis got their money.

Rachel Woroniecki told the campus newspaper that Jesus provided. "Seek Jesus not in the church or religion and not in the system," she said. "The system cannot save you because it is based in Satan. The world offers nothing else, and the world does not have the answers."

CHAPTER 17

Belinda Green felt that Rusty Yates pressured his wife to be the perfect mom. Andrea had reared three boys in the thirty-eight-foot travel trailer and talked about nothing other than her kids. She spent her hours playing with the boys and videotaping them.

May 3, 1998, Andrea Yates videotaped Noah and John outside their trailer.

"What are you young boys doing?" she asked as she taped.

"Shucking corn," Noah replied.

"What else do you like to do?"

"We like to run around and color," Noah said.

"What games do you like to play outside?"

Noah busily shucked, and John quietly shucked.

"What's the hiding game? What's that called?" she sweetly urged.

"Hide and seek," Noah answered with a big grin.

She turned the camera to John and complimented the three-and-a-half-year-old on his spic-and-span corn shucking.

Less than two weeks later, the Yateses took off for a trip to Florida.

Michael and Rachel Woroniecki had a Miami, Florida, address at the time. They also had a newsletter in which they'd advertised a renovated bus they wanted to sell.

The Yates family wanted to look at it.

* * *

With Noah's love for butterflies, they placed a cocoon and a few sticks in a plastic box and headed down the highway to Florida. While they drove, the cocoon hatched into a butterfly.

The family pulled off to the side of the road, and with the open Suburban door ringing and dinging in the background, they unfastened the plastic lid to set the monarch free.

"Here's our butterfly," Andrea said as the event was videotaped. "Aaah, look." Her voice was filled with tender awe as the camera moved close to the insect.

"Back, John. John," Rusty calmly instructed.

"Aaah, look. He wants to go," Andrea said, her voice soothing and deep.

Noah, wearing a Burger King crown, knelt close to the butterfly. "Are you ready to fly away?" he asked his charmed pet.

"Maybe," Rusty answered.

"Look, he's looking at me," Noah said in the excited, sweet voice that only children can have.

"Oh, he says bye-bye," Rusty continued.

"Thank you for taking care of me," Andrea said.

As the kids watched and giggled, Rusty softly said to Andrea, "That's neat."

"Um-hm," she replied, watching the delicate creature slowly lift its wings.

"Bye-bye," Noah said, waving his little hand good-bye.

"There he goes. He's trying," Rusty said, his voice lifting as if he were about to soar.

The kids giggled a high-pitched, joyous laugh.

"I think he's off on his own," Rusty continued.

And they silently watched the butterfly fly.

"Look at that. Wow," Rusty uttered in awe.

"Bye," said Andrea.

"Bye," said the kids.

"He's up on a tree," Rusty said as he watched.

"Bye, butterfly," Noah said.
"Bye butterfly," John echoed.

According to Rusty Yates, they looked at and considered buying the Woroniecki bus. Upon seeing it, he said, he wasn't keen on it. It was, he thought, rough around the edges.

But Rusty Yates was a man who liked to seek the advice of Andrea and Noah. Noah, he felt, was that smart. Noah liked the bus. Andrea, the woman who didn't ever want to be a burden and who was hard to read, told Rusty she liked the bus, he recounted.

They decided to buy it.

Eventually, Rusty and Andrea Yates returned from Florida, still in the travel trailer. Andrea Yates was pregnant again. Luke had been conceived in the trailer while they were on the trip. Green joked that every time Andrea showed up at Lazy Days, the young mother was pregnant, again.

"How many kids are you going to have?" she asked.

"As many as God gives us," Rusty answered.

Lazy Days was a calm, quiet place, with trees that whispered in the wind, and the roar of cars on the nearby highways drowning out their whispering.

Suddenly, the Yates family seemed to have whispered secrets. After their return from Florida, Rusty no longer visited in the evenings in the manager's office. In fact, when he drove home each evening and found the boys playing with Green's children, he yelled, "Get in the house, boys." He wouldn't let the Green kids go inside with the boys, either.

"Mommy, he hates us," Green's children cried. "He doesn't want us around."

Rusty Yates was downright cold.

In July, Rachel Woroniecki wrote Andrea Yates, saying

she was glad Andrea was taking to heart the things they shared.

She talked about how they hoped to move out of the bus by August. And the preacher's wife discussed setbacks they'd had, which had required much more work and expense than they had expected.

A few days later, Rachel wrote a letter to Rusty, dictated by her husband, thanking Rusty for his donation into the Woroniecki bank account.

To Andrea, she wrote that she thought about her often and was praying for her. "I'm so glad you're getting into the word & being diligent to seek Jesus. He alone will save you—not doing 'right' or being 'right' but coming to know Him."

According to Belinda Green, in September of 1998, the Yates family briefly left Lazy Days and took a trip.

Then Rusty was off again, back to Florida to work a bit and to purchase the bus. It was a bus *Rusty* wanted, Green said. He wanted to fix it up and travel the country, he said to her.

Rachel Woroniecki wrote Andrea and thanked her for a gift of edibles she'd sent. She said they were upset about a tape Rusty had sent them. She hoped Andrea's pregnancy and birth went well, and that Andrea could give "Jesus" to her boys.

She scratched at the bottom of the letter, "Remember the butterfly you watched. Become one!"

September 30, 1998, Michael Woroniecki and his family stood on the Penn State campus screaming their faith. "I don't care if you don't like me yelling and preaching at you like this today," Woroniecki proclaimed, the *Penn State Collegian* reported.

"I'm not really listening, but all I keep hearing are the

words 'Satan' and 'hell,' " the paper quoted student Gehan
Soliman as saying. "It's kind of disturbing."

In October 1998, the Yates family finally sold the Friendswood house that they'd leased out for years. And their rent
at Lazy Days went up, presumably to cover the camping
spots for both the travel trailer and the bus.

For a while, Yates parked both the new travel trailer and
the renovated Greyhound bus at Lazy Days. By then, the
rental price for a parking place was only about $250 a
month, utilities included. The Yates family slept in the travel
trailer, and Rusty worked on the bus, continuing its renovation. "He was very happy and seemed to really enjoy
working on it," Green recalled of the many hours Yates
spent working on the bus. He told her, too, of his "dream
of traveling and doing some kind of work so he could stay
at home with the family."

To Rusty Yates, a travel trailer was something that was
easy to buy and take care of; just pick out what you want—
the amenities look like everyone else's—then occasionally
clean the roof and wash the sides.

But a bus, now that was something different. It was personal—it was something that one built just like one wanted
it, with no thought to resale. And he'd bought somebody
else's bus, renovated to *their* dreams, which weren't his. He
needed to renovate it to his own.

Andrea Yates wrote Rachel Woroniecki and said they were
moving into the bus.

Woroniecki replied by saying she hoped Andrea was still
studying the Bible and that Jesus was a comfort "against
Satan."

She mentioned the butterfly Andrea, Rusty and the boys
had set free in Florida, and its change, she said, was a "sweet
witness" to Andrea of what she could become.

Woroniecki spoke of the grief and sadness they felt over

the students on college campuses and their personal woes—illness, a sore and strained voice for Michael, a blown radiator on their RV, followed by a transmission falling out. But God delivered them.

"I have no idea how things are going with you," she continued, "but I know you must get right with God before it's too late. The window of opportunity that God has opened up for you at this time through us will only stay open for a certain time." She listed a few scriptures. "All the rebuke, confrontation & sharing that went on between us was intended to effect your souls for salvation. If you allow Satan to come in and 'steal the understanding' the consequences will be tragic." She referenced Matthew 13:19.

Then whe returned to writing about the bus. "It was obvious God is wanting to break that yuppie, comfort-oriented mentality . . ."

The women at the RV park gave Andrea a baby shower, which she seemed to enjoy. Unlike Rusty, Andrea was friendly after their return from Florida. Well, friendly at first.

On February 15, 1999, Luke David Yates was born, again by natural childbirth. By then, Rusty had sold the travel trailer and the family had moved into the converted Greyhound.

Green changed the sign on Delaney Road to read, "Congratulations Rusty and Andrea. It's a boy."

"Here we are on our way home with our latest edition, Luke David," Andrea said as she videotaped the ride. Then she saw the sign and laughed. "Is there anybody behind us?" she said to Rusty.

"No," he answered.

She told him to wait, and he slowed the vehicle as she focused the camera on the sign. "What does it say, boys?" She read it to them. "That's so cute," she said in baby talk.

*   *   *

Green walked out to the bus to see the baby and mother.
Luke was beautiful. Andrea was proud and exhausted. But
it was the inside of the bus that struck Green. It was not
like a home at all. It felt cramped, confining, claustrophobic.
She wondered where everyone slept. But it was neat and
clean.

Suddenly, though, the park residents rarely saw Andrea
Yates. She no longer pulled the boys in the wagon when
she did her laundry. The bus had a washer and dryer. And
Andrea was downright busy with four little boys all under
the age of five.

The only people who ever seemed to see Andrea were
park residents Nina and Dan Ahlberg. Green got the feeling
that Andrea confided in Nina. And Nina and Green both
noticed, everyone in the trailer park noticed, that Andrea
was always exhausted.

Then, the Yates family was off again . . . on a trip to the
Grand Canyon and Lake Mead.

On their return, Rusty Yates pulled the bus into Cloud Croft,
New Mexico. The bus had felt tight for a family of six, he
noticed, but it was okay. And then there were the things that
a bus afforded that a home couldn't. At 2 A.M., he woke up
to rev up the generator. And as he did, he saw stars like
he'd never seen before. He woke Andrea to look at the stars
with him.

But it was in Cloud Croft, when they invited some friends
onto the bus that, according to Rusty, he suddenly realized
that a bus wasn't going to work in the long run.

After they pulled back in to Lazy Days, Andrea walked
into the RV camp's office and began telling Green about
Rusty getting the bus stuck in Flagstaff, after they'd driven
down the snowy, winding Grand Canyon roads, and how it
had frightened her. Then, she stopped talking.

Rusty had walked into the office.

Green took note; it was one of the most personal things the normally private Andrea Yates had ever spoken to her.

Once again, Andrea wrote Rachel Woroniecki, and Woroniecki replied.

"It is so very crucial for you to do whatever you have to RIGHT NOW before you are overwhelmed by things."

She preached on, "You must accept the reality that this life is under the curse of sin and death. There is nothing in you and your emotions. You are a daughter of Eve."

Then she spoke of the bus—she hoped the musty smell had gone.

She said she would pray for Andrea and give their love to Rusty, the boys, "and the tiny one 'in the hole.' "

Green had been told about a lift door in the Yateses' Greyhound. The door opened up to reveal a cramped compartment. It was the bus's wheel well. That was where two boys slept.

Then, one day, Green ran into Andrea and the four boys at Wal-Mart. She knew Rusty was at home, alone. She knew that when Rusty and Andrea had only two boys, that Andrea would get a mom's day out. She wondered what had happened to those days. It seemed that the more kids Andrea had, the less Rusty helped. Green felt as though Rusty believed it was *Andrea*'s job to rear the children, not his too.

All the people at Lazy Days observed that Andrea was getting more tired, and losing the happiness that she had once seemed to hold as dearly as her children. The Lazy Days residents wanted to help, but they didn't know what to do.

And Noah, who was always a likeable, yet nervous, child, appeared to be getting more nervous, Green noticed. He almost stuttered when he spoke, still trying to talk so very fast, like he just didn't have time to get all the words out.

Rusty never confided in Green anymore. Andrea had never talked about anything but the kids, and now she wasn't talking at all.

Suddenly, Andrea Yates was no longer in the trailer park.

CHAPTER 18

On Thursday, August 23, 2001, the Houston Area National Organization of Women announced the formation of the Andrea Pia Yates Support Coalition. The coalition planned to offer support for Rusty Yates, help raise money for the defense fund, and hold a candlelight vigil for Andrea the night before her competency hearing began.

Immediately, Houstonians penned emails in protest. "NOW has lost sight of what they are supposed to do. There is no common sense here," wrote one objector to KTRK-TV's Website.

Others griped that John Wayne Gacy and Timothy McVeigh didn't have defense funds, why should Andrea Yates? More complained that NOW supported "killing babies in the womb. Why should their support of Yates be any different?"

But one voiced a differing opinion: "As a society wouldn't it be incredible if we stood for this woman and everyone suffering from mental health diseases instead of condemning them? What she did is unforgettable but if she had cancer would we be blaming her and refusing her chemotherapy? I think not."

That same day, the *Houston Chronicle* reported that Harris County D.A. Chuck Rosenthal had received seventy-two emails and letters regarding his decision to seek the death penalty against Andrea Yates.

One of those emails was from Johnny Holmes, the former

Harris County D.A. who had mentored Rosenthal into his
current position. "It's the right call," Holmes wrote of the
decision to seek the death penalty. "That is why I had a
reputation of going for it so much. It is part of the range.
Amazingly the public went for it most of the times that we
included it in the range. I suspect your experience will be
the same."

Harris County proudly called itself the death capital of
the United States.

Rosenthal replied to some of the responses. "I do this
after seeking wisdom from God. My oath of office requires
me to follow the law without consideration for public opinion."

By the following Monday, twenty groups had joined the
Andrea Pia Yates Support Coalition—the American Civil
Liberties Union, the Texas Coalition to Abolish the Death
Penalty, and the Italian Coalition to Abolish the Death Pen-
alty among them.

On Tuesday, August 28, 2001, Assistant D.A. Joe
Owmby issued seven subpoenas to employees of the Mental
Health Mental Retardation Authority of Harris County, ordering their presence at the September 12 competency hearing. Psychologist "Dr. Phillip Rubenzer" and psychiatric jail
nurse "John Bayless" were included in that list. Owmby
meant Dr. Steven Rubenzer and John Bayliss.

August 30, *The Dallas Morning News* reported that a
telephone number provided by Devereux Texas Treatment
Network for Dr. Mohammad Saeed was disconnected.

It also reported that Andrew Kennedy, Andrea Yates'
brother, had said that Andrea was "a little upset about the
news reports, the negative stuff about Rusty. She thinks it's
unfair." He added that the Kennedy family was supportive
of Rusty. "There's a trial coming up. . . . Stuff will come out
that may be bad. We need to be united for Andrea."

That evening, Rusty Yates opened his door to a Harris
County Sheriff's Deputy. The deputy slapped a subpoena

Andrea Yates booking photo on June 20, 2001.
(Courtesy of the Houston Police Department)

Luke, Noah, Paul, and John in Medieval costumes made for them
by Andrea Yates, January 2001. (*Courtesy Rusty Yates*)

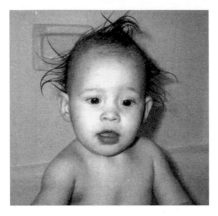

Noah getting a bath (TOP). John with his chalk portrait of the family and dog (MIDDLE). John, Luke, Paul, Noah, a pregnant Andrea, and Rusty Yates, fall 2000 (BOTTOM). *(Photos Courtesy Rusty Yates)*

Drawing by John of Rusty on a horse and Andrea in a wagon.

Luke holding newborn Mary.

Paul's birthday with NASA cake made by Andrea. *(Photos Courtesy Rusty Yates)*

The converted Greyhound bus, Rusty Yates' basketball goal, and his children's basketball goal at the Yates home, June 27, 2001.

The main office of Devereux Texas Treatment Network.
(both Suzy Spencer)

Mourner tent with coffin at Yates children graveside service, Forest Park East Cemetery, June 27, 2001.

Candlelight vigil coordinated by the Andrea Pia Yates Coalition, September 18, 2001. *(both Suzy Spencer)*

Prosecutor Joseph Owmby giving closing argument on September 21, 2001.

Prosecutor Kaylynn Williford giving closing arguments on September 21, 2001. *(Pool Photos, both Courtesy KTRK-TV)*

Dr. Steven Rubenzer, psychologist, testifying on September 20, 2001 that Andrea Yates was competent to stand trial.

Judge Belinda Hill at September 2001 Andrea Yates competency hearing.

Rusty Yates, Karin Kennedy, attorney John O'Sullivan, Brian Kennedy *(leaning forward)* and Andrew Kennedy hearing the competency verdict, September 22, 2001.
(Pool Photos, all Courtesy KTRK-TV)

Booking photo for Ruth Woroniecki (LEFT). Booking photo for Sarah Woroniecki (RIGHT). *(both Courtesy of Madison, Wisconsin Police Department)*

Rusty Yates at an anti-death penalty rally in Austin, Texas, October 27, 2001. *(Suzy Spencer)*

into Yates' large hand and said, "You have been served. You are under the gag order."

The following day, Andrew Kennedy was quoted more extensively in *The Dallas Morning News*, saying that his sister "makes jokes sometimes" and acted "completely normal."

"I've never seen her this happy—even ten years ago, she wasn't this happy," he stated. "Maybe it's a combination of the environment she's in and the treatment she's finally getting." He explained that his sister was getting better treatment in jail than she'd ever gotten on the outside. "They actually talk to her. They're helping her with her thinking." He noted, "She's opening up more than she ever has in the past."

He and his mother, he said, brought Andrea Bible verses about fear and worry, and Andrea asked for more, as well as reading material from their church. A jail chaplain had given her two Bibles, and she regularly spoke of reading them.

She told her best friend, though, "she could have all her craft supplies she had gotten over the years, because she doesn't think she'll ever get out," he said. "She's feeling a lot of guilt."

Upon his mother showing Andrea photos of the children, Andrea "started crying," Andrew recounted. "She said she was sorry for everything that happened."

He said he told her it wasn't her fault. "You had no control over what you did." And Andrea Yates "just kind of nodded her head."

That same day, Court TV filed a motion in the 230th District Court, petitioning Judge Belinda Hill for permission to air the Yates competency hearing. The motion claimed, "Televised proceedings foster public confidence in our court system." It also stated that Assistant D.A. Owmby took "no position on the Motion at this time" and Yates attorney George Parnham was unopposed to the Court TV motion.

Late that afternoon, the beginning of Labor Day weekend, Parnham and co-counsel Wendell Odom filed a 1,000-page stack of Andrea Yates' medical records with the court. Reporters stood waiting to receive them.

Wednesday, June 16, 1999, Andrea Yates phoned her husband at NASA. Soon, he was on his way home to their converted Greyhound bus, parked near the small town of Hitchcock, just past the dog track. It'd been raining for days on end. And for a week, Andrea had been feeling what she called "sad and depressed." Rusty opened the bus door to find out what the trouble was.

Andrea bit her fingers. Her leg trembled. "I need help," she said.

Other than that, she didn't talk much.

The next day, he took Andrea and Noah, John, Paul, and Luke to her mother and sick father's small home across from Glenview golf course. Andrea felt comfortable there. She just wanted to sleep forever.

So around 3 P.M. on Thursday, June 17, while everyone in the house napped, she reached for her father's medication, poured out forty to fifty tablets of 50 mg trazodone, placed them in her mouth, and swallowed them down. She knew psychiatrists used trazodone, a weak antidepressant that caused early stage drowsiness, primarily as a sleeping aid. She threw up, then fell asleep.

Later baby Luke started crying. Andrea's mother came into the bedroom, rustled Andrea, and said, "You need to get up. Your child's needing to be fed."

Andrea Yates was still breast-feeding Luke, but she answered, "I can't feed them, Mom. I've just taken an overdose."

Rusty Yates rushed his wife to Houston's Ben Taub General Hospital emergency room where she was lavaged and given charcoal to make her vomit, so that her body couldn't absorb the drugs. Andrea was quickly diagnosed as having a major depressive disorder and referred to nearby Methodist Hospital for inpatient admission with suicidal ideation.

Rusty Yates and a Ben Taub emergency room worker transferred Andrea to Methodist.

At 11:10 P.M., her first physician's orders were written at Methodist calling for Andrea's possessions to be searched and a social worker to conference with Rusty. Hours later, on June 18, Andrea Pia Yates had officially been transferred and admitted to Methodist Hospital's psychiatric unit, not far from M. D. Anderson, where she had once worked.

At 1:30 in the morning, as Andrea lay quietly in her hospital bed, a nurse reached for her pen to scribble down her patient progress notes. The patient's belongings had been searched and a bottle of pills had been locked away in the nurses' station, she wrote. She also noted that Andrea was very indecisive and not sure about staying at the psychiatric facility. "Nursing staff had reassured her frequently she would be safe and receive the help she needed."

The nurse wrote that a flat, quiet, depressed Andrea Yates who had poor eye contact could not tell anyone what was the cause of her problems.

Although Andrea Yates was considered alert with a steady gait, she was slow to respond to the nurse's questions, and when she did answer, her voice was soft and monotone. Her insight was limited and her judgment was poor, the nurse stated. "[Patient] understands she is on suicide precautions. . . . Patient admits to anxiousness and overwhelming thoughts, denies any suicidal ideation at present. [Patient] refused to sign any consent for meds but understands if she needs medication for sleep something was ordered."

In a psychiatric unit, as opposed to a typical medical floor, medical staff couldn't administer psychotropic drugs without the patient signing a consent form, even if the patient was mentally or emotionally impaired and couldn't understand his or her own need for the drugs. That was Texas law, which could only be overridden by a judge's order, in an emergency or involuntary detention situation. Getting that override usually took at least one week. Andrea Yates would be discharged in one week.

Just prior to the 7 A.M. shift change on Friday morning, Yates complained of fullness in her breasts and told her nurse that she had been breast-feeding her baby. She said she planned to continue breast-feeding after she got out of the hospital. The nurse ordered a breast pump. Two hours later, Yates was instructed in how to use the pump and said she felt relief. She also said she didn't have suicidal thoughts.

That afternoon, Yates was reported to be cooperative, pleasant, quiet, and guarded. As she sat in her hospital bed, she told her therapeutic recreation evaluator that she enjoyed reading, turning out arts and crafts for her children, and doing things with her children. She also enjoyed running, swimming, playing ball, and, again, her children.

Around 3 P.M., Yates sat in the day room while her social worker's notations were added to the file. The social worker, Norma Tauriac, had made several attempts to contact Rusty at every phone number that had been provided. There was no answer on Rusty Yates' cell phone, and there was a busy signal at home. Andrea explained that the phone might be off the hook. The social worker continued trying to reach Rusty.

Barely thirty minutes later, the social worker's notes were updated: Rusty had been contacted and a family session was scheduled for Monday at 2:30 P.M..

Tauriac sat with her new patient that Friday afternoon. Andrea wore shorts and a shirt; her hair was disheveled from lying in bed. When Tauriac asked Yates her vocation, she answered "Registered nurse." Tauriac noted that Yates was a housewife. She asked Yates what brought her to the hospital.

"I guess I was overwhelmed or depressed," she answered.

Tauriac picked up the phone and called Rusty again. Andrea simply wasn't giving her the information she needed, so she interviewed the husband over the phone while talking to the wife in person. She asked Rusty the same question— what brought Andrea to the hospital?

She's lost interest and has become withdrawn, he answered, and she'd phoned him at work due to anxiety. He explained the circumstances of Wednesday and Thursday— going to their "motor home," going to her parents' home, and the resulting suicide attempt.

Tauriac asked about Andrea's family history.

Rusty answered that her family was strict Catholic and "not very warm."

Andrea described her mother as "supportive, sensitive, caring, and nurturing."

Rusty stated that, because of Andrea's father's heart attack thirteen years ago, his current illness, and the fact that her mother was staying home to care for the father, there was stress on the parents' relationship.

"How is your relationship with your parents?" Tauriac asked Andrea.

She replied that she was close to both of them.

They talked about Andrea's brothers and sisters—the two oldest brothers were married and lived in Houston, worked in labor jobs, and helped their parents on occasion. One brother lived in California and was emotionally distant from his sister, while Andrea's only sister lived in Georgia with her children and had a troubled marriage.

Rusty stated that Andrea was closer to her parents than her siblings. And when asked about any physical or sexual abuse, Rusty answered that he did not think there was any history of either.

Tauriac asked Andrea if she'd suffered any significant losses as a child.

She said no.

She asked the wife and husband about their marital relationship.

Rusty said that Andrea saw their marriage as close, with

four beautiful kids. He said she relied on him to make a lot
of the decisions, and that sometimes he felt Andrea had lost
her identity. All of her energy, he said, is focused on the
children.

What are the strengths in your marriage? Tauriac questioned.

Our values are similar, Rusty said. We're both honest and
trustworthy.

What are the weaknesses in your marriage?

I could maybe treat her with more respect, Rusty answered.

Tauriac's questions turned to the children.

Rusty bragged about how all the children were born without medication.

Tauriac asked about parenting issues.

Rusty Yates replied that John, their second son, had difficulty focusing and staying with one thing for very long.
He said he and Andrea were both very strict with the children and they corrected them verbally and physically with
spankings. He added that they had Bible study at night with
the children.

The social worker asked if Andrea had suffered any significant losses as an adult.

She answered no.

Tauriac asked her about her sexual development.

In her family, Andrea said, sex was not talked about. Her
sexual education came from school. She didn't start dating
until she was 23 years old.

"How old were you when you became sexually active?"
the social worker inquired.

Andrea Yates refused to answer the question.

The social worker suspected the age was 25 or 26.

Andrea said she was a person who made friends easily
and had a few friends.

The social worker wrote that Andrea Yates had had a
few friends through the years, but that they had drifted apart.

Andrea said she was reared Catholic, but was now a

member of a non-denominational Christian faith. They didn't attend church services, though. They conducted Bible studies at home.

Why the change in church affiliation? Tauriac asked.

Rusty Yates answered that he had not found one he liked, and he thought that Andrea was struggling with the concept of salvation. She put a burden on herself, he added, then explained that he thought she had some guilt about showing anger.

The conversation switched to leisure activities. Andrea liked to make crafts with the family, particularly Noah, their oldest child, Rusty said. The family kind of keeps to itself, and Andrea doesn't seem to have the time or energy to pursue many leisure activities. One night a week, he said, he babysat the children while his wife went out and did the family shopping.

Eventually, alcohol and drug use were discussed. Andrea said she didn't use drugs, alcohol, or cigarettes. Rusty stated that Andrea's sister and one of her brothers had had a drinking problem in the past.

What are your plans once you're discharged? Tauriac asked.

Go home, Andrea stated. Then she said she had no real plans.

Rusty said they'd probably stay at Andrea's parents' and he'd like a list of suggestions that would help his wife from relapsing.

Finally, the social worker asked Andrea what she saw as her strengths.

"I can't think of any right now," Andrea answered.

Tauriac later wrote in her psychosocial assessment of Andrea Yates: "The patient's husband seems to be aware and accepting of the patient's problems except the patient's husband several times referred to the patient's diagnosis as postpartum depression, as opposed to regular major depression."

Rusty Yates had told the social worker, "The doctor said she is suffering from postpartum depression." He noted that

Andrea had been withdrawn since the baby's birth. And, regarding living in the bus, Yates told Tauriac, "She's been a real trouper moving around in the motor home."

Tauriac wrote, "The patient's husband appeared to be aware of the family's part in the patient's problem and was willing to be involved in the treatment process. However, the flavor of the phone interview with the patient's husband was that the patient's husband might be a little bit controlling."

The "Occupational Therapy Functional Psychiatric Assessment" filed that day on Andrea Yates said that Andrea had once been interested in running and crafts, but now had no interests.

"Her current difficulties may be related to the stress of raising her children," the therapist noted, and she mentioned Yates' recent move in with her elderly parents. Additional information, the therapist said, could not be obtained.

However, Andrea did agree to some goals: to initiate an exercise program to reduce her depressive symptoms, to state two reasons to be hopeful, and to be free of suicidal ideation at discharge.

Around 4 P.M., Andrea's nutritional assessment was written up. The main goal of the 5' 8", 130-pound Andrea Yates was to stay off any medication so that she could breast-feed her baby. She strongly felt she could not take medicine and breast-feed.

Just before 8 P.M., her patient progress notes were updated. Yates had been tearful that afternoon, and told her nurse that she felt guilty for attempting suicide. "I have my family to live for." And she said she was not feeling as hopeless as before.

The nurse then instructed Andrea to be sure and tell any of the staffers if she felt like she was going to harm herself. The nurse also tried to urge her patient to participate in group activities. She even went over the activity schedule with Andrea.

That day, Dr. James Flack, Andrea's psychiatrist, filed her treatment plan. He expected her to be inpatient seven to ten days. He thought the patient might need to stop breast-feeding, due to the antidepressant he expected to prescribe for her.

Saturday morning, Dr. Flack visited with his 34-year-old patient. She remained severely depressed and was essentially non-verbal. "She cannot discuss/verbalize any detail or even vague references to the overdose or her level of depression and hopelessness. She was only able to ask if she had done any permanent damage to her body from the overdose. We discussed starting Zoloft," the serotonin uptake reinhibitor antidepressant, "for her depression and she agreed."

Zoloft was to be started that very day. The order for sleeping pills was to be continued.

That afternoon, a withdrawn Andrea Yates sat on her bed and stared out the window in a daze. The nurse asked her if she was suicidal. Yates was slow to respond. Finally, she answered no. But the nurse noted that Yates seemed very "guarded." Yates read the medication consent form over and over. Finally, with great difficulty, she swallowed the prescribed Zoloft.

Andrea Yates slept seven hours that night.

For the next couple of days, she told the nurses that she was no longer breast-feeding and did not need the breast pump.

Just before lunchtime on Sunday, Dr. Flack wrote that Andrea Yates looked "slightly brighter and spontaneous." Her family had visited and that was "helpful" in instilling "self value and hope for future." But she still escaped to her room as often as possible, climbed into bed, and pulled the sheets over her head.

His final comment was that she was slightly improved, but still not verbal. Dr. Flack upped her Zoloft dosage from 50 mg to 100 mg.

By that afternoon, the nurses also noted a slight improvement in Andrea Yates' mood. She attended a group meeting, she was pleasant, neatly groomed, and said she felt her depression was decreasing. She said she was expecting a visit from her family that night.

But on Monday, the day her family meeting was scheduled, it was Andrea Yates' mood that was decreasing. She attended group therapy, but she was more withdrawn, vague, and guarded. Thirty minutes before the family counseling session with the social worker was to begin, the nurse wrote that Andrea Yates said she was worried about paying the hospital bill.

At 2:30 P.M., Rusty, Andrea, and the social worker sat down to talk. Andrea Yates didn't say much, despite attempt after attempt by the social worker to draw out her feelings. As usual, Yates was guarded and could not or would not say what had sent her over the edge, to the breaking point of trying to kill herself.

The social worker asked about their usual place of residence. Rusty answered, saying they lived in a converted Greyhound bus with 350 square feet of space.

She asked about parenting issues. Rusty said he was currently trying to teach his sons woodworking and allowed John, their three-and-a-half-year-old, to use a power drill. Repeatedly he stated that one of his goals as a parent was to teach his sons how to be quiet for longer periods of time.

The social worker talked to him about typical attention spans for children under five.

"Where is this therapy thing going?" Rusty asked.

Due to the time limitations of acute care, the social worker explained, therapeutic interventions were limited to identifying the patient's needs and problems and formulating a plan to address those needs after release from the hospital.

Not long after the family session started, Dr. Flack wrote, "Push Zoloft dose as fast as possible" and Yates "will probably need to remain inpatient through the week."

That evening, Andrea Yates spent a lot of time on the phone and told a nurse that her family meeting was "OK." When they talked about Yates' living condition—the 350 square feet of bus space—Andrea denied any need for more room for herself or her family. Andrea Yates spent most of the evening in her hospital room.

The following day, she talked to a nurse about the breast pump—she was worried that she was being charged for the pump despite the fact that she hadn't used it in several days. The nurse tried to assure Yates that she wasn't being charged for the unused breast pump. Andrea Yates, according to the nurse, appeared relieved.

Later that day, Yates told another nurse she was "doing OK."

Wednesday, June 23, 1999, Dr. Flack sat down with Andrea for forty-five minutes. She was still depressed, emotionally detached, and withdrawn with minimal verbal communication. The doctor later wrote, "She will not confirm nor deny any problems at home that she has not discussed with us. She was given multiple non-threatening openings to discuss these issues . . . She was able to ambivalently confirm that she would like to move into an apartment at least temporarily." While remaining "extremely withholding," she talked about home. But, he pointed out, she did not ask to be discharged.

Dr. Flack increased Yates' Zoloft to 150 mg.

That afternoon, Andrea Yates was "observed sitting on the fringes when not involved in activities" and had little socialization with her peers and nurses, but she went "off unit" with her husband.

Andrea's social worker filed a complaint with Children's Protective Services regarding Rusty training his young sons to handle power tools. CPS decided not to pursue the complaint.

Andrea's nurse asked if Andrea were hearing voices. She answered no. And she stared off into space.

The following day, Dr. Flack met again with Andrea and spoke at length with Rusty. The husband and wife both requested that Andrea be discharged to the family's care. "They have agreed to watch her around the clock and are aware that she is at risk of harming herself again. She has not been able to share much with either her [husband] or with me about her concerns. She has received little benefit from group therapy or individual therapy and her home and her children may be more therapeutic. I will refer them to Dr. Eileen Starbranch as a female psychiatrist."

That night, Andrea Yates was released from Methodist Hospital's psychiatric unit. Her discharge summary stated that Yates denied any previous psychiatric history for herself or anyone in her family. She denied any history of substance abuse. She denied hallucinations. But upon admission, Dr. Flack had noted "that there was possibly a component of delusional guilt" and her "memory was only fair."

Upon release, she was "discharged because of insurance restrictions." Her discharge summary said she was being released with 150 mg of Zoloft. But Dr. Flack's handwritten physicians' orders on that discharge date and the photostatic copy of his prescription pad stated that Andrea Yates' Zoloft dosage was reduced to 100 mg. Her final diagnosis was "major depression—single episode."

According to a Houston pharmacist, the maximum recommended Zoloft dosage was 200 mg a day. Rarely did he see a prescription for 200 mg of Zoloft. Most patients, he said, took 50 to 100 mg a day.

"As a pharmacist," he added, "I see a lot of patients who do not respond to SSRIs, which is what Zoloft is. And they became the rage when Prozac came out. And all the doctors now, they don't know anything else but these SSRIs, because that's all they're told to use. And I see so many treatment failures, because the SSRIs primarily target serotonin . . ."

Some people, he explained, don't have trouble with serotonin, but with norepinephrine, the main neurotransmitter, which is treated with tricyclic antidepressants, not SSRIs. "A lot of doctors won't prescribe tricyclics, the older type, because if you've got a suicidal patient you don't give it to 'em because those'll kill you. You overdose on that—bam. You're dead."

Soon, Andrea Yates' Zoloft prescription was upped to 250 mg.

And Yates did start seeing Dr. Eileen K. Starbranch on an outpatient basis. On July 1, 1999, she told the psychiatrist that the Zoloft was helping "a little bit." She also told the doctor, "I feel anxious."

Starbranch watched her new patient; she was nervous, shaky, suspicious, and extremely quiet. When Starbranch asked Yates about her sex life—had she noticed a decrease in her sexual desire, how often did she have sex, how many sexual partners had she had, did she use pornography?— Yates replied, "I do not want to answer these questions."

They moved on. Andrea was tired, she said. She worried about the children. "They are small—their needs . . ."

Dr. Starbranch recommended Yates switch from Zoloft to Zyprexa, an antipsychotic used for treating bipolar mania and schizophrenia. It is a drug reserved for the most resistant cases, as a last resort. A one-month supply cost $600–700, depending on the strength. Starbranch handed Yates a few samples of the drug.

Andrea Yates took the pills home and flushed them down the toilet.

Rusty Yates hid all other medicines, as well as guns and knives.

His wife heard a voice, then saw an image of a knife. *Get a knife.*

She raked at her legs, pulled on her hair, and picked at her head. There were deep scratch marks on her legs, bald spots on her head, and open sores on her scalp.

Get a knife. Get a knife. Get a knife, she heard.

CHAPTER 19

Four weeks after Andrea was released from Methodist Hospital, and two years and one month to the day before she claimed, "I killed my children," Rusty Yates walked into the bathroom of his in-laws' home to find his wife pressing a steak knife to her carotid artery.

"I'm about to cut my throat," she said.

Rusty Yates tried to wrestle the knife from his wife.

"Just let me do it."

He got the knife from her.

The following day, she was admitted to Memorial Spring Shadows Glen in Houston. It was an exclusive, private psychiatric hospital with a headline-grabbing past. Staffers, working for its former owners, who operated the hospital as Spring Shadows Glen, had been accused of insurance fraud and planting false memories of cult abuse in patients who had been diagnosed with multiple personality disorder.

But by July 21, 1999, the hospital was under different ownership and had been renamed Memorial Spring Shadows Glen.

Rusty Yates, and three of his four sons, sat with his silent wife as a registered nurse tried to ask Andrea questions. There was a mark on her neck from the knife, four sores on her head, a deep scratch on her nose, several scratches on her legs, and several yellow-and-brown bruises on her left arm. "I scratched myself," she explained about the bruises.

Once or twice, Andrea nodded her head, but Rusty had

to answer 98 percent of the questions. According to him, Andrea wasn't taking her Zyprexa and had "missed a couple of doses of Zoloft." She'd been in a good mood that morning, he said, but her moods were usually up and down. She did a few things around the house; she woke up at night and fed the baby. But he worried that she was suicidal. "I don't think she has much hope."

Finally, after much encouragement by Rusty, Andrea signed herself into the hospital. She refused, though, to sign a Consent for Medication form. And other than saying, "I'm here for postpartum depression," "to get new pills," and "my thoughts are really fast often," the only words she spoke were to say that she wanted to go to bed.

On July 22, 1999, a social worker tried to interview Andrea Yates.

As the youngest of five children, Yates said, she felt like she was an only child and that she had to take care of herself at an early age. That was all Yates said.

She refused to disclose any clinical information. She refused to sign a release so that the social worker could obtain the information from Rusty Yates. She refused all psychotropic medication.

She refused to dress for bed, even when female staffers tried to help her. Whenever a nurse approached, Andrea appeared frightened.

Dr. Starbranch called her "withdrawn and suspicious" and said, "She worries about her children."

The next day, Yates still appeared frightened. Once again, staffers attempted, unsuccessfully, to do a psychological evaluation on her. By 1:00 that afternoon, with Rusty Yates' complete support, Andrea was given an emergency shot of Haldol. Like Zyprexa, Haldol was a drug of last resort. It had too many potential side effects—including hallucinations—some that could be permanent, like liver damage and uncontrollable body movements.

A few hours later, Rusty called to check on his wife. Andrea actually walked to the phone and spoke briefly with him. That evening, Rusty brought Andrea flowers. He sat on a sofa, stroking her hair, as she lay next to him.

The following morning, Andrea again refused to answer interview questions and still refused to allow Rusty to answer the questions for her. Twenty minutes later, she drank a can of Ensure and simply said, "Can I go back to my room now?"

She was asked if she was suicidal.

She sat, with her leg shaking, and never answered.

She was asked if she was cold.

She denied being cold and finally signed a consent form allowing the staff to speak with Rusty and her mother. Still, she refused to sign a consent form for the antipsychotic Zyprexa. Later that afternoon, however, she said okay to the drug.

July 25, Andrea Yates stared lengthily at the pills before finally placing them in her mouth. "Patient appears almost catatonic," her nurse wrote. Yates was later observed holding and feeding her baby.

The following day, she was asked again for a psychosocial interview.

"Not today," she replied.

Yates didn't eat. She only drank a bit of apple juice or Ensure, usually at Rusty's coaxing.

By July 27, Andrea Yates was responding, "Yes," when her name was called. Other than that, she only shook her head. Rusty and the three older children came by for lunch with her. She barely ate. That evening, she didn't answer when asked if she was suicidal and her nurse noted that Andrea was "paranoid." Later that night, she said she still had suicidal thoughts, just fewer of them.

She was given another emergency dose of Haldol the next day. And she finally agreed to be interviewed by her social worker.

Yates was asked a question. She waited fifteen to twenty seconds. She asked for the question to be repeated. She waited again, before finally answering that she was angry with herself for not knowing how to commit suicide. "I'm a nurse. I should have known what kind of OD to take."

When her husband found her with the knife against her throat, she explained, "I was trying to find my pulse point in my neck."

The social worker talked to Yates about depression.

Yates acknowledged she'd been depressed for five years, since the birth of her first child. Her marriage wasn't a problem, she said, but Rusty was "helping more now with the kids since this," meaning her suicide attempt. She agreed that she needed even more help with the children, and some activities just for her. She confessed she didn't take her Zoloft.

After a week of trying to get Andrea Yates to talk, the social worker had to tell her that he had only two more days on the job.

That afternoon, she denied suicidal or homicidal thoughts; she denied having visions or hearing voices.

That evening, she ate all of her dinner, and Rusty asked when his wife could be discharged. The nurse told him that his question would be passed on to Dr. Starbranch.

The following morning, Andrea didn't respond when asked if she was suicidal. She appeared distressed. When her new social worker, Dr. James P. Thompson, tried to administer a Rorschach test to her, she said she was drowsy and couldn't do it. Her mother and father and four children came to visit her. After that, she denied any suicidal thoughts. "I'm just tired and sleepy."

Rusty Yates closed on a house at 942 Beachcomber on July 29. He eventually returned to the Lazy Days RV park and told everyone that they were moving into a house for Andrea. What he didn't tell them was that Andrea's mother had demanded to Rusty, "No more bus"—get a house for Andrea.

*   *   *

On July 30, Andrea Yates was being prepped to transfer
into adult services and group therapy. She seemed distressed. Lara Longo, M.D., noted that Yates wrung her
hands.

The next day, Andrea said she "did not particularly care
to transition and did not find it particularly useful," her nurse
noted. When Rusty and the children visited, Andrea was
quiet. He tried to get her to eat; she refused.

Her new social worker sat down with her over dinner. Andrea stared at and picked at her food. The social worker talked
about Andrea's overdose. Andrea abruptly stood and walked
out of the room. The social worker wrote that she appeared
"despondent."

On August 1, Andrea transitioned into adult services and
had her first group therapy session. She sat and listened. She
did OK, she said. She seemed perkier at noon. But by night,
she was disheveled, speaking in a monotone and in mono-
syllables, and refused to leave her room.

Her husband visited with her at length the next morning
and participated in a family therapy session. Andrea's therapist emphasized to him the necessity of follow-up therapy.
Rusty was agreeable. Andrea was unenthusiastic. She looked
to Rusty for approval. She said she'd consider follow-up
therapy.

By evening, Andrea resisted taking her prescriptions. "I
don't want to have to take medicine," she said. She also
refused food, saying, "I'm not hungry. I'm tired."

Social worker Dr. James Thompson filed his report on Andrea Yates.

"I intended to end my life," Andrea said of her June
overdose. She had suffered, she said, from postpartum depression. She refused to take the Zyprexa, she explained,
when she found out it was an antipsychotic.

Then she started hearing the voices and seeing the visions
of the knives. "I had a fear I would hurt somebody . . . I
thought it better to end my own life and prevent it . . . I had

a vision in my mind, get a knife, get a knife, get a knife . . .
I had a vision of this person being stabbed . . ."

She had the vision ten times over a couple of days, she
said. Later, she denied that it was that many times.

But Andrea Yates told the social worker that she had
tried to restrain herself.

She said she'd had the first vision right after Noah was
born, five years before. "I blew it off," she said. It only
happened in the early morning, she explained, and then
stopped.

"Who do you think you might hurt?"

Yates declined to answer, then changed the subject.

She said her father was a "disciplinarian" who had heart
disease and hypertension. "Possibly some siblings," she
said, have some difficulty with alcohol and might use "recreational drugs." She suffered migraines.

"My mood's kind of quiet," she said, ". . . periods of
nervousness." She was made nervous by "stressful situations."

"What's stressful to you?"

"The kids, trying to train them up right, being so young . . .
big responsibility . . . I don't want to fail."

"How did you used to be?"

"A little more outgoing, more cheerful, more helpful,
more patient, not so self-centered as I am now . . ."

She said she'd been depressed after her father's heart
attack, and while she cared for him. She'd also been depressed eleven years ago, after a failed relationship.

She'd lost thirteen pounds in the past month, she said.
She had low energy, memory problems, sleep disturbances,
and trouble concentrating.

"I probably am a worry wart," she said. She suffered
obsessive thoughts. "Most of them are over our children and
how they'll turn out." She picked at her scalp, she said, as
a "nervous reaction."

When asked about her level of anger, she answered,
"Probably not as mild as it used to be."

"Write a sentence spontaneously," she was told.
"I love my husband and kids," she wrote.

Dr. Thompson diagnosed Andrea Yates with "major depressive disorder, severe, recurrent, with psychotic features."

If psychotropic drugs were not effective, he suggested electroconvulsive therapy—electric shock treatment.

"Following completion of the inpatient program," he wrote, "she might benefit from involvement in a partial hospitalization program. Following completion of hospital programs, she needs to be followed for medication management and supportive psychotherapy on an outpatient basis.

"She needs help learning more effective strategies for coping with stress. She needs help learning to view herself more positively. She needs help developing a more satisfying support system. She needs help developing assertive behavior. She needs help learning to express her emotions appropriately. She is likely to need help organizing her thinking."

As Andrea Yates had said to her husband on June 16, "I need help."

August 3, 1999, Yates was quiet and refused to get out of bed. She was transferred to an adult services unit, but skipped group therapy. "I don't feel like talking," she said.

The next day, she got "teary" when she spoke to a social worker about Rusty.

The social worker quizzed her about abuse.

She denied any abuse, and claimed she "wasn't able to explain what she was upset about."

That same day, in group therapy, she said her husband had asked her to do more sharing.

On August 5, Rusty Yates, who had brought the children to see their mother, had to tell a nurse that Andrea hadn't taken a shower or changed clothes in four days. He also spoke with Dr. Arturo Rios, a consulting physician. Rios looked at Andrea and noted that she was "disheveled" and had "some disregard for personal appearance."

Rusty Yates told Rios that Andrea had improved significantly after taking the Haldol. The doctor studied Andrea's chart and felt that if there was any improvement, it was short-lived. Like Dr. Thompson, he recommended electroconvulsive therapy.

Andrea opposed it. Rusty preferred to wait and see if there was improvement with medication.

With much encouragement, Andrea Yates soon showered.

The following day, Andrea refused her medicines—"I just don't feel like taking them . . ." She refused them the following day, too.

August 9, 1999, Andrea Yates was discharged from Memorial Spring Shadows Glen Hospital inpatient care to day treatment at Memorial Hermann Health Center. Both locations were on the opposite side of town from Andrea's mother's house, and even farther from 942 Beachcomber in Clear Lake.

Yates left, with orders to take 150 mg of Wellbutrin twice a day, 75 mgs of Effexor twice a day, 2 mgs of Cogentin at bedtime, and 5 mgs of Haldol at bedtime. But Andrea Yates had a habit of "cheeking" her pills, hiding them in her cheeks and then spitting them out when no one was looking.

August 10, 1999, Andrea Yates began her outpatient treatment. When she met with her therapist that day, she said her return home had gone well, but was stressful considering she had four children and had moved into a new home. She also said she regretted her suicide attempt, because she'd forgotten she was needed.

She then mentioned that she wanted to get off her medication, because taking them made her feel like she was a weak person.

The following day, Dr. Starbranch decreased by half Andrea's Haldol dosage.

In therapy, Yates said that her children were a little detached due to her absence, and she felt guilt. The next day, she said she loved to watch caterpillars grow into butterflies.

August 13, Rusty and Andrea attended family therapy. Dr. Sonia Burlingame noticed that Rusty was "very eager" for Andrea to be discharged, and was "putting some pressure on her to leave soon."

Rusty said that Andrea was 90 to 95 percent back to normal.

Andrea reported that she was 70 to 75 percent back to normal.

But they had a plan to ease the stress on the young wife. Andrea's mother would help her with the kids in the morning, and Rusty would work half the day from home.

Burlingame wrote, "Nevertheless, stress level will remain high. The couple plans to have the [patient] home school their children. They also hope to have additional kids." The therapist suggested they consider Andrea's best interest in making their decisions. And she noted, "[Husband] expresses concern that [patient] still seems somewhat detached."

August 16, in group therapy, Andrea mentioned that Rusty Yates allowed her a couple of hours a week to do what she wanted. The group encouraged her to assert herself and increase those hours. She said she'd like to learn how to enjoy herself again.

But she also told Dr. Starbranch that same day that she wanted to get off all medications—she wanted to get pregnant again and home school the children. Andrea Yates' heart raced as she spoke.

"Anxiety?" Starbranch jotted in her notes. She prescribed Ativan for Yates, a sedative for anxiety.

Andrea Yates drove herself to therapy the next day and was shockingly open about herself and her family of origin. She described herself as an "eager-to-please" youngster. But she also admitted to getting stressed in her youth when her father lost his job for a year. She suspected that he had gone through depression then, and described him as a "very serious man."

In group therapy, she confessed that she wanted to be more communicative, but she mostly listened to her husband, who, at times, just turned on the TV. She was encouraged to ask him to turn off the TV so that they could talk.

On August 18, two days after prescribing Ativan, Starbranch wrote, "Apparently [patient] & husband plan to have as many babies as nature will allow! This will surely guarantee future psychotic depression."

August 20, Andrea Yates was discharged from outpatient care. On that last day, she told one of her therapy groups that she was sad she was leaving them, because she had found support and felt connected to them. She also said she planned to continue therapy in Clear Lake, but hadn't made an appointment and couldn't recall her recommended therapist's name. She again expressed her desire to get off all medications and admitted that she'd never taken the prescribed Ativan, despite still feeling anxiety.

By the time Yates left that day, she had psychiatric and therapy appointments scheduled for August 26 and a 100-mg shot of Haldol planned for August 27. And she'd asked, "Do you think I will have to continue the Haldol always?"

Karin Kennedy had given Rusty $7,000 to furnish the house. She told a supporter of Andrea's that Rusty spent the money extending the driveway to accommodate the bus and buying exercise equipment.

Soon, the old Greyhound and the Yates family were gone from the quiet of Lazy Days RV Campground.

On occasion, Rusty returned with the boys.

"Well, you know, Andrea's having some problems with depression," he said nonchalantly to Green, never mentioning a suicide attempt or any stay in a psych hospital.

And on even rarer occasion, Andrea herself returned. One

time, she returned with Rusty. Andrea, though, didn't get out of the Suburban, nor did she wave hello to anyone, or even acknowledge anyone's presence.

Belinda Green, the sweet blonde with the kind smile whom Rusty Yates had once interacted with as if she were a second mom, never even knew that his wife had been in the hospital.

CHAPTER 20

While Andrea had been a patient at Spring Shadows Glen, while she had been, in Rusty's words, "completely catatonic," he took her out of the hospital, placed her in their blue Suburban, and drove her to Clear Lake. He wanted to show her the home he'd picked out on Beachcomber. He wanted her to like it and approve.

He loved the way the home had a nice yard and was private. Fencing blocked the front door, side yard, and back yard from the view of any passersby.

At the time, Rusty didn't know whether his wife would ever get better. Her family, he said, had given up hope. But he dreamed a house would help her get better. Plus, it would give him a chance to finish renovating the bus while they lived in a more comfortable place.

Andrea, though, felt like a failure. She believed she'd let everyone down—that they'd been forced to move from the bus to a home because she wasn't able to manage.

By September 13, 1999, Paul's second birthday, Andrea was busy in the Clear Lake kitchen, cooking and designing an elaborately detailed homemade birthday cake that looked like a bright red, three-dimensional truck.

On October 14, Andrea and Rusty returned to Dr. Starbranch. Andrea wasn't getting her Haldol and Cogentin, they reported, due to a conflict with their insurance. They wanted to know if it was okay not to take the medications at all. Andrea, they said, was doing all right, even better.

Her appetite was good. She wasn't hallucinating or paranoid, they said. She had no thoughts of hurting herself, and wasn't depressed. Her concentration and short-term memory were both improved. Her energy level was good, but she said she wished she had even more. She was taking care of all four boys and home schooling them.

She wasn't exercising, though. She needed to run, she said.

Dr. Starbranch wrote that Andrea Yates seemed to be "doing OK," but she needed to be on her antipsychotic. Starbranch put Yates on Zyprexa, along with her Wellbutrin and Effexor.

Soon, Andrea walked up to Rusty and said, "In case you didn't know, I really like the house." He took that as a sign that she was recovering well.

In mid-November, Andrea's affect was "bright," she had "no bad thoughts," didn't want to hurt herself, wasn't depressed, anxious, or paranoid, and denied hallucinations or hearing voices. She was running once a week and seeing a therapist. Starbranch halved Andrea's Zyprexa dosage, while continuing her Effexor and Wellbutrin.

Effexor and Wellbutrin are often prescribed together, despite both being antidepressants. Wellbutrin counteracts Effexor's side effect of decreasing one's libido.

The day before John's birthday on December 15, Andrea Yates said she was "doing great." She was baking cookies and getting ready for Christmas. She was home schooling Noah, running a couple of times a week, and seeing a therapist.

Dr. Starbranch discontinued the Haldol, and continued the Zyprexa, Effexor, and Wellbutrin.

But when Andrea Yates returned to Dr. Starbranch's office in January of 2000, the psychiatrist learned that her patient had not been taking any of the prescribed drugs since the previous November.

Andrea said she was doing fine. The only problem she

reported was that she got a little restless during the day.

Rusty said he didn't like her going off her medications, but agreed that she seemed to be doing all right.

Andrea didn't want to be on any medication unless she was symptomatic, she said.

By the time Andrea Yates became pregnant with Mary, around early March, she was off of all medications.

On Good Friday, Nicholas Zeckets stood on his University of Arizona campus and stared at what stood before him—a ranting man in a sleeveless T-shirt with odd print on it, and jean shorts that had obviously been long pants in another life. To Zeckets, the man's clothing said, "Look at me."

The man stretched his vocal cords to yell, "You are all going to hell!"

Zeckets' gaze wandered to a girl who looked to be about 15 years old. She was maybe 5'7" tall, and blond with hints of brown that just touched her neck. *She's very cute*, Zeckets thought. Dressed similarly to the ranting preacher who was her father, she wore shorts, a white T-shirt with writing on it, white socks, and hiking boots. She looked like a girl who lived in the woods and hiked. She also looked too weathered for a 15-year-old. In truth, she was closer to 17 years old.

Zeckets studied her eyes. They seemed to show that she was battling within herself, fighting to be true to her father and his beliefs.

Zeckets looked at her younger sister, with whom other students tried to talk. She simply turned and walked away.

Zeckets barely noticed Woroniecki's wife, Rachel, who sat quietly behind her husband. She came across as simply the organizational lady with the pamphlets and fliers.

He moved his focus back to Woroniecki, obviously the leader of the pack . . . and the kids. *They seem to be thrown around, just kinda having to follow suit with their dad . . . simply because he's dad and they live in his house*, Zeckets thought.

He shouted to the preacher, "Have you ever given your

kids a chance to branch out and maybe look at other things, in order that they have more conviction, so that they truly believe in what it is you're teaching—if they find that other ideas, beliefs, ideologies, whatever aren't as true to their nature as what you're teaching them?"

Woroniecki seemed to wrestle with the question as if he'd been asked it many times, then sternly replied, "These are my children. I'm going to do with them what I want to."

The children were home schooled as they traveled the world with their father and mother. *I bet they don't have any friends outside the family*, Zeckets surmised.

He looked down at one of the pamphlets and saw an Oregon drop box, with mail to be addressed to Michael "Worneki." Other places, the pamphlets claimed they were the "Warnecki" family—Dad, Mom, Ruth, Sarah, Elizabeth, David, Joshua, and Abraham.

They're probably shut-ins in Oregon, and recluses, as they're bused to college campuses.

One of the fliers was titled "The Real Deal on Jesus." It boasted of the family being arrested in Casablanca because their preaching was against Islamic law. "We were not bombarded, as we are in the states, by 'Christian' hypocrites arguing to justify their self-centered lives," the flier read. "The Muslims dealt with THE ISSUE."

The flier condemned Christians, Catholics, the Pope, and football, which Woroniecki claimed to have played while on scholarship at Central Michigan University.

The preacher had recently been on college campuses in Pennsylvania and was then making his second stop on a tour of the Pac-10.

"What brought you to do this?" Zeckets asked.

Woroniecki said he was lost and then hit—like a brick in the face—by God.

Zeckets asked Woroniecki about the school system.

Woroniecki answered that the schools had open, liberal ideas that drew people away from the path of Jesus Christ.

With all those outside ideas, the preacher continued, the students were destined to get off track, and that's why university campuses were evil.

"You are all going to hell!" Woroniecki repeated, his words echoing up and down the university's grassy mall.

Zeckets had never heard anything so sick. *Surely,* he thought, *Woroniecki hates the government, too—anything that's organized.*

"You . . . are . . . all . . . going . . . to . . . hell."

"Do you realize the New Testament reveals nothing about praying to 'accept Christ as Saviour' in order to go to heaven?" Woroniecki's "Real Deal" flier stated. He claimed to have received a master's degree from Fuller Seminary in Pasadena, California. While there, he "discovered this modern day salvation formula did not come from God but from men. John Wesley and Charles Finney invented it to 'capsulize salvation' so the for the [sic] 'simplistic masses'. Today's fat-cat preachers don't have a clue to its origin."

Zeckets' freshman year, he nearly left college to join the clergy. He'd studied the Bible. He didn't believe there was one place in the Good Book that gave a human being the right to be judgmental. And here, standing before him, was Michael Woroniecki, who believed with every ounce of his football player muscles what he was telling the students— "You are all going to hell!"

Zeckets wondered. "If you're damning everyone who's here, what's the point of coming by and saying it?"

"I'm saving the few that are chosen," Woroniecki called.

The man is totally full of crap. He didn't quote Bible verses, or even refer to the Bible. *He can't, because what he's saying isn't in the Bible.* He spoke without ever holding up the Bible, like most traveling evangelists who hit the college campus did.

Zeckets asked Woroniecki where he got his financial support. The preacher skirted the question. In fact, most of the questions Zeckets asked over the next two or three hours went without answers. Woroniecki either didn't answer or he gave a roundabout response, which basically said he wouldn't answer the question.

Zeckets observed one of Woroniecki's sons, who looked about five years old. The child ran up and down the university's mall laughing and handing out fliers. *He's psyched.* The child stopped, glared into the eyes of a student, and said, "You are going to hell."

The student's buddies, all psychology majors, turned to the child. "I'm going to hell?" one of them said softly. "Why am I going to hell?"

Immediately, one of the child's sisters came and got him and walked him over to their family.

The psych majors walked up to the older sister. "You are a beautiful person," they said, hoping to let her know that she wasn't there to damn them all, that they weren't damned, that she was a good person, and that she didn't have to live up to what her father was telling her was the truth.

Zeckets watched the students' words eerily resonate in the girl's mind. He saw in her eyes a yearning to say, "I know." He didn't know what to do, how to save her. It made him sad. She spoke eloquently. He just didn't think she believed the words she spoke. *Not at all.*

Each morning, while pregnant with Mary, Andrea rose before the sun came up and slipped into the community pool on nearby Diana Lane and swam, lap after lap. On July 2, 2000, she celebrated her thirty-sixth birthday with a store-bought cake.

Luke dove into the cake and painted his face with its chocolate frosting.

Andrea laughed as she videotaped him. Then, as though guilt had struck, her voice turned panicked and she began apologizing on the tape's soundtrack. "That's chocolate cake. It's this thing." She panned the camera down to show the half-eaten chocolate cake. "It's not dirt."

*   *   *

A few months later, Andrea's father's health spiraled downward. Andrea Yates, though, seemed to keep her spirits up.

Fifteen days after Mary was born on November 30, 2000, Andrea threw a birthday party for John. She and Noah had baked and decorated a brightly colored hot-air balloon cake for John's fifth year of life. As the partygoers—the Yates family—laughed and yelled around her, Andrea held Mary in her lap.

The next month, she taught the kids about Medieval times, creating a king's wardrobe for Noah, a knight's outfit for John, shields, swords, helmets, crowns, and a throne . . . and writing a play that was performed for Rusty. Andrea's normally enthusiastic voice was flat as she fed the children their lines.

February 15, 2001, Luke's second birthday, she baked a train cake, with an individual boxcar cake for each child. Nine days later, it was Noah's birthday. Andrea filmed the family event, while Rusty held Mary.

"What kinds of things do you like to do, Noah?" she asked in their regular interview format.

"I love going to Radio Shack." He giggled. "And I love playing with my electrical stuff and making new things every day."

When Mary was three months old, Andrea still seemed happy as she videotaped Paul and Mary, while Paul recited his ABCs. By March, Andrea's father was admitted to the veterans' hospital.

He "bounced back" for a day or two, according to Rusty, but was returned home with a "do not resuscitate" order. By then, Andrew Kennedy was neither eating nor drinking. His five children gathered around his bed. Less than a week after coming back from the hospital in March 2001, Andrew Kennedy passed away, his children by his side.

*   *   *

March 31, 2001, Andrea Yates was admitted to Devereux Texas Treatment Network in League City, a pleasant, neat facility of red brick, modern Georgian buildings with wood accents painted white. A canopy of crape myrtles stood by the *porte cochere* of the main building. Clusters of pink and white crape myrtles and oaks dotted landscaped grounds that were sliced by a blacktop road weaving past volleyball nets and basketball goals and around the adult acute care unit.

Telephone Devereux Texas Treatment Network, and they say they have facilities all over the country and deal primarily with children and adolescents. Indeed, Devereux contracts with several states to house and treat youth who have been convicted of crimes, such as murder. But that's not mentioned on the phone . . . or on their Website.

They tell callers they have a twenty-two-bed acute care unit for adult patients who are suicidal or "going psychotic" and "need to calm down." Usual treatment, they say, is two to three days. A one-week stay is "historically unusual." Anything longer than that is "like unheard of."

Telephone the Texas Department of Health and ask about Devereux and one learns that the facility had twenty-nine pages of complaints logged against them from September 1, 1996, to August 31, 1999, the last day such complaints were made available to the public. The complaints involved everything from neglect to abuse to death. Just over twenty-eight percent of those complaints were found to be valid.

In comparison, Methodist Hospital, Andrea's first facility, had only six pages of complaints during that same time period. Less than eight percent of those complaints were found to be valid.

Rusty Yates checked his Blue Cross Blue Shield preferred provider list. Devereux was on it.

Physician Ellen Allbritton admitted Andrea, diagnosing the young mother with major depression, recurring.

CHAPTER 21

Andrea sat quietly, infrequently nodding her head as the nursing supervisor completed an admission assessment.

Rusty Yates told the nurse about the death of Andrea's father, that she'd gotten more and more depressed since then, and stopped sleeping and eating. She slept only one or two hours a night, and had lost five pounds in the past three weeks. And, Rusty stated, she seemed overly concerned with caring for their new baby. "She always needs to hold her."

The nurse asked Andrea if she was suicidal.

Andrea didn't answer. A vacant look covered her face.

The nurse marked on her assessment sheet that Yates suffered "extreme suspiciousness (paranoia)."

Andrea Yates, though, smiled when she was approached.

The nurse's assessment was based on what Rusty Yates had told her. She also checked that Andrea suffered hallucinations, then noted "unable to assess, but appears to be attending to internal stimuli."

The patient strengths, the nurse wrote, "supportive husband, good physical health, desires treatment." However, Andrea Yates refused to sign herself in for psychiatric care at Devereux Texas Treatment Network.

At 12:14 P.M., physician Allbritton put Yates on Effexor, Wellbutrin, Restoril, Tylenol, and Mylanta.

At 12:26 P.M., she was seen by another doctor, who wrote

that there was a risk of Yates developing catatonia. The doctor also noted, as per Rusty Yates' information, that Andrea was becoming "needy" toward the baby and "does not want to put her down."

Andrea Yates had not seen a doctor since Mary's birth.

At 3 P.M., an application for emergency detention was completed. Dr. Allbritton wrote that Yates needed "stabilization for safety of self and others."

Yates was assigned to the Devereux's unit 3.

The following day, the attending nurse checked that Andrea had lost twenty pounds in the past one to two months. She was additionally described as "catatonic, unable to assess thought process/content, depressed, blunted, poor historian." That was written in one handwriting. The report was signed in what appeared to be another handwriting by an MD and a licensed social worker, neither of whose handwriting seemed to match the assessment.

On other notes, someone simply said "psychotic break."

April 1, Dr. Mohammad Saeed scribbled below the bottom line of Andrea's progress notes that she was "almost catatonic." She'd answered only about one-third of his questions.

She told a staffer, though, "I am not a good mother." The children and Rusty visited her that day.

On April 2, 2001, Andrea sat down with Dr. Saeed, the doctor Rusty had been told was "a good one." A lawsuit for alleged wrongful death against him and Devereux, though, had been filed in Galveston County. It is still pending.

Saeed noted that Andrea didn't shake his hand. She sat slumped in her chair. The always dapperly dressed doctor noticed that Andrea was dressed in hospital clothes, with her pajamas not particularly well-tied.

As if she were a prisoner of war reciting her name, rank, and serial number, Andrea Yates stated her name and marital status to Saeed. She mutely stared into space for all other questions, her body motionless.

Rusty Yates told the doctor that he'd brought Andrea to

Devereux because he didn't think she could survive another night at home. She had become distressed, he said, because she had "dried off" and was unable to nurse. She'd lost ten pounds, he said.

Saeed's typed psychiatric assessment stated, "The patient appeared dressed and groomed casually. Her hygiene could be better. The patient seems unmotivated."

Her chief complaint, he wrote, was "I have been like this for months."

His game plan was to try to engage Yates in voluntary treatment, get her involved in family therapy, and put her on Effexor and Wellbutrin, since they'd worked for her in the past.

Despite the fact that the admitting nurse had written in her assessment that one of Yates' strengths was her desire for treatment, that day, April 2, 2001, Dr. Saeed and Devereux program director Jan Clemens wrote Galveston County Probate Judge Gladys Burwell, requesting that Andrea Yates be committed to Austin State Hospital.

"She is catatonic and is refusing to talk, eat or drink fluids. She is also refusing to take her medications," Saeed's letter said. She refused her Effexor and Wellbutrin that day. Her urine output was so minimal that she was at risk of kidney failure.

In his "physician's certificate of medical examination for mental illness," which was filled out for the Galveston County Probate Court, Saeed scribbled that Yates was diagnosed as having "major depression with psychotic features (postpartum)."

He also petitioned the court to allow him to administer psychoactive medications.

Dr. Saeed put Yates on Risperdal, an antipsychotic, and Cogentin.

Her progress notes that day were written on another patient's chart. That patient's name was x-ed out; "Andrea Yates" was handwritten above it.

*   *   *

When Rusty and the children visited Andrea that night, she sat on the couch and minimally interacted with her family.

The next morning, Andrea Yates voluntarily signed herself into Devereux.

A new letter from Dr. Saeed to Judge Burwell was drafted regarding "Amanda Yates." He meant Andrea Yates, but "Amanda" had been the first name of the patient whose chart had briefly been Andrea's. Saeed wrote, "We should like at this time to discontinue the court proceedings."

Rusty phoned the hospital, concerned with his wife's fluid intake and hygiene. He also worried that she wasn't taking her medicines. He suggested dividing the meds into smaller doses and offering them to her more frequently, since she only seemed to take fluids when she swallowed her pills.

The nurse assured him that his suggestion would be passed on to his wife's "treatment team."

Eventually that day, Andrea drank some Ensure, at Rusty's persuasion.

On April 4, Andrea put on her street clothes, Saeed noticed, and attended her first group session. It was a video on alcoholism.

That evening, Rusty and the children visited Andrea, and Rusty got her to drink some chocolate milk.

The next day, Yates answered a few of Saeed's questions, until he asked her about any suicidal ideation. Yates became mute.

April 6, Saeed doubled her Risperdal dosage. She went to group; it was another video on addiction. She spent the evening pacing, until Rusty came for a visit. With his help, she drank a bit of instant breakfast.

April 8, she finally ate some solid food. April 9, Saeed scribbled that Yates "looked much better today." April 10, she paced in her room and refused food. April 11 she "ate a good breakfast," her "eye contact improved," but she spoke "only to have her needs met." She watched a video on depression and "seemed very interested in video. [She] watched it all the way thru [sic]."

Saeed thought Yates "appeared more spontaneous."

She told him she felt 90 percent better, and asked to be discharged. She agreed to partial hospitalization.

So did her husband.

According to Saeed, Rusty felt that Andrea was 65 percent improved and wanted her discharged "so he can organize home so [patient] does not get overwhelmed."

April 12, 2001, Andrea Yates was released from Devereux Texas Treatment Network inpatient care to partial hospitalization, PHP, wherein the patient stays at the hospital during the day and goes home at night. "I'm not suicidal," she said. She was released with prescriptions for Risperdal, Effexor, and Wellbutrin. Her condition was marked "improved." She was considered "alert." Her discharge status was "routine."

Dr. Mohammad Saeed's typed discharge summary stated, "On the day of discharge the patient appeared dressed and groomed casually but carefully and hygiene was good. The patient waved at me and seemed much more interactive today. . . . No delusions or hallucinations. No suicidal or homicidal ideation."

"Condition on discharge" was initially left blank. At some point, Saeed scratched in "improved."

Her next appointment with the psychiatrist was scheduled for almost one month later, on May 4 at 6:30 P.M.. Yet her drug supply was for two weeks.

At 8:30 A.M. on April 13, Andrea Yates showed up for her first day of partial hospitalization at Devereux Treatment Network and sat down at a table. Her affect was "flat."

April 13 was also her last day of Andrea's partial hospitalization program—PHP. According to Rusty, she told her husband she didn't see any reason to continue. He agreed, since all his wife had done that day was watch a video on addiction.

But Saeed scrawled onto paper that his patient had no complaints, was maintaining progress, and he saw no "decompensation" since her discharge—of one day.

Three days later, Saeed reportedly paged Rusty Yates. According to the doctor's annotations, Yates told him that Andrea was improving, she was more involved with the children, and was talking more, but was beginning to have problems sleeping. They discussed Andrea's medications and talked about increasing her Effexor.

Saeed said he "encouraged" them to participate in partial hospitalization, but noticed a "reluctance." He said he would keep her chart open for one more day. If she didn't return then, she would be discharged.

At 6 P.M. on April 18, 2001, Andrea Yates was completely released from Devereux. According to Dr. Saeed's notations, Andrea's compliance was poor—she stopped attending PHP. Her condition upon discharge was "improved by report."

The following day, consulting physician Brian Doeren dictated: *Yates suffered postpartum depression and was on Effexor, Wellbutrin, Restorial, Tylenol, and Mylanta. Both her Effexor and Wellbutrin dosages had been reduced. Indeed, the prescriptions matched exactly those prescribed for Yates by admitting physician Allbritton on March 31. The doctor made no mention of the antipsychotic Risperdal.*

Dora Yates, Rusty's mother, had arrived from Tennessee and was helping with Andrea and the children. Purportedly, she didn't know Andrea was sick when she came for her visit. But on May 3, 2001, Noah told his grandmother that Andrea was filling the bathtub with water. It was the middle of the day. Dora approached Andrea and asked her why she was doing that.

"In case I need it," Andrea answered.

Debbie Holmes, Andrea's friend, rang the doorbell. She held food in her hands, which she was trying to deliver to help Andrea. But Andrea wouldn't let her good friend in the house.

On May 4, 2001, Rusty drove Andrea to Dr. Saeed's office. He was worried that Andrea wasn't eating or drinking enough, and he mentioned that she'd filled the bathtub with water. His wife had been "nearly catatonic," but she was not suicidal, he said.

Andrea did not deny that she was suicidal; she simply stared into space looking exceedingly depressed.

Rusty extensively discussed with Saeed the medications that had previously, successfully worked for Andrea—Haldol and Cogentin and, later, Effexor and Wellbutrin.

Saeed reportedly talked to the Yateses about electroshock therapy—that it was recommended in such a situation.

Rusty wouldn't consider it.

Saeed agreed that Risperdal wasn't working and said he would put Andrea on Haldol.

Rusty agreed to readmit his wife to Devereux.

At 6 P.M., Andrea Yates was once again signed in to Devereux Texas Treatment Network, Unit 3. Andrea Yates was "sad, depressed, tearful, not talking." In a photostatic copy of a picture taken of Yates upon admission, her head was down, her eyes appeared closed, her broad shoulders were hunched, and she appeared emaciated. She looked like a dead woman.

Andrea was assigned to a two-bed room. She walked into the room, climbed into bed, and stared into space.

Her 31-year-old roommate watched her. *There's nobody in her body*, she thought.

The next day, staffers coaxed Andrea Yates out of bed and to group therapy. She didn't even voice her name.

Again she did not answer when asked if she was suicidal.

Staffers were also always supposed to ask if she were homicidal. But none of the Devereux records indicated that she was ever asked that.

Rusty visited her that evening and expressed his optimism for her condition and said he "would always be there for her."

May 6, 2001, after Rusty had begged and begged Saeed to look at Andrea's previous medical records, the doctor finally had his patient sign a consent form releasing Dr. Eileen Starbranch's medical records of Andrea to Saeed.

That same day, Saeed dictated his psychiatric assessment of Yates. He said that Andrea had not continued "partial hospital care after a couple of days of attendance."

In truth, she hadn't continued after one day of attendance.

"They started following up as an outpatient with me on a once a week basis."

She did not see him from April 19 to May 4, a time span of two weeks.

"The patient was noticed to improve slightly during this course, but on the second to last visit the patient had begun to deteriorate. The patient seemed less energetic and was not eating well but denied suicidal ideation," he dictated.

There were no holidays during that two-week period to prevent him from seeing his patient who "had begun to deteriorate."

On May 6, he continued dictating, saying that Andrea had not communicated with anyone "her intent" on filling the bathtub with water. Regarding his lengthy conversation with Rusty over the medications Starbranch had successfully used on Andrea, he said, she was treated "with some kind of injectable cocktail including Haldol and Cogentin."

Saeed's notes left blank her strengths, diagnosis, and discharge criteria. Her immediate goals and objectives were designated as "see above." But the above was the blank discharge criteria. He later scribbled in a few words such as "postpartum depression."

On Andrea's daily report for May 6, Saeed said she "did not answer any questions" and she was "alert."

The following day, he wrote that he'd met with Rusty Yates on the evening of May 6, and had once again discussed electroshock therapy, which Rusty Yates had again rejected.

However, nurse's note after nurse's note pointed out that Yates was "supportive" of his wife. Indeed, Andrea only ate when prompted and urged by Rusty. Nurse's note after nurse's note also stated that Andrea was in bed and was isolating.

Saeed reported that Andrea Yates was "up and about."

That night Andrea climbed into bed, with the same clothes she wore day after day. All Andrea wanted to do was stay in bed. She changed clothes only when she was encouraged to do so. She stood in line to get her meds only after the nurses had urged her out of bed. But as a general rule, staffers left Andrea Yates alone to sit and stare.

Time and again, Saeed wrote that he'd discussed Andrea with the staff. On May 9, Saeed's records indicated that he hadn't even seen his patient the day before because she was asleep. Instead, he talked about her with the staff, who said she'd been "withdrawn."

On May 10, staffers described Yates as "non-responsive." Saeed described her as "doing a little better." She answered a few questions, he said.

By then, he'd also received Yates' medical records from Dr. Starbranch. He wrote, "no new info noted."

That evening, Rusty and Andrea were physically present for family therapy. Andrea didn't speak. Rusty spoke for them. He said Andrea was non-verbal with him, too, that he felt he had to guess what she was thinking, feeling, and wanted. He described his wife as a "pack rat," said she was the "baby" of her family of origin, and that Andrea's mother was "hard on her."

He also told the social worker that he'd taken time off from work to stay home and help. The staffer described the time off as "a good bit." She wrote, "The spouse seems to be doing everything possible." He was, she said, considering getting a housekeeper.

May 11, Andrea Yates shuffled into group therapy, found a seat that was away from everyone else, and sat down. She did not seem to be one bit engaged in what was going on. Her fellow patients called her "the quiet one." She left group early to see Saeed.

Saeed wrote that day that Andrea Yates "denied hallucinations."

Rusty Yates joined his wife in family therapy the following evening. Andrea said she had no issues to discuss. Rusty participated, but stated that they had no issues to discuss as a couple.

A 54-year-old patient watched the young couple. Again, the children played around them as they talked. The patient then overheard Rusty Yates tell his wife that the doctor said she was well enough to go home the next day.

Andrea Yates did not react.

Andrea, Rusty, and the children walked outside and sat in the courtyard where there was a swing. Mary rested in a carrier seat.

The patient still watched them.

Everyone seemed happy but Andrea. Her hair was long and oily. She looked like a "zombie."

After about an hour, Rusty and the children left. The husband and wife never hugged or kissed each other.

The patient got up and walked over to Andrea. "Are you here because of postpartum depression?" she asked.

Andrea mumbled and stared into the evening.

"My cousin had postpartum depression, and it was very hard to live with the pain."

Andrea Yates got up and went to her room.

The patient thought Andrea followed Rusty "like a puppy would follow its owner."

May 14, Andrea told Dr. Saeed that she was not suicidal, she had thought of suicide off and on in the past, but she did not dwell on it and had no intent or plan.

No records indicate that she was asked about homicidal ideation, as required.

She also told the doctor that she wanted to go home and participate in partial hospitalization.

Saeed decided to discharge the still-depressed patient, unless Rusty Yates objected. His physician's orders stated, "Husband can call and talk to me."

That evening, Rusty Yates was stunned, he said, to find his wife with her bags packed and ready to go home. According to Rusty, he questioned the nurses why. They turned and meekly walked away.

The "discharge plan" for Andrea Yates that had been completed almost ten days earlier had an "anticipated discharge date" of May 14, the very day she was released.

Andrea Yates possessed prescriptions for 2 mg of Haldol, 45 mg of Remeron, and 450 mg of Effexor, up from 300 mg when she was admitted on May 4.

Strangely enough, there was one page of Andrea Yates' daily progress report with a May 4, 2001, date that indicated a staffer had asked her if she were suicidal or homicidal. According to the report, Rusty had answered that she was neither. And Andrea had agreed, not by answering verbally, but by nodding her head.

Whereas all Yates' other progress notes were in relative chronological order, that page did not have another notation until May 13. That note was written by Dr. Mohammad Saeed.

The very first day of Andrea Yates' partial hospitalization, she arrived without having taken her morning medications. Reportedly, she was "improved" over the previous week. The next day, though, she was back to one- and two-word answers.

May 17, Saeed said that she "appears stable." He also wrote that she reported "depression."

In therapy, she said she had no issues to work on.

After all, the topic, as usual, was addiction.

The therapist suggested communication.

Andrea Yates stared into space.

Eventually, she participated a bit and shared that her own negative self-image influenced her relationships.

The next day, she was asked what she enjoyed most when she returned home each night.

She sat silent for a long time, then answered, "Being back with family."

She slept the last half of the session.

Saeed wrote that day that Yates was "slightly more improved."

May 21, 2001, Yates sat in one spot all day. Her voice was emotionless. Her lips were dry and cracked. Saeed wrote that she was sleeping and eating well and "tolerating meds well." They discussed, he said, her possible discharge from PHP the following day.

The next day, her posture was "constricted," her affect was flat. Yet, she was reported to be "much improved compared to last week."

On May 22, 2001, three days before her planned release from PHP, Andrea Yates was discharged from partial hospitalization. The registered nurse signing that discharge wrote "patient not here for discharge." She also wrote "patient not suicidal" as the reason for discharge.

According to Rusty Yates, Andrea attended every single day of PHP, and *he* wanted her to go to PHP for two weeks. Devereux wanted her to attend for six days.

Dr. Saeed's discharge summary stated that Yates had continued with severe depression until her Wellbutrin "was tapered off" and Remeron started. "Patient began slow and steady recovery. Husband noticed 70 percent improvement."

She was to be in Saeed's office the following week.

Two weeks before June 20, 2001, the day Andrea Yates called Houston police to her home, Dr. Saeed took Andrea off of her antipsychotic.

Two days before June 20, Rusty Yates drove his wife to Dr. Saeed's office. They were barely through the appointment, Rusty recalled, when he looked over at Saeed's notes.

Saeed had filled 60 percent of the page with comments, according to Yates. But when Rusty later saw Saeed's official notes from the meeting, there was much, much less writing. Rusty Yates didn't believe they were the same notes.

He left the doctor's office with new prescriptions for Andrea and took his wife to Burger King. He got her a Whopper, Jr., fries, and a Coke. She ate nothing, not even one sip of soda.

CHAPTER 22

"Those people are nuts!" A psychiatric nurse who once worked at Devereux Texas Treatment Network, sat in her home and railed against her former employer. But her former employer couldn't respond to the charges. Neither could Dr. Saeed. Both were bound by the gag order. She used the code-name Jane.

The ideal way psychiatric treatment works, she explained, is that there is a team of doctors, nurses, therapists, even the insurance company, functioning together and agreeing on patient care, goals, and time frames. And if that plan doesn't work, the team has an alternate plan. Her experience was that that didn't happen at Devereux.

"The therapist doesn't talk to the doctor." Protocols aren't always followed, she said, not even when patients are on suicide watch. Jane referenced a patient who was supposed to be on one-on-one suicide watch, meaning he was to be watched every minute. Yet, he hanged himself in a Devereux bathroom. Staffers took so long to check on him that his body was cold when he was discovered, she said.

Many of the twenty-nine pages of complaints filed against Devereux at the Texas Department of Health, from September 1, 1996, to August 31, 1999, involved patient rights. Specifically, out of 181 total complaints, 106 involved a violation of patient rights. That equated to almost six out of every ten complaints. Thirty-two percent of those patient rights complaints were found to be valid by the Texas Department of Health.

If anyone tried to correct Devereux's practices, she heard, " 'This is the way Devereux has always done things. That is the way Devereux does things now. That is the way Devereux will always do things.' " Her voice was almost monotone, as if she'd heard the phrase so many times that it had become a hypnotic recording.

It didn't make sense, Jane said, and it had made her feel like she was in *A Clockwork Orange* or *The Twilight Zone*.

"The only central form of communication that you had was the patient's chart. That was a place you could go, even though you hadn't talked to the therapist or talked to the nurse or talked to the teacher or talked to the recreational therapist or the doctor, you could go to that chart and find out exactly what everybody was doing." In her experience, that didn't happen.

"They were understaffed . . . Many of the nurses' morale was so poor that all they could do was sit behind a desk and talk about how bad things were." She never saw a patient being abused; she simply thought the nurses were "burned out."

In Jane's experience, Devereux didn't care about quality assurance. A member of the nursing administration, a friend of hers, left her job at Devereux after telling the hospital leadership that she was concerned about Devereux's meeting patient/staffing ratios set by the Texas Department of Health.

In her experience, Dr. Saeed had difficulty following protocol.

She found he had "difficulty" showing up for staffings— once-a-week meetings to discuss patient treatment—despite the fact that staffers would wait forty-five minutes just for him. "He wouldn't be there for critical calls." Repeatedly, Jane recounted, she phoned his office about the needs of his patients. "And I could not get a response. He didn't answer his pager. His office didn't reach him. And then he would show up at an inadvertent time and be angry because we paged him. And that's when I said I had had enough."

She told the Devereux administrators that she would stay at the facility if she didn't have to work with Saeed.

In her dealings with him, he often spent only five minutes with patients and that was it, she stated, and, in her view, never "adequately listened to his patients as far as their signs and symptoms." His notes about patients were sparse.

"I don't think I ever saw him make eye contact with a patient. I saw him do a session with a patient in the hall, they were sitting in chairs, side-by-side, and he has his little book—his little chart out and he's making notes, and he's 'uh-huh, uh-huh, uh-huh.' And I don't think I ever once saw him look up at that patient. And after about five minutes he says, 'Okay,' " and Jane clapped her hands as if a notebook were slapping shut, " 'Thank you very much,' and that was it."

In one instance, she asked him, she said, to sit down and tell her what he planned to do regarding a patient. "Well, the rule is, if it's not in the medical records, it never happened." She handed him the chart and told him to write down his instructions.

An hour later, she checked the chart, "and there [was] a two-line note that said nothing of what," she recalled, "he'd just told me."

Her voice eased into breathy compassion, "I don't know how in the world Dr. Saeed ended up with this child," meaning Andrea Yates. "Not that I have any love lost for Russell, but Russell can't be held responsible for treatment, because he's not a trained professional. And he might have balked at her treatment, but can you really say you blame him after dealing with somebody like this?"

Jane recalled having discharge and aftercare plans ready for a patient ready to leave. The family was waiting to take the patient home, and all she needed was Dr. Saeed's signature. "And the man wouldn't show up. Then he'd come up with some excuse that the patient had to stay another three days, but he wouldn't tell us why!" Her impression, she said, was that "his thing was that, 'I don't have to, I'm the doctor.'" Jane's attitude was, "You may be the captain to the ship, but without the sailors, the ship don't move, buddy."

She thought about a photograph on her refrigerator door—a photo of Andrea Yates' nurses, women who did care deeply for their psychotic patient. She then recounted how one nurse in particular had said that Rusty Yates "just flat said no" when it came to putting Andrea in partial hospital.

There were other doctors at Devereux, she thought, who would have given Andrea Yates better care.

A Devereux staffer, she said, told her that Andrea kept mumbling something about a religion and "they had to live on this bus in Florida." And it was when they were living on the bus in Florida, Andrea said, "that that's when she knew that the devil had gotten her."

Jane said she asked her friend, "What are you talking about?"

"Well, that's the part that never made any sense," her friend answered.

"And it was real sketchy about this religious thing," Jane continued.

They asked Rusty about it. "Have y'all ever lived on a bus in Florida? We never could get anything out of him about some bus in Florida," she quoted her friend.

Jane supposed there was probably something in the medical records about "patient living on a bus in Florida." There was.

"I don't know what the preachings or the teachings were," Jane said of Andrea Yates' exposure to the devil on a bus, "but it would not have taken much to work that child's mind." Somewhere along the line, she said, a very weak psyche was destroyed. "This is beyond postpartum depression. This is far beyond."

*   *   *

Maybe Andrea Yates wasn't verbally telling staffers what
they needed to hear, but she was telling them in other ways.
"She obviously had an eating disorder. She was anorexic.
She was pulling out her hair. There were some real obvious
signs and symptoms there that something was real off-board
that nobody was looking at." As psychiatric professionals,
she stated, one should hear the words *and* see the symptoms,
and hear what's not being said, too—which sent her back
to discussing Saeed.

When you have somebody who has a history of mental
illness, some doctors, Jane stated, assume that there's nothing they can do that will make a permanent difference, that
they're going to keep coming back, and coming back, and
coming back.

"Everybody who had anything to do with Andrea said the
same thing—they felt such tremendous pity for her because
here she had this domineering husband that . . . took over
everything. And here was this sweet, almost childlike person. And I know that in their minds, that would have been
the furtherest thing from anybody's mind that she could
have done that to her children." Andrea Yates, she said,
"was the most unaggressive person you would ever meet.
She seemed like a frightened deer . . ."

Her friend told her, "Those children would walk in that
door and you could just see her face light up. She was such
a wonderful mom."

She fired off, "I do believe Rusty had a part to play in
this, but not near the part that Dr. Saeed [did]. I think that
that man"—Yates—"was so frustrated with the lack of response he was getting from his treatment team that he didn't
feel it was necessary."

She continued, "If Russell couldn't get the response he
needed from his own treatment team, why would he have
been led to believe that day hospital would have done any
better for Andrea?"

But Jane stuck by her belief that Rusty Yates didn't do

all that he should have done for his wife. "Russell would show with the kids, and the nurses would have to watch the children, which is really inappropriate, very inappropriate. First of all, you don't bring children into a psychiatric unit like that. Secondly, there's all kind of nasties running around. And third, it's totally inappropriate. He should have gotten a babysitter."

She added, "See, I'm hearing two different stories, from the therapeutic group and then from what Russell is saying. And then with Dr. Saeed in the middle, I can see it both ways. I can see Russell getting frustrated and say 'To hell with this,' but I can hear from the therapeutic side that, you know, his push was to get her home because he needed a babysitter. And that was her job.

"We all leave wanting to tell the world what's going on there, but we realize in the medical profession, doctors don't do it, nurses don't do it, we don't tell on each other because once you're blackballed, you're blackballed forever. They make sure you don't talk out of school. . . . You love giving the information as long as nobody knows it's you. . . . God knows, plenty of people have tried, and plenty of people have ended up in the unemployment line doing something like selling newspapers because they can't get jobs as nurses. Some of those have chosen to go quietly into the night, like myself.

"There are a lot of people who want to talk, but out of fear, don't . . . And what ends up happening is that the people who are innocent get hurt to protect the people who should be to blame. It doesn't matter what you say; a nurse's voice will never be heard over a physician's, or an administrator's."

CHAPTER 23

Tuesday, September 4, 2001, Harris County Assistant D.A. Kaylynn Williford subpoenaed Andrea Yates' mother, three brothers and one sister, and Rusty Yates' mother and one brother, ordering them to appear at the September 12 competency hearing.

By then, prosecutors had issued a search warrant for blood and hair samples from Andrea Yates. They wanted to compare her DNA to the scrapings taken during her children's autopsies.

Her attorneys objected, saying that the search warrant was "nothing more than a veiled effort to underscore and sensationalize the facts and circumstances of the drowning so as to arouse and inflame the community that will ultimately judge whether or not Andrea Pia Yates was insane at the times of the deaths."

Mid-morning of September 5, Michael Woroniecki and family parked their red mini-van near the University of Oklahoma campus, unloaded their worn banners from PVC tubes atop their vehicle, and marched onto the campus mall to preach and convert the overwhelmingly Christian students of OU.

Everyone was outdoors. The day was warm, with just a few puffy clouds in an otherwise blue sky. It was the kind of day that made students love going to OU.

According to OU student Jeremy Tate, the signs the Woronieckis carried looked at least a couple of years old, and were two or three words from different Bible verses, put together to say what Woroniecki wanted them to say.

"What's going on?" Tate asked one of Woroniecki's grade-school-age sons.

"You're not saved." The boy handed Tate a pamphlet.

Tate quickly read the material: "False Christians have the same goals of any pagan; go to college, get a job, make money, get married and settle down. Their false preachers breed such delusion because they themselves are blind leaders of the blind."

"They're tools of the devil," Michael Woroniecki loudly proclaimed, without the aid of a loudspeaker. Computers are bad, he called, they take you away from what you really need and what you should really be doing. His belly hung over too-tight shorts. His sleeveless T-shirt was on the tight side, too, and showed off the muscles in his arms.

"Well," Tate responded, "I mean, you say computers are bad, technology is bad, cars are bad, but yet I'm assuming you came here in a van that was designed by people who went through college."

Tate had already seen the Woronieckis' red, mid-1990s mini-van with Texas plates parked along the Oklahoma University street. On the back glass, stenciled in white letters, was a saying to the effect that church wasn't going to get one to heaven.

"Yes," the boy answered, "but you don't have to do that. You can drop out of college and follow God and do what God wants you to and let God work in your life."

No matter what Tate said to the young, blue-eyed, blond boy in blue jean shorts and a Texas T-shirt, the boy's answer was always that God would provide for him, he didn't have to worry about anything.

"Look at these flowers," the child quoted, pointing to a Bible verse, "they do not worry for tomorrow, for God will take care of them. Look at the birds, they do not worry about what they wear, for God takes care of them."

"Have you ever been to a doctor or a hospital?" Tate asked.

The boy answered that he'd once broken his arm.

"That doctor who treated you, in essence, saved your arm, and maybe your life, because if any infection had gotten in . . . What about him? . . . Can he not use the gift from God of being able to heal people and to practice His words, can he not use that for good? Is that not good enough?"

"That's not the point," the boy replied, expressionless. "The point is that you're not going to heaven, because you're not following God's word and God's path. School is bad. God will take care of you. You don't need all this. All this will not get you to heaven. That's not the point. The point is you don't need this. All you need is Jesus Christ in your life to get to heaven."

Other students tried to ask one of Woroniecki's college-age daughters a question.

"You're going to hell until you're saved," she replied simply. "You're not saved until you quit going to school and start living according to God's plan and God's word." She then turned her back and ignored the students, staring into space with glazed-over eyes.

None of the children ever smiled.

"You hide tremendous depression. You smile on the outside but deep within you are full of anxiety," read one of the fliers the children handed to the students. "Satan tells you to blame a job, a spouse, even God Himself for your problems. THE TRUE REASON IS BECAUSE YOU ARE SEPARATED FROM YOUR CREATOR GOD! You live by FEELINGS and MOODS, not FAITH. So Satan easily manipulates your life. God says your heart is 'desperately sick.' (Jer. 17:19). You don't know the JOY of spirit-life."

And farther down the flier, Woroniecki had written, "Satan owns you."

Like his children, Michael Woroniecki never smiled.

A couple strolled by with their baby, and Woroniecki

informed them that their child wasn't going to heaven because of them.

By afternoon, the campus trashcans overflowed with discarded pamphlets and fliers. The lawns were littered with them, too. As the Woronieckis packed their banners and pamphlets into their red mini-van, Eric Webb, of the *Undercurrent*, OU's underground newspaper, approached Woroniecki and asked more questions, which he later published in the paper.

Like everyone else on campus, he wanted to know why Woroniecki was there.

"To tell them they're going to hell," the preacher answered.

Noticing the Oregon drop box address, Webb asked if Woroniecki was from out of state.

"From out of this world. Whole 'nother kingdom. Another realm." And later Woroniecki said to the student, "Oklahoma is a horrible college. It's a horrible school, because it's right in the Bible Belt. It's one of the worst campuses to go to."

"Horrible because they think?" Webb responded.

"Horrible because they're all Christian. It's outrageous. . . . This place is just sick with Christianity."

That same day, Rusty Yates walked into the Four Seasons Hotel in downtown Houston to sit down with Ed Bradley of *60 Minutes*. Rusty Yates answered 130 questions posed by Bradley, bobbling only one, Yates later boasted. They had to repeat that one only out of concern that he may have crossed the gag-order line.

The CBS crew then traveled to the Yates house for a bit of additional filming. Rusty provided them with a home video of the kids and a video of the funeral.

Soon, Rusty was on a plane headed for Nashville, to mark his thirty-seventh birthday with his mother and fifteen or twenty friends from DuPont High. It was like a mini-reunion with love and support for Rusty Yates. To the

NASA engineer, it was so pleasantly different from Houston's constant harsh judgments. It was a time of compassion. With his high school friends, he could share his feelings and not be persecuted, as he felt he was in Clear Lake.

It was also a time of caring by his mother. Rusty Yates and his brother, Randy, had a running joke—Mom loves me best. "She gave me a thousand dollars," he'd brag with a grin to Randy, knowing that the gift was really $100. "What'd she give you?" he'd crack. She gave them both unconditional support.

September 7, 2001, the day after Rusty's birthday, a stack of subpoenas were issued for the competency hearing. George Parnham once again subpoenaed his client's medical records from Methodist Hospital, Memorial Hermann Prevention & Recovery Center (Spring Shadows Glenn), Devereux Texas Treatment Network, and Dr. Michelle Ferguson of Harris County Sheriff's Department Jail Facility Psychiatric Unit, Yates' admitting doctor.

Prosecutor Joe Owmby subpoened MHMRA jail employees Beatrice Carroll, Fannie Turner, Leila Harris, B. Bohmann, Jean Garcia, and John "Bayless." As he had weeks before, Owmby meant John Bayliss.

Rusty Yates got back to Houston on Sunday, September 9, just two days before jury selection was to begin for his wife's competency hearing. He caught a ride that evening with the two leaders of his Clear Lake Church of Christ small group. He rode with them from his house, just a few blocks from the church, to Alvin, Texas, and the home of Byron Fike.

Fike was leading the small group at his own home, and the group wasn't so small that evening. There were visiting missionaries and other guests ready to talk about faith. Members expected Rusty Yates to say something about his faith. Instead, with many children in attendance, he talked about his family, his Website, his new criminal attorney, and his publicity plan.

Yates explained part of his strategic plan to save his wife—his interview with *60 Minutes*, which he said would air on September 23, a week after Andrea's competency hearing. Bam. He planned for that interview to be followed the very next day with a *Time* magazine story. Bam. In essence, it would be a one-two public relations punch. Rusty grinned. He'd thought it out, he'd planned it out, he'd timed it out, and that's the way it should be . . . just perfect for affecting the trial. He'd even told *Time* magazine that they couldn't run their Yates article until *after* the *60 Minutes* interview had aired.

A *Time* reporter had told friends and neighbors of Rusty Yates that she *was* writing a story on him, and she was trying to entice them to talk with lures of lunches at Houston's Ritz-Carlton Hotel. Money, budget, was no problem, she told the folks.

In truth, Rusty Yates hadn't yet sat down with *Time*. He told the small group that he thought the *Time* reporter—a different one from the woman trying to lure sources with Ritz-Carlton lunches—was "shifty." But that wasn't going to stop him from talking to *Time*; it was part of the plan. And it didn't matter that Rusty Yates was under a gag order; he and the judge hadn't quite gotten together on that, yet, he said.

He's not supposed to talk about the trial, or his feelings about the trial, he said, so he's just talking about Andrea's history and their history. He said *60 Minutes* asked him, "Will you ever forgive your wife?" He said he had answered, "She doesn't need to be forgiven." She has a good heart; she just had a bad mind at the time, he explained. Even when she was killing the children, he said, she thought she was doing the right thing, because she believed she was a bad mother.

If he did decide to talk about the trial, he told the small group, he thought he could get by with it, because the district attorney had repeatedly talked to the media. The D.A.'s been talking, he said, why can't I?

In fact, Rusty Yates felt that the gag order violated his First Amendment rights, and his new attorney—Edward A. Mallett, president of the National Association of Criminal Defense Attorneys—had been hired, at the suggestion of George Parnham, to fight that for him. Indeed, Yates was ready to hire the attorney on Parnham's recommendation alone. But Edward A. Mallett provided Rusty with references—a magazine cover story about himself.

After the meeting wrapped up, Rusty Yates stayed and talked. Church member Becky Morris walked up to him and listened. He looked her in the eyes. She tried to urge him to come to the church's Sunday-school class taught by Byron Fike, which Rusty had never attended. Yates said he'd been "thinking about it."

She later said, "I'm glad I'm not you."

Rusty started laughing. "That's funny."

"No, that's true," Morris replied.

Rusty Yates continued to laugh so hard that Becky Morris thought he was going to fall down.

Rusty was one of the last ones to leave that night.

The next day, Parnham and Odom filed three motions before Judge Belinda Hill. One was a motion for discovery, requesting the State's "evidence or information of medical records" and its competency hearing witness list, with a specific request for the names of the expert witnesses that the State planned to call. Another was a motion to determine the competence of the State's MHMRA expert witnesses.

A third motion requested that Article 16.02 Section 1A (a) of the *Texas Code of Criminal Procedure* be set aside as unconstitutional. It argued that the article stated "the defendant must have sufficient present ability to consult with the person's lawyer with a reasonable degree of rational understanding" and "a rational as well as factual understanding of the proceedings against the person," but that the U.S. Supreme Court had expanded that standard to include the prerequisite that the defendant be able to "assist in his defense."

The defense additionally requested that the jury receive specific instructions "on the issue of whether the Defendant is competent to assist in her own defense."

That same morning, Owmby filed a "supplement to State's motion to order defendant to submit to examination by mental health expert—statement of nature and scope of the examination."

It explained that a mental health expert chosen by the prosecution would examine Andrea Yates as to whether she was insane at the time of the crime. The expert would not question Yates regarding whether she was a future threat to society, a matter the State had to prove to make Yates eligible for death by lethal injection.

"However," the motion read, "any information developed during a mental status examination has the potential to become relevant to an issue in the punishment phase of the trial. Consequently, the State may be forced to call the mental health examiner as a rebuttal witness on the issue of Future Dangerousness."

Owmby requested that the expert have three days of unfettered access to Andrea Yates. "The nature of any psychological examination, including this one, requires an unhindered relationship between the examiner and the subject. For that reason, a Defendant does not have the right to have an attorney present during a psychiatric examination."

Tuesday, September 11, 2001, dawned with beauty in Houston, Texas. The air was stunningly clear, the sky autumn bright. The temperature was almost crisp as Bay Area residents walked out their doors and picked up the *Houston Chronicle* from their driveways. They opened the paper and saw a front page headline: "Yates jury selection is today." Reporter Lisa Teachey wrote, "National attention will be focused on a Harris County courtroom today as 120 citizens are culled down to the 12-person jury who will make a ma-

jor decision regarding Andrea Pia Yates—whether she is fit
to stand trial."

Teachey's words seemed accurate. The night before, six
satellite trucks had searched for prime parking places in
front of the Harris County Courthouse, ready to flash across
the world the images of Rusty Yates, George Parnham, and
Joe Owmby as they entered and exited the courthouse.

Visitors staying in the hotels surrounding Johnson Space
Center, Rusty Yates' workplace, woke to find a 5½"-by-
7½" color photo of Andrea Yates centering the front page
of *USA Today* with the headline, " 'Psychotic,' but is Andrea Yates legally insane?"

By 9 A.M., reporters had their press passes for the hearing,
and 120 potential jurors were lined up ready to enter the
courtroom. But soon, the CNN satellite truck drove away.
It was 10 A.M. in New York, and the nation's eyes, even
Houston's, were *not* on Andrea Yates. They were on the
crumpled and smoking World Trade Center in New York
City. Terrorists had struck.

The jurors were sent home to hug their living children.
The competency hearing was postponed until September 18.
Suddenly, the deaths of five children in Clear Lake, Texas,
didn't seem important.

Rusty Yates may have had a publicity plan, but so did
Osama bin Ladin. And bin Ladin's proved more powerful.

With constant replays of the burning and collapsing World
Trade Center playing on a large-screen TV, Andrea Yates'
Starbucks friend, fan, and fellow nurse wanted to study Andrea's medical records. She read out loud from the Methodist Hospital records, as Katie Couric described the falling
buildings over and over again.

"Patient's husband also stated several times that one of
his main goals as a parent right now is to teach his sons
how to be quiet for longer periods of time."

"Rusty was a little different," the woman's husband
spoke over her. "Nice guy," he said, munching chips. The

husband, who hadn't wanted to talk or get involved, was talking, as he continually cocked his head toward the TV. "He's pretty much to himself. He's not the type to go out and talk a lot."

Suddenly, the man's wife got up from the medical records, rushed around the kitchen, and jabbered about Andrea. Finally, she sat back down to the medical records. She noticed that Andrea rarely answered when asked if she were suicidal or homicidal. Patients who were suicidal, she stressed, weren't going to tell you they were; you had to go by their body language. She read farther down—Child Protective Services called over Yates' living arrangement, Yates hinted she wanted to move into an apartment.

The psych nurse and friend stopped. "I know Rusty didn't drown those kids. She did." But she believed that Rusty Yates was an accomplice because of the living arrangements. "He slowly killed her. I *mean* he slowly killed her."

Her husband tried to stand up for Rusty, pointing out that Andrea was severely depressed. The husband and wife bantered back and forth, she defending Andrea, he defending Rusty.

"Rusty was to himself, but then to somebody he knew, he would just be a chatterbox," the husband commented.

The wife broke in and emphasized that Andrea was a plain Jane who felt like she'd married a Prince Charming.

The husband recalled, "I just remember saying, boy, you know, 'She's kinda thin, but she's muscular.' She could use one of those makeovers, you know, where you fix the makeup and the hair and put you in a decent dress and suddenly you go from 'Aiieh' to 'Hey, look.' She just never did anything to improve her looks. And probably she never cared about it. . . . She probably had this ideology that 'I've got Rusty and that's all I need.' " She smiled and laughed regularly, he remembered.

"That's the Andrea I knew," his wife said wistfully.

The woman's husband was a man who knew drugs, depression, and how they worked together on one's body. Andrea Yates, he said, got so horribly depressed that her brain's neurotransmitters no longer fired. "She couldn't help the way she did. And it led to psychosis."

He thought Yates' attorneys would try to paint Rusty Yates "as a real mean husband to try to get her off. And I don't think he was. Rusty—he's a pretty good man."

"You can say that," the wife interrupted, then argued that Rusty knew Andrea suffered postpartum depression, kept having babies, had her living in a bus. "He's keeping her confined 24/7 and she's having no interaction with anybody else but the kids and him. . . . That's evidence right there. You can be a good guy, but you can be neglectful and not intimate. To me, that's controlling behavior. He was more worried about the kids than he was her."

Theirs was the typical heated discussion over the Yates family that happened in homes all over Houston. The difference was that this family actually knew Rusty and Andrea Yates.

The woman read in the medical records about Andrea taking an overdose of her father's medicine.

"That's very desperate. That's extremely desperate," the knowledgeable-about-drugs husband commented. "She being a nurse, too, to take her father's medication . . ." He explained that one doesn't do anything to "get" depression; it's a biochemical imbalance. And that it took Andrea Yates a long time to get that severely depressed.

Event after event—having child after child, her father dying—"they were more fuel for the fire. Depressed people can't concentrate. They can't think right. They get eating disorders, sleeping disorders. . . . You get up in the morning, you're severely depressed, you can sit in that chair all day and not do anything, because you just don't have the get-up-and-go. And can you imagine feeling like that and getting up and having to take care of five children? It was all she could do, probably, to do anything."

The wife read in the medical records about Andrea's leisure time—that one night a week, Rusty Yates babysat the children while Andrea went out to shop for the family. "That's really leisure activity?" the woman remarked, her voice rising with incredulity. "I don't know," she sighed. "I don't know. I just think he's really responsible for her deterioration."

In the background, on their big-screen TV, a reporter at Ground Zero in New York City watched a gray cloud speed toward her. She frantically ordered a woman with a child, "Get out of here! Get out of here! Look out for your baby!"

But the woman in Houston, Texas, staring at Andrea Yates' psychiatric history, turned to her husband and said, "How can you say this is such a good guy when he's stupid?"

"He doesn't have the knowledge that we do."

"He's controlling and selfish."

The psych nurse read down and saw that Andrea Yates was pulling her hair out when she entered Spring Shadows Glen. The pain was so severe, she explained, that pulling out her hair felt good—it dulled the other pain.

One of the last things the psych nurse emphasized on that September 11 was that one should never talk religion or introduce religious thoughts to a psychotic patient. Andrea Yates, she had read, was worried about her salvation.

Friday, September 14, 2001, was a gorgeous, autumn day in Madison, Wisconsin, perfect for tossing a football. By one in the afternoon, 20,000 persons had gathered on the Library Mall of the University of Wisconsin, not to pep their team for a football game—all games had been cancelled—but to pray and grieve for the victims of the World Trade Center, the Pentagon, and Pennsylvania.

Ten police officers stood together and leaned in to listen as Professor Joseph Elder rose to address the crowd. They needed comforting words.

A stage and loudspeaker had been set up on the steps of the west entrance of Memorial Library. A fifteen-foot-wide

sidewalk separated the stage from the crowd. Professor Elder had just barely started speaking when one of those ten
officers, Detective Bruce Carroll, noticed three sixteen-foot
poles mysteriously moving toward the stage. The carriers of
the poles were not visible through the crowd, but he saw
that those poles held rolled-up banners. The poles stopped
near the sidewalk. The banners were unfurled.

"ALL THAT MATTERS—YOU ARE HEADED FOR HELL," one
banner screamed over a span of eight feet by sixteen feet.
Another cried, "JESUS SOON TO JUDGE" in a smaller six-foot–
by–ten-foot banner. The banners began moving again,
through the crowd and closer to the sidewalk. Then the hold-
ers of the banners became visible. Two young, blond females carried the larger banner; one younger, blond female
carried the smaller one. They wore shorts and short-sleeved
tops.

The three girls moved directly in front of the stage, using
their banners to block one side of the crowd's view of Professor Elder. Thousands booed. The eldest blonde yelled
back, "You're all going to hell!" Her unamplified voice was
louder and more powerful than the amplified voice of Professor Elder.

The girl continued shouting, the crowd continued booing,
and the three girls slowly began to move their banners and
their "You're going to hell" taunts along the stage.

A white female in her mid-forties jumped from the
crowd, grabbed one of the poles of the largest banner, and
yanked it to the ground. The throng of grievers roared and
rose to its feet, as more mourners for the U.S.A. moved
toward the girls. The oldest blonde, whose banner had been
ripped from her hands, still yelled at the crowd.

The police officers moved toward the three females, fear-
ing that the girls were in danger. But a male onlooker beat
them. He grabbed the eldest blonde's arm, spun her around,
and twisted her into his control, marching her away from
the onlookers.

"Drop your pole," Detective Carroll ordered the middle

blonde. He grabbed her upper arm and yelled, "You're under arrest."

Miraculously, the eldest blonde appeared at the middle blonde's side and said, "Okay, we're done now. We'll leave."

"You're under arrest," Carroll informed her, too, and grabbed her by the arm. With the aid of three other officers, he escorted the two girls away from the mall, found the youngest blonde, and told them all that they were under arrest for disorderly conduct. The girls were handcuffed and searched.

Their identifications showed that they were Sarah Woroniecki, who was going to turn 21 years old in just twelve days; Ruth Woroniecki, who was 19; and 17-year-old Elizabeth Woroniecki. Sarah held a Texas driver's license. Ruth held a Florida license. They said they traveled with their father.

Their father was Michael Woroniecki, also known as Michael Worneki and Michael Warnecki, and a few other names.

"We are definitely not Christians!" said one of the girls, upset that she and her sisters would be construed as such. "We would rather have been killed at the hands of the crowd than be arrested by Christian police officers."

And the girls implied to the captain that they'd been arrested many times, and a simple arrest wasn't going to stop them.

Eventually, they were booked. Bail was set at $242.75 each and a court date of September 28, 2001, was established. The Woroniecki girls were released without posting bail. They left in a Volkswagen van with Texas license plates. As they drove off, slogans referring to Jesus were visible on their van. But Michael Woroniecki had never shown his face.

Neither of the girls made their initial court appearances, according to the Madison Police Department, and arrest warrants were to be issued.

*   *   *

Write the traveling evangelist at the Oregon drop box, and
one receives a calligraphically addressed packet. It contains
an audiocassette, carefully wrapped and taped in paper tow-
eling, and labeled by hand, "How to Study the Word of
God," as well as a handwritten, personal letter inviting one
to "share more personal things." There are also musty news-
letters and brochures—"The Perilous Times," which claims
"God says the source of sin's power is **the Law** and your
deep anxieties and fearfulness can be traced to **the Devil's
right to your soul when you die**," and a "Hi! How ya
doin?" pamphlet explaining that the Woronieckis have lived
full-time in an RV for twenty years, going through three
buses, all renovated themselves. "All six of our children
were born 'at home' in a different state. My wife is not a
contemporary 'witch' sacrificing her children for a career."
Michael Woroniecki adds, "She is awesome and submitted
to me."

A brochure called "The 'Witch', The 'Wimp' " is also
included. "Before I obeyed God," Woroniecki writes, "I too
accepted the teachings of darkness from this 'advanced' culture on 'womens [sic] rights'. I was stunned, but thrilled, to
discover God's 'light.' At birth a woman inherits the con-
tentious nature of Eve and a man is born with the passive
nature of Adam."

Women, he teaches, are witches, while men are wimps.
"The fury, for being labeled a 'witch' only serves to further
expose the blinding power of your arrogant self-image. (I've
never seen a guy furious over the label a 'wimp'.) . . . Unless you face this SIN NATURE you will be tormented and
blinded by its' vexations. Your blindness renders you STU-
PID to the obvious. You are an emotional 'basketcase'!"

CHAPTER 24

The notice for the rescheduled candlelight vigil for the Andrea Pia Yates Support Coalition—Tuesday, September 18, 8 P.M., in front of Yates' new home, the Harris County Jail—had warned: "Be prepared for protestors against us. We need peacekeepers to act as monitors. Major media will be there."

By 7:30 P.M., one lonely TV van was parked curbside at the jail. A pleasant wind blew. Deborah Bell, president of the Texas chapter of NOW, smoothed a cloth over a small table pushed as close to the jail wall as possible. She laid out press kits. Sheriff's officers glared. Don't block the sidewalk, they ordered.

A coalition participant suggested they move the vigil across the street. A cop muttered disgustedly, "I'm glad to hear that."

Moments later, Andrea's supporters were setting up in front of Bail America Bail Bonds, a weathered house trailer located on the edge of a $5.50 self-serve parking lot. Bell's table was close to the trailer's steps. Any photos taken of the vigil would have "Bail Bonds" just above the five purple candles Bell was setting up in honor of the dead children.

Texas NOW claimed they were holding the vigil to bring attention to postpartum depression. Bystanders, though, handed out fliers protesting the death penalty. Buses and vans drove by. Drivers rudely roared their horns. Passengers stared with confused faces.

Participants started to light their candles and then were ordered not to. Signs went up and down, "Andrea Yates should receive treatment, not punishment." "Breaking the Silence, Post-Partum Psychosis & Depression." Folks milled aimlessly back and forth. "Post Partum Depression is Real." "We support Andrea Pia Yates."

There was an occasional flash of a NOW sign. A *Houston Chronicle* photographer and reporter showed. A senior citizen posed for photos with her posters. "Treatment, Not Death Penalty." Associated Press finally arrived, and a couple of other TV stations meandered in. A mother and child posed for photos with their candle, as Deborah Bell and crew repeatedly lighted the candles in honor of the Yates children. The candles kept blowing out.

The gathering grew to maybe thirty persons. A microphone was set up. An announcement was garbled over the sound system. A guitarist played while a young girl sang *Andrea's Song*. "As five my one, a calling thee, home to find another me." A bus engine groaned. And the chorus lost itself in the wind, "Deep, deep in my mind . . ."

A sign flashed from near a fence. "In Memory of Noah, John, Paul, Luke, and Mary Yates. Prevent Another Tragedy. Learn About Postpartum Psychosis." "Andrea, You Are Not Alone."

Three small groupings of deputies vaguely watched, looking bored.

"Shame on You, Mr. D.A." a poster read.

The sun shined, and the temperature was moderate for Houston on Wednesday, September 19, 2001.

Three rows of mostly local media settled into Judge Belinda Hill's fifth-floor courtroom, comfortably seated with lots of space between them. A pool video cameraman waited.

With high ceilings, dark wood-toned paneling on its walls, and dark wooden church-pew–like benches in its gallery, the courtroom had almost a sanctuary feel to it. But there were no windows and no hint of a breath of fresh air, only the scent of bleakness. The lighting was low and dark, like sitting in a fog at night. Some of the spectator benches were padded with plastic, dark turquoise cushions that squeaked with any movement.

Joe Owmby stood near Judge Hill's bench with his arms crossed and a cup of coffee in his left hand. George Parnham, arms also crossed, studied notes on a yellow legal pad.

The morning before, as Parnham and Wendell Odom had approached the building for jury selection, TV camera crews had rushed the lawyers, begging for a comment.

Parnham, with his glasses on the tip of his nose, carrying a huge, black briefcase, turned to the cameras and waited for Odom. Odom, holding an easel, told the reporters that jurors might be distracted by world events, "but all in all, they will pay attention." The attorneys then slipped inside the building. The terrorist attacks of the past week had hit Parnham & Associates. Their receptionist, Sheryl Steele, had lost a cousin in the World Trade Center.

To the 120 potential jurors crammed inside the courtroom, Judge Hill had clarified the difference between competency and guilt. Competency, she'd explained, referred to Yates' state of mind at that moment in September, not to her state of mind at the time of the crime in June. Guilt referred to whether she had committed the crime or not. The jurors were there to decide competency, not guilt, she'd said.

Hill had then explained the difference between competency and insanity. Insanity meant that Yates did not know the difference between right and wrong at the time of the crime, due to a severe mental disease. Competency referred to Yates' present ability to help attorneys with her case— today, not three months prior—and rational and factual understanding of the proceedings against her. The burden of proof was on her attorneys, not the State, based on a preponderance of evidence, not reasonable doubt.

That evidence, she'd instructed, did not, could not, and

would not include what the jurors had already read or heard, because that information might be inaccurate. She'd asked for a show of hands of those who had *not* read or heard anything about Andrea Yates. Two hands went up.

The judge had explained that if found incompetent, Yates would go to a mental health institution and could stand trial later. Listen to the evidence, decide the credibility of the witnesses, and weigh the evidence, Judge Hill had said.

She'd asked if anyone had already made up his or her mind about Andrea Yates' competency. Twenty-five percent of the 120 potential jurors said they had.

George Parnham had stood, his Santa Claus eyes twinkling, and explained that since the burden of proof was on the defense, the defense went first in a competency trial.

He'd placed a large white poster with black lettering on the easel. The poster outlined the two-part definition of competency: (1) sufficient ability to consult with the person's lawyer with a reasonable degree of rational understanding and (2) a rational and factual understanding of the proceedings against the person.

Andrea Yates must meet both standards to be found competent to stand trial, he'd said. If she did not meet either standard, she was found incompetent.

He'd asked the jury pool if they or a relative had been diagnosed with a depressive disorder. Nearly 23 percent of the jury panel answered yes.

Joe Owmby's mouth hung open.

Almost five hours after they started, twelve jurors had been picked—eleven women and one man.

Yates had sat quietly next to her attorneys, staring forward, slightly turning in her swivel chair during the process.

Afterwards, the defense made a motion. Last Friday, Odom explained, he'd learned that Dr. Steven Rubenzer, the psychologist who had found Yates competent, had met again with Yates . . . without the defense's knowledge.

An enraged Owmby had argued that that was routine, since thirty days had passed since the evaluation and competency hearing. They'd needed to see if anything had changed.

Judge Hill stopped the arguments to excuse the jurors.

Once they were out of the room, Odom argued that Rubenzer's visit had violated Yates' Fifth and Sixth Amendment rights. He felt blindsided, he'd said, and told the judge to hold Rubenzer in contempt.

Get a disinterested party to examine her *today*, the judge ordered, and stated that it "was wrong" for Rubenzer to see Yates without the Court's permission.

Eventually, after speaking on the phone with Rubenzer, the judge learned that the psychologist had had two meetings with Yates without the judge's knowledge—September 10 and 17.

With that, Odom had asked that no other experts be allowed to use any underlying data from those exams.

Until one side or the other wants to have it revisited, Judge Hill said, the State could not tender any of the information from those two exams.

The State next made a motion to prohibit the introduction of Yates' mental history during the competency hearing.

It would be best to handle this as it came up, Hill had replied.

Andrea Yates had still stared, and she had rocked.

Parnham said he didn't have copies of all the State's interviews with witnesses and if they were exculpatory, they needed to be turned over.

A witness felt sorry for her, she was out of it, and from time to time he felt sorry for her, Owmby had replied.

Feeling sorry for her was no big deal, the judge had found. But out of it from time to time was exculpatory.

Owmby had stomped out the door fuming, "Bullshit. Bullshit."

Just after 10 A.M. on the first day of the competency hearing, Judge Hill entered the courtroom. She looked up. There were many spectators, but there was ample room for more.

Andrea Yates twisted almost imperceptibly in her chair and stared blank-faced.

At 10:18 A.M., Judge Hill called Yates' case. She ordered all those testifying to stand. Five did. She swore them in, then sent them out of the room. Two witnesses were allowed to stay. Rusty Yates was not. At 10:25 A.M., the jury was brought in. Some jurors carried notepads; some studied the spectators.

George Parnham set up his poster outlining the legal definition of competency and began his opening statement. He stated that the "legal definition" of competency refers to being competent "at this time." And he repeated, "At this time." He said he does not believe Andrea Yates "yet" meets that legal standard. And he said the jurors would decide if she is competent by hearing doctors testify about "evidence of the internal workings of her brain."

He talked about the birth of her five children, and he splayed his hand to show five fingers as he mentioned the five children. He said the jurors would hear about Andrea Yates' attempted suicide.

Joe Owmby objected and Parnham backtracked, saying that in 1999, after the birth of Yates' fourth child, she was taken to Houston's Ben Taub hospital, then transferred to Methodist Hospital. "You will hear that Dr. Starbranch diagnosed her with depression with postpartum onset with psychosis." He went on to say that Andrea Yates later took a knife to herself, and "her husband had to forcibly wrestle the knife from her." Admitted to Spring Shadows Glen Hospital, she was prescribed the antipsychotic drug Haldol.

In 2001, approximately nine days after the death of her father, Andrea Yates was admitted to Devereux Texas Treatment Network, Parnham said, where the admitting physician said she was a danger to herself. She was taken off Haldol at the doctor's orders.

You will hear the testimony of two psychologists, he went on—Dr. Gerald Harris and Dr. Steven Rubenzer. The doctors disagreed about Yates' competency, he said, but both agreed that it was important "to keep an educated eye on her during the course of these trials." The stress of hearing "what she is" would trigger her back into a psychotic state, he explained.

Dr. Lauren Marangell was to testify that if Andrea Yates got better, then she wouldn't need to be watched for a relapse, Parnham added.

Owmby objected twice, once angrily. Both were sustained.

Lastly, said Parnham, the jurors would hear about Andrea's last stay in the hospital—

"Your Honor," Owmby interrupted.

"Approach the bench," Judge Hill said.

When the attorneys returned from the bench, Parnham stood again before the jury, his voice was so soft and low that his words were inaudible to the gallery. Quickly, he ended his opening statement.

Joseph Owmby passed on making an opening statement— the burden of proof was on the defense.

At 10:41 A.M., Andrea Yates' attorneys called Dr. Gerald Harris, a clinical psychologist, licensed in the State of Texas since 1983. He had obtained all of his degrees from the University of Houston, and done his internship at the University of California at Los Angeles (UCLA). He said he was currently an associate professor at the University of Houston teaching doctoral students in clinical psychology, and he evaluated treatments for children who were victims of violent crime.

Dr. Harris, with thinning, graying hair and a moustache, always turned to the jurors when answering a question. He said he worked with the Harris County District Attorney's Office and testified as an expert witness for them.

He said he'd met with and examined Andrea Yates on four different occasions. On June 25, 2001, he said, he saw her at the Harris County Jail and had a one-and-a-half- to two-hour visit with her.

Parnham suggested that the doctor check his notes.

"I'm sorry," Harris replied, after looking at his notes. "It was an hour."

He described Yates as having "overt psychosis" and "hallucinations" and "delusions." It took her up to two minutes to process and respond to a question. "She told me," he said, "that Satan was talking to her."

Parnham asked whether she had visual hallucinations.

"She said she had seen images of Satan in the walls, in the cinderblock of her cell."

On June 29, Harris saw her again. "I saw almost no change in her," even though she had started taking Haldol. She spoke again about talking with Satan. Sometimes, he said, she stared as if she was seeing and hearing something else, someone other than him.

On his third visit with Andrea Yates, on August 31, she looked much better "on the surface." She moved better. She was quicker to respond. She said hello back to you. She made some eye contact. She was not experiencing any more auditory or visual images.

But when he asked Andrea Yates about messages Satan sent her through the television, she seemed like she was talking in the present, he said. "She still had some belief about these delusional ideas." He then added, "Oh, every time I see her, she tells me she's not mentally ill."

Harris then talked about giving Andrea Yates an IQ test— to study her level of memory. Andrea Yates, he said, tested out with an IQ of 113, well above average and placing her in the 81st percentile. He then tested Yates for four different types of memory—visual recognition, where something looks familiar; recall, where one remembers facts; immediate memory, for something one heard; and memory a half hour later for something one heard.

Why is memory important in legal competency? Parnham followed up.

She needs to remember information she's given and to

provide information to her attorneys, the doctor answered.

Parnham asked where Andrea Yates fell into the memory tests on August 21?

"It was actually very interesting," Harris responded. For visual recall, Andrea Yates scored in the 40th percentile, which, he said, was about average. But for immediate auditory recall, she plummeted to the 6th percentile. For delayed auditory recall, Yates slipped even more, to the 4th percentile. And she slipped even further when she was asked to recall something she'd been told repeatedly—down to the 3rd percentile. "So telling her something repeatedly still doesn't stick."

Parnham asked Harris to compare his first meeting with Andrea Yates to his August 31 meeting with her.

"Oh, she was much better," the doctor answered. She did her hellos "fairly well."

Dr. Harris went on to say that he'd seen Andrea Yates in the holding tank on this first day of the competency hearing and had asked her what today was about, but she didn't really answer him. She would ask him a question, he said, and three or four minutes later, she would ask him the same question. And regarding the fact that she's mentally ill, he said, "She's a little more accepting of that."

Harris testified that he was "really concerned about" Andrea's memory and how it would affect her ability to work with her attorneys. He said he was also worried about her residual delusions. He wasn't sure that she wasn't still delusional. And he added, "She's just recovering," and he was concerned that the stress of a trial would break her again.

Parnham began to ask Dr. Harris about Dr. Steven Rubenzer's report.

Owmby stood up and objected. The objection was sustained.

Dr. Harris' report was entered as Defense Exhibit 1. And Dr. Harris said, "She's rapidly getting better."

Owmby objected.

"Sustained."

Parnham asked Dr. Harris if Andrea Yates would regain legal competency in the future.

"I think that's extremely likely."

Parnham then asked Dr. Harris if Andrea Yates was malingering—faking her illness.

She's not malingering, Harris replied. In fact, she tries to act like she's functioning better than she is, he said.

Does she try to please? Parnham questioned.

"Yes, she does," Harris said. "She wants you to be happy with her."

Parnham pulled out his competency definition poster and showed it to Dr. Harris.

On the first part of the definition, said Harris, Andrea Yates' abstract thinking appears to be impaired, which is due to her mental illness. "And I think that makes it hard to work with your attorney."

Referring to the second portion of the definition, Harris stated, "She does have a rational understanding of the legal system and how it works, as well as anyone." But, he added, he was concerned about her delusions—the fact that she said if she died, she was getting rid of Satan.

At 11:50 A.M., after a brief recess, Owmby began questioning Dr. Harris. Owmby emphasized that Dr. Harris was a psychologist, not a psychiatrist, and was not authorized to prescribe medicine. Dr. Harris, Owmby stated, was not even a forensics psychologist. Forensics psychologists, Owmby said, conduct competency hearings. Dr. Harris, Owmby stressed, focused on family matters, not forensics.

Owmby then tried to prove that Dr. Harris wasn't doing continuing education on forensics.

But Dr. Harris replied that he was. So Owmby asked about criminal forensics.

And Dr. Harris replied that he currently taught it at the University of Houston.

Dr. Jerome Brown was asked by the defense to look at Yates, and he's a forensics specialist and he's not testifying today, Owmby said.

Harris simply stated that he was asked to report his impressions to Yates' attorneys.

"Like all experts, you are paid for your time?" said Owmby.

So far, Harris quickly replied, he hadn't been paid.

Rusty Yates' mother frantically scratched notes.

Owmby grabbed Parnham's poster and berated the doctor, saying that he certainly implied that Andrea Yates had a rational and factual understanding of the proceedings.

Harris calmly responded that Yates didn't understand the proceedings against *her*, and she didn't understand the possible outcomes against her.

Have you always understood everything explained to you by an attorney? Owmby quickly countered.

"No," Harris answered.

So it's understandable that Andrea Yates doesn't understand, Owmby retorted.

Owmby queried the psychologist about whether Yates displayed a rational and factual understanding of the proceedings against her.

Dr. Harris paused for a very long time, and then answered "to some degree." He added, "She does not have a complete understanding of the proceedings against her."

She's anxious about what's going to happen to her, Owmby asked.

She's not anxious, the doctor replied.

You just told the jury she was, Owmby retorted.

"She appears remarkably unanxious about that," Harris responded.

Andrea Yates blankly stared at Joe Owmby.

How many competency evaluations have you done by order of the court? Owmby asked.

"Zero," Harris responded.

At the order of the Harris County District Attorney's Office? Owmby asked.

"None."

At the order of other district attorneys' offices? he continued.

"None."

At the request of defense counsels? he argued.

"Several."

Andrea Yates' main problem, Owmby proceeded, is her lack of memory?

"Yes," Harris answered.

Owmby then quizzed the psychologist about the memory tests the doctor had given Yates, immediate versus delayed, "delayed" meaning thirty minutes to an hour later. "What tests memory of two months ago?" he then asked.

The test Harris gave Yates, explained the doctor, "does not test that type of memory."

At the time of the testing on August 31, Owmby said, Andrea Yates had been in jail for about forty days.

Two months, the doctor replied—from June 20 to August 31.

Owmby did not flinch at his own inability to remember time frames.

He walked all around the courtroom, stepping up to the witness, and back again. Could Andrea Yates have been distracted by being in jail for two months after drowning her five children? he asked. Maybe that's why she couldn't remember numbers.

She didn't seem distracted by that, Harris answered.

Owmby emphasized that Andrea Yates could remember the names and dates of birth of her children, and asked if she were better able to do that two months ago than she could today.

Yes, Harris said.

She could remember her husband's birthday, said Owmby, and she could help other inmates and call her mother for help for them . . .

Parnham objected.

Sustained, said the judge.

When Owmby again asked the question, Parnham quickly objected again, and Owmby objected to the objection. The attorneys carped back and forth, nattering over each other until nothing either said was intelligible.

"Excuse me. One at a time," Judge Hill interrupted. The objection, she repeated, had been sustained.

Andrea Yates' abstract reasoning is poor, Harris said. Her ability to comprehend complex questions is poor—

Owmby began speaking over Dr. Harris.

Parnham objected and asked that the witness be allowed to finish his answers to his questions.

Sustained, said the judge.

Harris went on to explain that the first time he tested Andrea Yates' memory, she failed the test. The second time, he said, she hit the minimal level.

So, that's a pass, Owmby emphasized.

"Yes." But she had problems comprehending when her specific case was discussed, Harris explained.

Judge Hill suddenly asked the attorneys to approach the bench. It was 12:30, and court recessed for lunch.

Outside the courtroom doors, Rusty Yates stood with Byron Fike. Though parts of the sky were clear, rain clouds were scattered in places. Outside the courthouse doors, one could stand in the sunshine and be touched by raindrops.

CHAPTER 25

Rusty Yates stood just outside the courtroom and talked with a stranger about his Website. Tears crept into his eyes.

Family members, reporters, and spectators walked past them and filtered into the dimly lighted, windowless courtroom. Andrea Yates already sat in her chair. She looked up at a woman leaning down to her and they spoke, Andrea with a soft smile on her face and loving pats for the woman. Then the woman walked out of the courtroom.

Dora Yates walked in with Byron Fike and took her seat close to the wall and away from the Kennedy family. Sitting on the front row next to the Kennedys was Mary Alice Conroy, a professor at Sam Houston State University, and a witness for the prosecution. Her physical closeness to Mrs. Kennedy seemed like a cruelty even the prosecution could not ignore.

At 1:40 P.M., Owmby resumed his cross-examination. He asked Harris to talk again about Yates' IQ.

A person who functioned at the level Andrea Yates once indicated that she had would certainly have a good memory, Harris said.

What if she'd always been that way, said Owmby, with this level of impairment?

I cannot imagine that, the doctor answered.

He stated that Andrea Yates spoke in the present tense about messages she received from the television—as if the messages were still true.

How does that affect competency? Owmby retorted.

This all has to do with a complicated scheme between Satan and the State, the doctor explained.

The State would destroy her and Satan, right?

Owmby seemed to try to get Harris to admit, and the jurors to comprehend, that since the State of Texas was pursuing the death penalty against Andrea Yates, she was not delusional, because, indeed, the State was trying to destroy her.

Owmby asked if Yates was still incapable of helping her attorney with her defense.

Yes, Harris said, based on her memory and her inability to accept her mental state.

Owmby then talked about malingering and what he perceived as a paradox. We don't expect one who is functioning normally to say they are mentally ill, but you are saying that Andrea Yates is not competent because she won't admit that she is mentally ill . . . when most people don't want to admit they're mentally ill because of the way society looks at mental illness, the prosecutor explained.

Quickly, Joe Owmby passed the witness to the defense.

The prosecutor talked to you about religion, about Andrea's desire to be punished, the existence of Satan, and good and evil, Parnham began. In your conversation on those subjects with Andrea, is that what she meant?

Harris stated that Yates' thoughts went beyond the conventional ideas of Satan, that Satan was actually having conversations with her, that Satan was inside her, that the media had cameras everywhere to watch her.

If Andrea Yates had, at that moment, turned her head slightly to the left, she would have spotted the media pool video camera staring toward her.

Parnham asked about the exam Dr. Melissa Ferguson, Yates' first jail psychiatrist, had given Yates.

Objection, Owmby called. Hearsay, he said.

Judge Hill sustained his objection.

Parnham asked Dr. Harris if he'd found anything that indicated a religious belief in Andrea that Satan lived inside her.

Records indicated that she believed Satan lived in her and Andrea Yates' plan to kill Satan was to kill herself, Harris answered.

Owmby objected that Parnham was leading the witness.

Judge Hill, as usual, sustained the prosecutor's objection.

Did you find anything to suggest that her memory lapses were intentional? Parnham said.

"No, I did not."

At 2:45 P.M.. Dr. Harris, a kind, wee little man in cowboy boots, was excused, and a recess was called.

After a lengthy consultation at the bench between the judge and the attorneys, the jurors were led out of the courtroom. George Parnham looked stressed.

I am ready to testify that if Andrea is not competent, if she continues her treatment, Dr. Marangell calmly said, her trajectory to be competent is good.

Dr. Lauren Marangell, an associate professor of psychiatry at Baylor College of Medicine, sat in the witness chair. She was an expert the *Houston Chronicle* had quoted in the days just after Yates' arrest.

At 3:21 P.M., a slide screen was set up, the jury was brought in, and Dr. Marangell sat in the witness chair. The jurors saw a heavyset woman with a kind, round face. She wore a dark business suit over a white shell, and pearls. She quickly stated her qualifications—knowledge of psychopharmacology, experience with bipolar patients, and her development of new treatments for them.

Psychologists go through a Ph.D. program, she explained, whereas psychiatrists go through medical school and learn to deal with physiology, the brain, and how medications work. The doctor said that she did her undergraduate work at Trinity University in San Antonio, Texas, went to Baylor College of Medicine for medical school, and served her residency at Albert Einstein College of Medicine in New York.

She reeled out a long list of organizations she belonged to and awards she'd received so quickly and so nonchalantly that it seemed as though all those awards were simply expected of her. She mentioned twenty-seven publications she had, including pieces in *The New York Times* and *Newsweek*. She said she lectured to doctors and at scientific meetings in the United States and throughout the world. And, she said, she was an expert on depression.

You're an expert witness, Wendell Odom said.

Dr. Harris sat in the courtroom and watched.

The previous week, Marangell continued, she'd reviewed Yates' hospital records, her medical records from Harris County Jail, Dr. Harris' reports, and Dr. Rubenzer's reports. Based on those records, Andrea Yates suffered major depression with psychotic features.

Odom then asked the doctor to discuss the levels of major depression.

Objection, Owmby called. Relevance.

Sustained, said the judge.

Odom started to ask about chemical changes in the brain.

Like a jack-in-the-box, Joe Owmby popped up with constant objections.

This time the judge overruled him.

Marangell said that when a person is depressed, there are physical and chemical changes in the brain, and she could show the jurors photographs of those changes.

Objection, Owmby cried, unless those photos were of Andrea Pia Yates' brain.

Judge Hill once again overruled the prosecutor.

Dr. Marangell stood and walked over to the slide screen, which sat just behind Andrea Yates. As if she were in the classroom, the doctor started to lecture.

Brian Kennedy leaned forward in his seat as though he was learning with the jurors. Some of the jurors looked fas-

cinated. Some looked as though the lecture was over their
heads and they had traveled to another atmosphere. Andrew
Kennedy stared intently at the slides. The doctor seemed to
be just an arm's length away from him.

Judge Hill immediately stopped her and ordered the M.D.
to answer the questions only.

Upon questioning, the doctor explained the various treatments for depression and the resulting changes. For psychosis, she said, the drugs Respiradol and Haldol work, but
weeks and even months must pass before they take effect.

Andrew Kennedy's daughters touched, patted, and comforted the family.

Using Andrea Yates' medical records, starting in 1999,
Marangell had mapped out a life chart for the alleged killer.
It showed psychotic episodes, how long they lasted, and
their severity with the prescribed medications mapped on
top of them.

Odom showed the jury Yates' life chart and entered it as
Defense Exhibit 2.

Odom asked the doctor whether, if Andrea Yates continued to improve, she would eventually be well enough to be
competent to stand trial.

Yes, the doctor answered—a qualified yes. Like cancer,
she said, you want to get rid of all of the symptoms. And
if one is not completely well, the chances of relapsing increase.

You don't know where Andrea Yates is now in her recovery? Owmby asked in cross-examination.

No, the doctor said.

So this is all irrelevant today?

"I am not in a position to say whether she is competent
today," Marangell replied.

"Really?" Owmby responded with mocking disbelief.

Now Odom was constantly objecting.

Judge Hill sustained all of his objections.

After two or three months in recovery, Marangell stated,

and two more months of being psychosis-free, Andrea Yates would be rational.

Psychiatrists and neurologists cannot tell the difference between the mind and the brain, Owmby said. They have to look at the way people act. Right?

Wendell Odom objected.

The judge sustained his objection, and Owmby passed the witness to Odom.

"Is there any question at all that Andrea Yates has a mental illness?" he asked.

Objection, Owmby called.

Sustained, said the judge.

But the usual bickering between the attorneys started up, and the judge, also as usual, instructed the lawyers to stop speaking over one another. She further ordered them to stop making sidebar comments in front of the jurors. Williford stood by with a stern look on her face, which was actually the norm for her.

If Andrea Yates is not competent today, Marangell said, finally returning the attention to where it was supposed to be, she will be competent in the foreseeable future.

At 4:30 P.M., the attorneys stood before the judge's bench. Moments later, Wendell Odom called George Parnham to the stand. Jurors and reporters alike perked up their heads and straightened their torsos.

Parnham stated that he had been sworn in to the bar on September 11, 1969, was raised in Georgia, attended undergraduate at Loyola in New Orleans, dropped out of law school to join the military, finished law school at the University of Texas in Austin in 1970, and had specialized in criminal law since 1983. And, he said, he sees 100 clients a year, which, he qualified, was a conservative estimate.

He said he was testifying about the attorney–client privilege as it related to the definition of competency.

Andrea Yates briefly placed her hand over her mouth.

On June 22, 2001, Parnham said, he'd been retained as
Yates' counsel and had seen her a "number of times"
since—more than ten, fewer than fifty. He discussed attorney–client privilege and how he was bound by that, but he
said he could talk about whether Andrea Yates could communicate with him in a rational manner. He did not feel that
his client met a level of competency to consult with him on
a matter of this import, he stated.

Are you able to have a typical attorney–client relationship? Odom asked.

"I can talk with Andrea," Parnham said.

Can you advise her about taking the stand? Odom asked.

Indignantly, Owmby objected.

Odom managed to get Parnham to say that there were
matters he couldn't discuss with Andrea to her understanding.

If I thought Andrea Yates were competent, Parnham continued, I wouldn't be here today.

Parnham was calm. Owmby was hot-headed and began
his cross.

Is Andrea Yates not conversing with you because that's
what she thinks is in her best interests, the prosecutor asked,
not what you think is best?

Parnham said he felt he owed it to his client to get her
where she needed to be.

Again, Owmby said, is it what you think is best versus
what she thinks best?

"To a degree, yes."

Then he asked if Parnham had or would ever lie under
oath.

I haven't ever lied under oath, Parnham responded.

Did you take an oath to seek justice? the prosecutor demanded.

I don't think that word is in the oath, the defense attorney
answered.

And Owmby passed the witness.

You just have to support the law of the Constitution? Odom asked.

Right, Parnham answered.

The defense rested.

CHAPTER 26

The Houston heat and humidity rose with each passing day of the competency hearing. Around 9:30 A.M. on Thursday, September 20, Dora Yates slipped into the line with the Kennedy family to go through security and enter the courthouse, all unnoticed by the three video cameramen stationed outside the glass doors.

Brian Kennedy, a head higher than those around him, stared over the long line at the oblivious photographers. Brian's sister was on the front page of the local paper, below the fold, in a semi-smiling photo cut from the pool videotape. She could have been the Mona Lisa. It was surely a photo that the defense did not like. It did not reveal an accurate picture of Andrea Yates' usual courtroom demeanor—motionless, emotionless, and empty.

Suddenly, she was in direct line of her mother and no longer in the direct line of the video camera lens. And she would not be in the direct eye-line of the jury. But she would be sitting much, much closer to the jurors where they could see the tension in her jaw and the blankness in her eyes.

As the jurors entered, they seemed to purposely turn their eyes away from Yates.

Quickly, the first witness for the State was called—John Bayliss, a nurse with Mental Health Mental Retardation Authority (MHMRA) of Harris County. Dressed in royal blue scrubs, he was a rotund man with gray hair and wire-rimmed glasses who, as second-shift charge nurse, interacted with Andrea Yates almost every day.

As he sat down, he had to move the microphone from grazing his belly. He said that he worked on the third floor of the county jail, with those with mental illness.

Kaylynn Williford questioned him. Her cheekbones were etched into her thin face, giving the pretty woman a hard look, in sharp contrast to Bayliss' caring appearance.

Andrea Yates had a psychiatrist, a psychologist, a case-worker who was a liaison for the jail staff and the family, and the inmate's physician in the outside world, he rapidly mumbled. She also had one-on-one therapy, and a nursing staff that administered the prescribed medications and made sure she kept herself clean, ate, and did the daily nursing assessment.

Williford instructed her witness to speak more slowly.

He said he had contact with Yates at least once a day via observation. He said Yates was always within eyesight because she was on suicide watch.

He held the microphone with his left hand, occasionally gesturing slightly with his right. He had chipmunk cheeks that looked like they were holding nuts, as if that were the reason he mumbled so.

Dora Yates moved away from her wall and closer to the witness as she strained to hear and understand him. She busily scribbled notes.

Bayliss said he observed Yates talking to other inmates, reading, and playing dominos. It was only in the last month, he said, that she had started interacting with the other patients. When she first arrived at the jail, he said, she stayed to herself.

Every day, he asked Andrea various psych assessment questions—how are you feeling, are you hearing voices? In the last month, he said, he'd had no problem getting answers from her.

Kaylynn Williford passed the witness.

Wendell Odom asked Bayliss about his education.

The nurse said he went to Texas Women's University Nursing School, that he did undergraduate work in Indiana, and he'd done a great deal of forensic nursing, working with mentally ill patients who had legal problems. He'd spent ten months working in the medical department of the Harris County Jail.

When Bayliss first saw Andrea Yates, he testified, she was catatonic, had no idea where she was, but did follow directions. When she was first placed in the jail, he said, she sat down and started talking to the walls and picking at her head. If he called her name, he said, she briefly looked at him, then looked down and began mumbling to herself.

The prosecution began a tirade of objections before Odom could finally ask, is she better today?

"Very much better, yes." He added that she now smiled when he approached her, and answered his questions in a soft voice, but he felt as if her answers were always trying to please him. "She'll do exactly what you say when you say it," he explained. When he asked her how she was doing, he said, she'd reply, " 'I'm fine.' " That, he said, had been her answer from the very first time she entered the jail. But, about a month later, he said, she started talking.

At that moment, Andrea Yates sat directly in front of Bayliss.

"Do you know if she's able to comprehend what she reads?" Odom asked.

"No."

Do you know if she understands what's being said, or if she understands dominos? the attorney queried.

"No."

The distracting clinking, squeaking noise of days past began again in the courtroom with a vengeance.

"Does she still appear to be sick?"

"Yes," the nurse replied. Her answers are always the same, her mouth smiles, but her eyes don't, he said. There's no brightness to them.

Odom passed the State's witness. The State excused him. And the spectators in the courtroom muttered that the prosecution's witness sounded more like a defense witness.

At 11 A.M., the State called Dr. Steven Rubenzer, the previously much-talked-about psychologist with MHMRA. A tall, well-turned-out dresser, Rubenzer had the gallery muttering about, of all things, his facial hair.

It outlined the bottom portion of his jawbone, but on his cheeks and sideburns, he was completely clean-shaven, leaving large spaces of white with a few dark slashes of accent—as though he were a kid in a school play who had painted on whiskers with a dark Magic Marker.

His job, he said, was to administer competency/insanity evaluations for the court, which he'd done for six years. He had specialized training, he said, in forensic psychology, pointedly undermining Dr. Harris' testimony.

Rubenzer held the microphone with his left hand and turned to the jurors every time he spoke. He said he conducted about two competency evaluations a day. Seventy percent of those he evaluated, he said, were found competent. And he emphasized the numbers again by clarifying that that was seven out of ten people.

For Andrea Yates' competency evaluation, he said, he studied documents prepared by his office, her medical history, and her police report.

Rubenzer testified that he had met with Andrea Yates on seven occasions—July 19, 20 and 25, August 2 and 3, and September 10 and 17. At the July 19 meeting, he said, he took her social history.

Also on July 19, Rubenzer said, he met with Andrea Yates for one hour and forty minutes and gave her the MacArthur Competency Assessment Tool (MacCAT) test. There are three different scales to the test, he explained—understanding, reasoning, and appreciation, which appraises her situation in the court system. On understanding and reason,

Andrea Yates tested acceptable or competent, stated Rubenzer. On appreciation, he said, Andrea Yates scored very low.

Dr. Rubenzer also did a personality assessment on Yates, which involved 344 questions. It showed no evidence that she was malingering, or faking her illness, he said.

Of the 344 questions, Yates left ten or eleven blank.

On June 20, Rubenzer said, he met with Andrea Yates again and conducted a second type of competency assessment. This one, he testified, was more of an interview guide than a test.

After a brief recess, Rubenzer testified that he had asked Yates short, simple questions, and sometimes waited a full minute for a response. He said he'd ask her to say her name, he'd wait, she'd finally say, "What?" and he had to repeat the question.

But regarding the 344 questions that Andrea Yates answered for his test, he said, he did not read those questions to her. "Presumably," he said, "she answered them." And she answered them in one hour's time.

When he met with Yates on July 19, Rubenzer stated, he explained her legal rights, then told her he was there as an investigator, not a doctor. It was a concept that Andrea Yates initially had difficulty understanding. And when he asked her to explain in her own words her understanding of her rights, she answered, "Don't talk about it."

During their August 3 meeting, the doctor executed a brief assessment of Yates' intelligence and memory. "She did reasonably well," he reported. She had a problem with attention and concentration, but could stay on task, and could remember a sequence of three numbers on her second try, he said.

Rubenzer and Williford then began going over thirteen points that Andrea Yates needed to understand to be found competent for trial, points like whether she appreciated the charges against her, whether she appreciated the pleas available to her, her appraisal of the roles of the judge, jurors, prosecutors, and the like.

Andrea Yates, Rubenzer said, did not initially understand what a no contest plea meant, and she indicated that she did not want to answer certain questions when he asked her about events leading up to the crime. " 'I want to talk to my lawyer first,' " he quoted her as saying. And on other questions, he stated, she said she'd rather not discuss that.

On "appraisal of likely outcomes," he said that Andrea Yates understood and responded.

Rubenzer turned to speak directly to the jurors and said he had asked Andrea Yates about her knowledge of privilege and the judge's role.

She did understand the roles? Williford asked.

"For the most part, yes," he replied. To a limited extent, he qualified, she understood the judge's role. But she was "hazy" on her answer regarding what a witness did. She was confused, he said, whether a witness would be called to help her. He then said he asked her, "What about the police officers who were called?" Would they be helpful to her?

She told him, " 'No.' "

He said he asked her if any witnesses would be called against her. No, he said that she'd answered. What about police officers? No, she again replied.

He said he'd talked to her about the planning of her legal strategy. Had she thought about representing herself? he asked. Had she thought about whether a judge or jury would decide her case? And they discussed plea bargains, he said.

Andrea Yates answered in the negative regarding representing herself, he reported, because she said she did not know the law. Regarding taking her attorney's advice, "She said she would have to think about it."

When they discussed her appraisal of legal defenses, Rubenzer said he'd asked Yates if she disagreed with the way her lawyers were handling her case. He said he wasn't necessarily pleased with her answers. Indeed, he was concerned. He asked her if she had confidence in her attorneys. " 'For the most part, yes,' " she answered.

When they discussed "unmanageable behavior" in the courtroom, Yates explained that that meant she should " 'be quiet and listen,' " he said. If she misbehaved in the courtroom, " 'They would take me out,' " she answered.

"I tutored her a little bit on that," Rubenzer said.

They also talked about challenging the prosecution's witnesses. " 'They're not supposed to tell lies,' " Yates told the psychologist for the State. He then asked her what she would do if she heard a witness lie. "Tell her lawyer," he said she replied.

He then tried to discuss self-defeating and self-serving motivations. But there was a very long pause by Yates, he said. He finally called her name. "Andrea?"

" 'Huh?' " he said she'd answered. And he'd repeated the question, he said.

The monotony of the testimony was tiring and Williford was losing her audience. Still, she charged on, asking Rubenzer about Andrea Yates' ability to discuss pertinent facts of the case with her attorney.

"Would you like to tell me your side of what happened?" he said he'd asked her. She then told me a little of what happened, he testified, then said she wanted to talk with her attorney.

Judge Hill apparently realized that Williford was losing her audience, and called for recess for lunch.

As spectators and Andrea's loved ones exited the courtroom, they passed Rusty Yates sitting on a hard wooden bench, with a big, thick black manual in his lap, speaking animatedly to his mother.

CHAPTER 27

As the clock ticked toward 1:30 P.M., Rusty Yates, his mother, and reporters crammed shoulder to shoulder in the security line, waiting for their bags and bodies to be scanned. Rusty held his thick, black manual in his arms and turned to a reporter standing a couple of persons behind him in the line. They nodded hello, and Rusty said he'd been studying the manual while waiting outside the courtroom.

"Something for work?" he was asked.

No, he replied, it was Andrea's medical records from Devereux. They were meticulously, copied, neatly stacked, and bound in the black binder. As Rusty, his mother, and the media pack crowded onto an elevator, the reporters leaned in even closer as Rusty opened up the folder and instructed, "Look at this."

It was a page where a tiny box had been checked saying that Andrea Yates had a chemical dependency and stating that her goal was to learn to lead a drug-free life. "She was the biggest teetotaler ever," Rusty remarked incredulously. That showed how crazy they were at Devereux, he added.

As the reporters and Rusty Yates stepped off the elevator, Yates continued to talk.

"I don't want to get you in trouble," the reporter responded and moved away.

Judge Hill's media orders prevented the press from asking any questions while in the courthouse.

But another reporter whispered, "He wants to get in trouble."

At 1:45 P.M., the attorneys stood at the judge's bench. Rubenzer took his chair in the witness box. And by 1:47 P.M., the jurors padded in.

Williford abruptly abandoned her point-by-point questioning.

Instead, Rubenzer testified that he spent one and a half hours going over the thirteen points with Andrea. Then, on July 20, he spent one and a half hours with Karin Kennedy and two and a half hours with Rusty Yates.

On July 25, he said, he asked Andrea Yates about the prescription drugs she had reported in her statements to the police and the jail psychiatrist, about her home life, about her youth, and about her life with Rusty Yates.

On that date, he said, Yates was more alert, more animated, and "less confused and perplexed." She was aware of the date and the charges against her, he said. But on July 25, he added, all of Yates' responses were rational and coherent.

He was then asked to look at his notes.

He reached for his notes and continued. On August 2, he said, they discussed the sequence of her marriage, the birth dates of her children, and "bad thoughts" she had been experiencing.

Rubenzer said he advised her again of her rights and asked how often she had had "bad thoughts" prior to June 20. He said she had difficulty expressing what forms the thoughts came in—voices, visions, and so forth.

A month before the murders, he testified, Andrea Yates had had thoughts about killing her children and did not act on them.

At one point, Rubenzer stopped Yates from talking when she was expressing the sequence of events because, according to Williford, the doctor was "looking out for Mrs. Yates"—he knew such information could affect her case.

He continued on, saying that he readministered the appreciation scale of the competency exam to Yates. "She did considerably better." She scored only "mild impairment" that day, and he felt it was sufficient enough to find her competent to stand trial.

On August 3, he testified, he pulled Yates aside to make sure she was not hearing voices before her August 8 arraignment. By that time, he reported, he'd spent eight to eight and a half hours with her.

Williford showed Rubenzer the competency definition poster and asked him to answer both parts of the definition: (1) sufficient ability to consult with the person's lawyer with a reasonable degree of rational understanding and (2) a rational and factual understanding of the proceedings against the person.

He answered yes to both criteria and stated that he'd tendered a report to the court saying Andrea Yates was competent to stand trial.

On September 10 and September 17, he said, he readministered the competency exam.

How was Andrea Yates on September 10 as compared to August 3? Williford queried.

"For the record—" Odom interrupted.

Owmby, Odom, and Williford approached Judge Hill's bench.

Williford returned to questioning her witness—How did Yates' score on September 10 compare to her scores in July?

"She scored better," he said. Previously, he added, she'd scored a nine or ten. On September 10, he said, she scored an eleven. Overall, she scored in the 77th percentile in understanding, in the 90th percentile in reasoning, and in the 30th percentile in appreciation.

State's Exhibit Three was entered—Andrea Yates' September 10 test scores, scores that resulted from the very visits the defense had objected to just after jury selection.

She's still competent? Williford asked.

"Yes." However, he noted, Andrea Yates would have

trouble following the trial unless it was not complicated. She could testify, but he wasn't sure how stable she would be.

On September 17, he said, he met with her because her competency hearing had been postponed and he wanted to make sure his previous assessments were still accurate. On that date, he added, he tested her again. By then, he said, he'd spent in excess of ten hours with Yates.

Again, Williford showed the doctor the definitions of competency.

Again, he answered yes to both precepts. "She is competent to stand trial."

The witness was passed.

Under Parnham's cross-examination, Rubenzer admitted that he did find that Andrea Yates had a "serious mental illness." It was, he said, a severe depressive disorder with psychotic features in *partial* remission.

There was nothing in Andrea Yates' behavior, the psychologist pointed out, that indicated she was psychotic, except the fact that she seemed distracted. And he felt that that was due to her being preoccupied—not hearing voices—despite the fact that she had said she heard voices when she first got to jail, and had heard voices prior to being incarcerated.

Parnham began to question Rubenzer about his observations of Andrea Yates compared to the observations made by psychiatrist Dr. Melissa Ferguson, Yates' admitting psychiatrist at the jail.

Williford objected time and again.

Every objection was sustained.

Parnham turned back to Rubenzer and stated that Andrea Yates had no evidence of any psychotic features.

This time, Rubenzer referred to Yates as having psychotic features in *full* remission . . . at least, he said, that's what he had thought until he saw last night's news.

Stop, Judge Hill ordered, and she banished the jurors into their jury room.

Once the jurors were tucked out of hearing, Judge Hill asked Rubenzer what in the world last night's news had to do with the answer to Parnham's question.

Rubenzer turned meek and mild like a schoolboy caught with his hand in the cookie jar.

In no way, Judge Hill demanded, was Rubenzer to comment on someone else's testimony.

The jurors were returned to their seats.

Parnham returned to his questioning. Did you hear anything that made you think her psychotic features weren't in full remission? he asked.

Yes, the doctor answered, on TV.

You cautioned the court to watch her during the trial process because the stress of the trial could kick her back into psychosis? Parnham said.

Yes, Rubenzer responded.

A stressor such as hearing about June 20? Parnham continued.

Yes, the psychologist said.

A stressor such as hearing that she had drowned her children? Parnham asked.

"Potentially, yes," Rubenzer answered.

Rubenzer then added that he still believed Andrea Yates was suffering a major depressive disorder. In early August, he said, he found Yates to be depressed, mildly confused, slow to process information, and *starting* to become aware that she is perhaps mentally ill. Usually, he said, she avoided the question when he asked her if she were mentally ill. Rather, in August she answered that she was "a little depressed." Due to "lack of insight," he said, she couldn't understand that she was ill.

On July 20, Rubenzer continued, he discussed the insanity defense with Yates. "She said she didn't talk to her lawyer about that."

Parnham backtracked. When you tested her for appreciation on July 19, he said, she failed. What was her score?

"It was below the first percentile." The exact score, Rubenzer said, was a four—"clinically significant impairment."

On August 2, Rubenzer said, he tested Andrea Yates again because he didn't think the previous score was valid.

But Judge Hill called for a break, and the concentration was broken.

Rubenzer stepped out of the witness box, walked over to two MHMRA attorneys, and said, "How bad did I do?"

During court recesses, in a sweet, childlike manner, Andrea Yates had begged Parnham for forgiveness for not being able to help her attorneys—as she kept hearing in the courtroom—and pled with him for understanding as to how she could help him.

Parnham patted his client and tried to comfort her with assurances that she was doing just fine. Andrea Yates was a person who was grateful for the smallest of kindnesses, like Parnham bringing her a sandwich.

The break-time gossip in the hallway answered Rubenzer's question—he was a better witness for Andrea Yates than for the State. Supporters of Yates smiled when they talked about his testimony . . . and the way he shaved his beard into a chin outline sans sideburns.

Reporters also talked about Rubenzer's beard, his testimony, and how they were ticked that no sound was allowed on the pool video. They wanted to run the clip where Rubenzer said he'd thought Andrea Yates was in full remission, until he saw last night's news. But the video, they griped, was unusable without sound.

At 3:47 P.M., Parnham continued his cross-examination of Dr. Steven Rubenzer. He quickly established that on July 19, his client had failed the appreciation portion of her competency exam and that on July 20, Yates had asked for her attorney.

Joe Owmby looked disgusted.

Rubenzer looked stressed and strained. "I'd rather not talk about the kids and what happened," the doctor quoted Yates as saying. According to Rubenzer, Yates also said it was time for her to be punished. That phrase, he added, is in the offense report as something she said to her husband.

Why was it time. Parnham asked.

She said, "I wasn't a good mother. I neglected them. . . . I guess I got overwhelmed."

Did you ask her what the phrase "it was time" meant? Parnham followed up.

He'd asked her that about four times, Rubenzer replied.

At that moment, did you feel "it was time" was based on a delusion? Parnham asked.

The State's witness said he didn't have enough information to know that.

Parnham then laid out that Rubenzer had referred to "bizarre statements" on page one of Yates' competency report, and that Rubenzer did not feel that "it was time" fell into that category.

Rubenzer stated that Yates' bizarre statements were not the basis of competency.

Williford stood and objected—since the questions and answers did not have to do with competency.

Rubenzer acknowledged that Yates had said she was Satan and that Satan would be destroyed by Governor Bush. But, he added, that that had nothing to do with competency, because that was three months ago, not now.

Williford objected again. Her objection was denied.

"Dr. Rubenzer, let's talk about depression," Parnham said. Did the test deal with depression? he asked.

Yes, Rubenzer answered.

Parnham asked if the doctor was familiar with a 1997 study on depression in jailed women, and how that depression affects the women's competency.

No, he answered.

The doctor was beginning to lose his concentration and couldn't follow the questions.

But he continued on and, once again sounding like a witness for the defense, not the prosecution, Rubenzer said that the MacCAT was not a complete assessment of com-

petency. He added that if one had a serious, untreated disorder, that that would affect competency.

Williford objected. They were delving outside the scope
of this competency hearing, she said repeatedly.

Parnham asked Dr. Rubenzer what he, Parnham, as a lay
person, should look for in psychosis and competency.

Objection, Williford called.

Sustained, said the judge.

Parnham asked if the court had asked Rubenzer to return
to see Yates for his most recent visits with the young
woman.

Objection, Williford proclaimed, again, and asked to approach the bench.

By then, every Kennedy family member had exited the
courtroom.

And as Joe Owmby left the bench, after the sidebar, he
threw up his hands.

On July 19, 20 and 26 and August 2 and 3, Parnham
established, Rubenzer saw Andrea Yates. Normally, he
asked the psychologist, you don't spend that much time with
someone when testing for competency?

No, he didn't, Rubenzer replied.

Rubenzer testified that he'd met twice with the prosecutors
to prepare for the case, and on September 17, he said, he
told the prosecutors he was going to see Yates. But, he
stated, he didn't tell the defense.

Most times, said Parnham, you're on the witness stand
for the State?

Right, Rubenzer answered.

Are you motivated to find her competent due to your role
with the State? the defense attorney asked.

"No, not at all," Rubenzer said softly.

As the afternoon wore on, more and more spectators
eased out of the courtroom. Indeed, by late afternoon, spectators were sparse.

Rubenzer appeared very, very tired.

What do you think about you using the phrase to her "the lawyer getting you off"? Parnham inquired.

The psychologist said he didn't recall using that phrase, but he admitted that it might have been similar to something that he had said.

As George Parnham continued his cross-examination, his tiredness also seeped through—he had difficulty finding and pronouncing words. But Parnham pushed on.

Did you take into account the fact that she killed her own children in assessing the extent of her mental illness? he asked.

Not to evaluate her mental illness, Rubenzer replied, but to evaluate her competency.

A mother drowning her children, Parnham said, don't you think that'd have some impact on her ability to come back?

Objection, Williford said.

Overruled, the judge responded.

"Yes, I do," Rubenzer answered.

Parnham leaned and rocked in his chair and asked whether killing five children affects competency.

Judge Hill interrupted, as if she were the prosecution objecting. Asked and answered, she said.

Rubenzer then admitted his concern about Andrea Yates' ability to stand trial. If Andrea Yates perceived herself as mentally ill, the psychologist testified, she might work better with her attorneys. If she didn't perceive herself as ill, he said, she might overlook things that would be beneficial to her attorneys.

The better she gets, the more fully she will appreciate what she did? Parnham asked.

Yes, Rubenzer answered.

She doesn't yet fully appreciate what she did? Parnham inquired.

I don't think so, Rubenzer said.

And the courtroom was very, very quiet, not even a creaking in the seats . . . until Williford objected.

Parnham relinquished and passed the witness. He'd made his point anyway.

What was it you heard last night in the media? Williford asked.

That Andrea Yates had heard Satan talking to her, Rubenzer replied. He said he'd spoken with Williford about that in the hallway and had learned that that wasn't a recent development. And, he said, he had no other information that might change his opinion about her competency.

Williford asked Rubenzer about a question in the competency exam that Yates "chose" not to answer. The question related to her punishment for the crime—how Yates perceived she would be punished in comparison to others charged with the same crime.

Rubenzer agreed that Yates "chose" not to answer and that was why she failed the appreciation portion of the exam.

The score, he continued, isn't based on one's answers, but on how well one can explain one's answers. In July, Yates couldn't explain her answer. In August, he said, she explained that answer by saying, "because they have lots of evidence against me."

He testified that she didn't answer questions such as "I need some help to deal with important problems," "I used to lie a lot to get out of tough situations," "I have had some horrible experiences that make me feel guilty."

Rubenzer stated that during his conversation with Andrea Yates about her statement that "it was time" for her to be punished, she'd said, "I guess I got overwhelmed" and admitted that she had had thoughts about killing her children for a couple of months.

He said he asked her about Satan and she replied, " 'I am Satan. . . . George W. Bush will kill Satan' "—meaning that Bush would kill Satan by executing her.

Rubenzer did not state the obvious—that Andrea Yates had no concept of time, George W. Bush was no longer governor of Texas, he was President of the United States.

Is Andrea Yates competent to stand trial? Williford asked.

Yes, Rubenzer answered.

Williford passed her witness.

Andrea Yates wanted to be executed so that Satan could be put to death by the governor of Texas, Parnham said. "Isn't that a bizarre statement?"

Yes, Rubenzer said, again never pointing out that Bush was not the governor and had not been for months before Andrea Yates allegedly drowned her five children.

The State said she "chose" not to respond to certain questions, Parnham stated.

Rubenzer finally clarified that he didn't say she "chose" not to answer; he simply said she "did not" respond.

Rubenzer was excused from the witness stand.

The lawyers were asked to approach the bench. Soon, Judge Hill turned her attention to the jurors and instructed them to bring an overnight bag the following day. They might be sequestered and have to spend the night, she explained, if they couldn't reach a verdict by Friday evening.

At 5:30 court recessed for the day.

Joe Owmby walked down the gallery aisle and out the courtroom door mouthing, "Fucking shit."

George Parnham stood hugging Andrea Yates repeatedly, as she sat in her orange county jail jumpsuit, bare-legged in matching orange rubber slippers, in a courtroom that everyone complained was too cold.

Parnham was concerned that if Yates ever truly realized what she had done, that she'd kill herself. "She's the sweetest," he said.

CHAPTER 28

The morning after President George W. Bush sat in front of the cameras to reassure the nation, Americans woke to a crashing stock market. Houstonians woke to an even hotter and more humid day. And courthouse lawyers and workers walked past the TV trucks, which were fewer in number on that Friday, September 21.

But on the fifth floor of the courthouse, people seemed oblivious to world events. Andrea Yates was their only focus. Rusty Yates sat outside the courtroom with his mother. Spectators munched muffins from overpriced hotels. Prosecutors sat at their table. Kaylynn Williford wore navy blue. The day before, she'd worn American blue.

Around 9:50 A.M., Judge Hill took the bench and began dealing with other cases. She wore an orange scarf tied at her neck that perfectly matched the inmates' orange jumpsuits.

"Quiet in the courtroom," the bailiff yelled.

The courtroom barely quieted.

His face stern, the bailiff's shoulders sagged. The tattoos on his forearms somehow managed to gleam in the court's dull lighting.

Karin Kennedy, dressed in black, walked up to her usual front row pew and looked miffed and frustrated. The row that was reserved for her was filled with spectators waiting on other cases. She and John O'Sullivan walked out.

The bailiff bellowed again, "Have quiet in the court-room!"

Judge Hill seemed oblivious to the noise.

Joe Owmby stood and strutted near his table, looking angry, his arms crossed against his chest.

At 9:57 A.M., Mrs. Kennedy got her seat.

Parnham stood nearby, smiling and looking relaxed.

The jury entered and took their seats at 10:31.

"Good morning," the judge said to them.

Like schoolchildren, they obediently responded, "Good morning."

State's witness Mary Alice Conroy, the clinical forensic psychologist at Sam Houston State University who had been sitting for days on the front row with Mrs. Kennedy, took the stand.

Joe Owmby began to question her, repeatedly stressing that the psychologist was a doctor, and emphasizing that Sam Houston was renowned for its criminal justice department, and that she was director of its clinical training for the Forensic Clinical Psychology program. She additionally stated that it was the only program of its kind in Texas, and only one of seven such programs in the nation.

Ironically, Dr. Conroy testified that she'd gotten her Ph.D. from the University of Houston, the very school where Dr. Gerald Harris taught in its Ph.D. program. She said she'd worked for the Department of Justice and with the Federal Bureau of Prisons. She'd also worked with women, administering competency evaluations.

Finally she stated that she'd worked to develop the standards and training programs for forensic evaluations, and was in the process of trying to get the Texas legislature to turn those regulations into laws. She was, in essence, doing a dandy job of undermining Dr. Harris' credentials.

"In a general way," she said, Harris County worked just like the federal system in that a staff regularly performed competency exams.

The staff is sometimes called non-partisan? Owmby

asked, trying to refute Parnham's words that Rubenzer was pro-State.

"I think that's fair," Conroy answered, then said she'd been hired by the Andrea Yates prosecutorial team to consult on what goes into "a good, solid forensic evaluation." She stressed that she was not there to evaluate Andrea Yates' competency.

In a quality competency assessment, she explained, the evaluator must warn and explain to the defendant the parameters of the evaluation, and who will be privy to that information.

She did not mention that someone who was incompetent probably could not understand and retain such explanations.

She did say that the competency evaluator needed to review as much collateral information as possible—talking with those who knew the inmate, reviewing the inmate's medical records. She explained that the tests are instruments, not tools, and that there aren't any pass/fail grades on the competency exam.

Dora Yates scribbled furiously on a borrowed notepad.

Owmby bounced forward and back with each question he asked.

Parnham objected regularly and was overruled.

Owmby then stood up and walked around the room as he said, if a lawyer says he's having difficulty with a client, does that mean she's incompetent? Or, could it be capability versus choice on the part of the defendant?

Dr. Conroy said that Dr. Rubenzer's methodology would have passed the board exam and met the standards in his field.

Owmby walked over toward Mrs. Kennedy to pick up a brown folder from the bench on which she sat, placing him next to the mother of the woman he hoped to convict and have sentenced to death. The information he was retrieving was the article on competency in jailed women previously referenced by George Parnham.

Women, Dr. Conroy pointed out, have different psychopathologies from men, but, to be adjudicated, they need to have the same capabilities as men. And because of that, she stressed, women would not need to have a different competency evaluation than men.

Depression without psychotic features, she said, rarely leads to incompetency. But being psychotic highly correlates to incompetency, she said.

Owmby passed his witness.

George Parnham stressed that the doctor had been hired by the prosecution and that every day she had sat in the courtroom and listened to *all* previous testimonies. He emphasized that she'd advised the prosecution on the types of questions to ask and the follow-up questions to ask. "You became a part of the State's team."

"I certainly was assisting," she replied. But Conroy insisted that she was not part of their "team," despite the fact that she was, in her own words, not an impartial observer. And she admitted she had no way of knowing whether Dr. Rubenzer's assessment that Andrea Yates was competent to stand trial was correct.

Parnham tried to emphasize that the finding of competency was subjective, not objective.

Attorney and witness then returned to the article on psychosis and competency in women. Conroy stated that the article correlated psychosis with competency, not depression with competency.

While the jury was out of the room, Parnham asked Conroy if depression affected one's thinking.

"Of course," she answered. Depression could put one into an "almost vegetative" state.

Psychologist Mary Alice Conroy was excused, but Owmby said he wanted her to remain in the courtroom.

The State rested.

Parnham called Dr. Melissa Ferguson, Andrea Yates' admitting psychiatrist at the Harris County Jail.

Kaylynn Williford declared that the State objected to Dr.
Ferguson testifying, explaining that Ferguson was Yates'
doctor only from June 21 to June 29, and then saw her only
two other times. So there was no relevancy to Dr. Ferguson's testimony, which did not, Williford emphasized, address Yates' present competency.

"Do you know what it is they are going to ask her?"
Judge Hill responded, and the judge explained that Dr. Ferguson was there to rebut Dr. Rubenzer's testimony that Andrea Yates was in full remission.

The State then argued that Rubenzer didn't testify that
Yates was in full remission. And Owmby pointed out again
that Ferguson was not Andrea Yates' treating physician
now.

That certainly goes to the weight of her testimony, Hill
commented. But the judge also noted that the last witness
for the State had testified that there was a correlation between psychosis and competency. Therefore, she said, Dr.
Ferguson could testify as to whether Andrea Yates was in
full remission. And she said the court reporter would search
her transcript to determine whether Rubenzer had stated that
Yates was in full or partial remission.

So you have no objections? the judge asked.

Yes, we have objections, Owmby replied.

With that, Judge Hill instructed the court reporter to review her record.

Owmby asked to be excused and left the courtroom.

Frantically, reporters flipped through their notes, searching to determine whether Rubenzer had stated that Yates
was in full remission. In truth, Rubenzer had first testified
that Andrea Yates was in partial remission. But later, when
he talked about the TV report he'd seen the night before,
he testified that she was in full remission.

Owmby reentered the courtroom, muttered angrily, sat
down, and pouted.

At 12:12 P.M., court was brought to order. This time,
George Parnham and Owmby weren't in the room. He was

retrieved from the hallway, and soon all the attorneys again stood at Judge Hill's bench. Bring in the next witness, she ordered.

At 12:15 P.M., Dr. Melissa Ferguson stepped into the witness box. With short blond hair and glasses, she had a pleasant face and a pleasant demeanor. She said she was a Houston Baptist University graduate who'd attended the University of Texas at Houston Medical School, graduated in 1986, became a general psychiatrist, and then earned a fellowship in forensic psychiatry.

Currently, she said, she was medical director of the MHMRA psychiatric unit and had admitted Andrea Yates to the unit in the early morning of June 21. She was, she said, Yates' treating physician for the next one and a half weeks, and had also covered for Andrea's other doctors. Her last clinical conversation with Yates, the doctor stated, was on September 19.

Based on her September 19 meeting with Yates, and on the assessments done on Yates toward the end of August, Ferguson testified that the defendant suffered major depression with psychotic features in *partial* remission.

The doctor of psychiatry was then asked the definition of *complete* remission.

Totally free of symptoms for at least two months, she answered. And Andrea Yates does not meet those conditions, she said.

The witness was passed to Owmby, who immediately mentioned Dr. Jerome Brown.

Most people in the room had forgotten who Dr. Jerome Brown was, despite the fact that Owmby had often tried to slip the name into his questioning. Brown was the forensic psychologist who, according to Owmby, had been asked by the defense to "look" at Yates, but was not testifying.

Owmby appeared to hope the insinuation would convey that Brown had found Yates competent, and that's why her defense team had not brought him to the stand.

Jerome Brown, Owmby told the psychiatrist, had administered competency evaluations in the past. Then Owmby asked Ferguson if the State had had the chance to have a psychiatric assessment done on Andrea Yates.

Dr. Ferguson told Owmby she did not understand his question.

Repeatedly, he asked her whether the State had had the chance to have a psychiatric evaluation of Yates.

"I don't know," Ferguson finally answered.

Owmby spouted to the judge that he wanted a "judicial notice."

After some argument, Hill stated that there would be judicial notice that the State had not made a request for the psychiatric evaluation.

At 12:35 P.M., court broke for lunch, with closing arguments set for the afternoon session.

At lunch, Rusty Yates' hands shook so vigorously that one of his lunch mates feared his chicken-fried chicken wasn't going to make it from the fork to his mouth without falling to his lap.

When she mentioned that, Dora Yates responded, "I've never noticed you shaking."

But Rusty Yates blew it off, saying that his father shook, too.

He spent much of the lunchtime reciting the Bible verses he'd spoken at his children's funeral.

CHAPTER 29

Just before 1:30 P.M., Andrea Yates was brought into the courtroom.

Moments later, her husband walked in. Rusty stopped at the front row and asked, "Where's my mother?"

Karin Kennedy gestured and replied, "Oh, anywhere."

Yates sat down on the front row, about six feet from Mrs. Kennedy. Dora Yates walked in and sat on the same row, on the opposite end from her son's mother-in-law.

At 1:45 P.M., Judge Hill brought the court to order.

At 1:50 P.M., the jurors entered the courtroom and sat down.

Five minutes later, in a soft, melodic voice, Wendell Odom began Andrea Yates' closing argument. He brought up the ever-present definition of competency. "You've heard that 100 times," he said. But doctors, lawyers, or judges, he continued, don't decide what that means.

You decide what's a rational and reasonable degree, Odom pressed on, referring to the definition, and he encouraged them to use common sense. He then emphasized that they had only heard evidence that Andrea Yates would indeed recover; they had heard nothing to the contrary.

"Do we do it now or do we do it later?" he said. "That's what we're really talking about."

Dr. Rubenzer said she was in full remission, Dr. Harris and Dr. Ferguson said she was in partial remission, and Dr. Marangell testified that Andrea Yates' mental illness was

treatable with medicine, Odom stated. One can look at the
history of the patient and can see that if she continues to
get better, she will get well, he said that Marangell had
testified. But if she is in partial remission, he said, still para-
phrasing Marangell, if Andrea Yates is under stress, she will
relapse. If that happened, he pointed out, the trial would
have to be conducted all over again. "Believe me, I don't
know if I can handle it one more time. . . . We only want to
do this once."

Dr. Harris, he said, used his own tests, plus Dr. Rubenzer's tests, and found that Andrea Yates' memory is
"messed up." But Rubenzer kept retesting Yates until she
passed the tests, Odom stated. "I don't care what you say,
these are both subjective opinions." And, he quoted Rubenzer, " 'She's not quite there yet.' "

Odom moved to Dr. Mary Alice Conroy's testimony that
psychotic features have a major impact on competency.

Objection, Owmby called, claiming that that wasn't what
Conroy had said.

Judge Hill turned to the jurors and instructed them that
closing arguments aren't evidence.

"If I heard it wrong, shame on me," Odom replied to the
jurors, and soon ended his closing argument.

Kaylynn Williford walked over to the jury box. Dr. Rubenzer, she said, was ordered by the court to be independent
and to do a competency evaluation. Dr. Rubenzer, she
stated, found Andrea Yates competent to stand trial.

Rubenzer, she argued, was the one person who has spent
the most time with Yates, knows her abilities to consult with
her attorney, and her factual understanding of the proceedings.

On July 20, after explaining her rights to her, Rubenzer
found that Andrea Yates "had the presence of mind and
capability" to say, I want to be punished, I guess I was
overwhelmed, and I want to consult with my attorney.

According to Dr. Harris, Williford said, Andrea Yates did

poorly on memory, not on events but on numbers and stories. Do you really think these things are important to her?
the prosecutor asked. Then she pointed out that Harris didn't
have the ten hours with Andrea Yates that Rubenzer did.

Most of the jurors watched Williford. One juror wrote
hard and fast notes.

Everyone, she said, agrees that Andrea Yates is getting
better. But getting better, she stated, doesn't matter. "It matters that she's currently competent."

Twice, Williford used the phrase "killing her children,"
then noted that Yates had thought about killing her children
the night before the drownings.

Think about the facts, she said, and that Dr. Rubenzer,
"an independent appraiser of the court," says she's still competent. "And that's the issue, and nothing else."

"I feel a little tense now," Owmby said, as he looked at the
jurors at 2:20 P.M.. So if I talk colloquially, he said, or use
"far out examples," I'm just trying to get you back to where
you were before today—ruled by common sense, justice,
and fairness.

If you were sitting out there, he said, indicating the gallery, think: Andrea Yates has a problem, a serious offense,
with serious consequences, and she should stand trial.

And like Williford, he mentioned the deaths of five children.

He spoke of Yates' 113 IQ and noted that she was valedictorian at Milby High, and that in jail she reads and plays
dominos. She has a factual understanding, he stated. Even
her lawyer concedes that, he said.

But does she have sufficient, present ability to consult
with a lawyer? Yes, he answered. She's not delusional about
the sequence of events, but she can't remember numbers a
half hour later. And he reeled off a long list of numbers to
show the jurors that they, too, couldn't remember a list of
numbers.

The juror who had been taking fastidious notes leaned back in her chair and rocked.

"If you were out there where the air is better," Owmby dramatically stated, "you would say she's competent."

Then he noted, "But you're not out there." You've been here for days, he said, and lawyers are asking you to put away your common sense.

Andrea Yates appeared to be watching the well-dressed Owmby in his dark, three-button suit.

We all have emotional problems to a varying degree, he said. And, pointing his finger right at Andrea Yates' nose, he added, and hers are severe.

The defense implied that Dr. Rubenzer always testified for the State, he said, but Rubenzer finds three out of ten incompetent. So for those three, he stressed, he doesn't have to testify.

Then he declared that Dr. Jerome Brown would find Andrea Yates competent.

Wendell Odom flew out of his chair, "Objection!" screaming from his mouth. He demanded that the judge ask the jurors to disregard that statement, because Jerome Brown never testified.

Sustained, Judge Hill said as she glared toward Odom.

He looked around and realized why—Parnham was also standing and only one member of each team was to voice objections. Odom quickly apologized to the Court and said that his emotions "got to" him.

Owmby continued, saying that Rubenzer had testified that Yates was in full remission with regards to her psychotic features. He did not acknowledge that previously Williford had stated that Rubenzer had testified that Yates was in partial, not full, remission.

Rusty Yates, sitting on the front row, shook his head nonstop.

Owmby talked about residual psychosis and again mentioned that "she killed her five children." Because she has the possibility of relapsing, she's incompetent, he said in a tone of voice insinuating that he found that ridiculous. "Let's say you accept that that makes her incompetent—"

And Rusty Yates still shook his head, his arms defensively crossed over his chest.

"She will always have some residual psychosis," he noted, claiming that defense witness Dr. Marangell had testified to that. "This indicates a cycle into the future. . . . She goes away and never has a trial" because the conditions will never change, he said.

Rusty Yates shook his head no.

"If they bring her back, what will the doctors say?" Owmby asked. She's in partial remission—

Judge Hill halted Owmby's closing and firmly warned spectators to stop gesturing and commenting.

Rusty Yates quit shaking his head.

"If you don't find her competent," Owmby continued, "she will never be put to trial."

Objection, Odom and Parnham cried. That was a misstatement, they argued, and the judge should order the jury to disregard it.

Sustained, she answered.

The defense asked for the statement to be struck, too.

Denied, Judge Hill replied.

The issue, the prosecutor said, is whether Andrea Yates is presently competent to stand trial. If she is incompetent, he asked, is it because of sympathy, or because you don't like the prosecutors?

He did not include the option that the jurors might find Andrea Yates incompetent based on the facts.

"She has to have a trial, and she is competent to have a trial today," he said. He then told the jurors to let in some of that common sense air.

At 2:44 P.M., twenty-four minutes after Owmby began his closing argument, George Parnham faced the jurors. Owmby had ranted; Parnham's voice was almost inaudible.

Do not decide Andrea Yates' competency based on the

unsubstantiated charge by the prosecution that she will never face trial for the deaths of her five children, Parnham began. "It's unsupported. It's a fear tactic."

He quoted Owmby: "Mental health is not relevant to competency." Every expert, Parnham claimed, said that was a factor. "That's the testimony."

"Show me one person in this courtroom," he commented, who said, " 'I am Satan. . . . It's time I am punished, and George W. Bush should kill me.'

"Her mental illness is severe, severe as it gets." He went on to say that the prosecution's own witness stated that psychosis affects competency. Dr. Rubenzer, he pointed out, says she's fully recovered. Dr. Ferguson, who saw Yates two days ago, Parnham noted, said she's in psychotic remission.

Dr. Rubenzer said he was a disinterested expert, Parnham continued, and he had visits with Andrea Yates that were known to the State.

But before Parnham could say that those visits were not known to the defense, Williford objected, claiming that Parnham was assuming facts that weren't in evidence.

Judge Hill turned to the jurors one more time and again explained that closing arguments weren't evidence, and for them not to take it as such.

Rubenzer had seen Yates on September 10 and 17, Parnham commented, and talked to the State about the visits, but not the defense. Put that in perspective, he said. Rubenzer, he claimed, was a neutral, disinterested party in name only.

Parnham again emphasized that Yates was in partial remission. And, he stated, that's a fact—not an old attorney zealously defending his client. He talked about how the prosecution said that Yates "chose" not to answer questions and that Rubenzer answered that she didn't answer certain questions and he didn't know why she didn't answer those questions.

"Failed," Parnham said, was Williford's word. "He failed

her," Parnham said, quoting Williford discussing Rubenzer. He failed her, he said, until she got the right answer.

"An absolutely unimaginable act," Parnham called his client's crime.

"Is she where she ought to be?" he soon asked. "I don't think so," he answered. "What's the rush? What's the rush? Give her the benefit of the best Texas has to offer."

Parnham looked to the jury, and in a voice so soft that the gallery couldn't hear, he spoke his closing words.

At 3:15 P.M., the eleven-woman, one-man jury exited to the eliberate Andrea Yates' competency. The two-part definition of competency boiled down to one question—did they believe the State's witness, forensic psychologist en Rubenzer?

Andrea Yates was led out of the courtroom, looking healthy as she walked.

Her brother, Brian Kennedy, turned to a spectator and said, "Thanks for coming."

Rusty Yates and his mother turned to the press and listened as the reporters compared notes and quotes.

Karin Kennedy smiled.

Quickly, a reporter out of New York was at Rusty's feet, introducing herself to Yates and his mother. Rusty then turned his attention to another national magazine reporter.

Parnham talked with a Texas newspaper reporter.

Kaylynn Williford watched it all.

And hours slowly ticked by.

Mrs. Kennedy kept an eye on her adult sons, making sure they didn't say anything to the press that would break the gag order. Brian—charming and self-effacing—simply said that he used to wear Italian clothes and joked about his own "research" visit to the Harris County Jail.

Parnham and Odom eased around the room, making sure to treat each reporter with politeness, making sure not to say anything about the case. Odom spoke of the property he owned in East Texas. Parnham lay down on one of the courtroom pews. Minutes later, he rose, rubbing his eyes as if he'd slept for a few minutes.

At 4:30 P.M., Parnham and Odom stood in the hallway when they were instructed to gather at the judge's bench—there was a question about the definition of competency. "All this means we're going to be here for a while," Odom muttered to no one in particular. And all the attorneys but Joe Owmby stood before Judge Hill. The issue resolved, Hill stepped down.

Five minutes later, the judge stepped up to the bench again, this time waving a piece of paper.

"Another one?" Parnham said.

The New York reporter asked Rusty Yates if he was going to write a book.

"Where'd you hear that?" he responded, then said he was going to write down a few things about the kids and post them on his Website. He talked about his concern that people would download the photos on the site and do cruel things with the pictures. That worry, he said, was why there were no photographs of Andrea on the site.

After *The Dallas Morning News* mentioned yateskids.org in one of its stories, he said, his Website got one gig of hits, an extraordinary amount for a personal Web page. Then, when the Web address appeared in the *Houston Chronicle*, he said, it got three gigs of hits.

Quickly, the conversation turned to NASA, the panels on the shuttles, computers, LINUX operating systems, and on and on about science and technology. Rusty Yates grinned when he showed his intelligence, and his tech knowledge flew over the heads of his listeners.

Brian Kennedy chatted with a spectator and said he knew what depression was, and he'd seen it in Andrea's eyes just a day or two before the murders. But he never dreamed she'd be capable of such a thing.

"Andrea is the sweetest person," he said, as he sighed.

"If you knew her—I mean, I doubt if she's ever even told a lie in her life."

Mrs. Kennedy strode past with long steps, just like her daughter's. She appeared a strong, determined, and agile woman. But as she returned to sitting on the front row waiting, her thinning hair shining in the dark, she seemed a worried mother in grief. She told a spectator, who she made sure wasn't a reporter, that just last night, Andrea had said she'd killed two of her children because she'd damaged them by nursing them while on Haldol.

She told Claire Anderson of Capacity for Justice the same thing, adding that Andrea had never nursed her children while on Haldol. She was in the hospital, not nursing the babies, and by the time she was released from the hospital her breast milk had dried up. Andrea, Mrs. Yates told Anderson, has false memories.

Outside the courthouse, Owmby rushed by and mentioned that no matter what the jury decided, Andrea Yates couldn't go on trial for another ninety days. He'd wanted the jury to know that, but he couldn't tell them that.

At 7:06 P.M., Andrea Yates was brought back into the courtroom.

In the back of the room, like a vulture waiting for its prey to die, Dianne Clements watched Andrea. Clements, the spokesperson for the pro–death penalty group Justice for All, wore a blood-red blazer and held a Stephen King novel. Just a day or two before, she'd been on the news professing her desire that Yates be found competent and ready to face the death penalty.

Two minutes later, Judge Hill walked into the courtroom. Two minutes after that, all the attorneys stood at her elbows. As they turned to go to their tables, Owmby and Williford stepped away laughing.

At 7:12 P.M., the jury entered, and reporters noted that the jurors had been dancing and partying when their door opened. Spectators hoped for and expected a verdict.

A portion of Dr. Steven Rubenzer's testimony was read instead.

"Parnham: 'She's not quite there yet?'

"Rubenzer: 'I don't think so.' "

At 7:13 P.M., the jurors exited.

Dora Yates looked bedraggled and admitted she was tired.

Circles showed under her son's eyes as he stood next to Brian Kennedy, who sat on the floor. Then Rusty turned and walked over to talk to his mom.

At 7:57 P.M., the attorneys and Andrea Yates were again brought before the judge. George Parnham didn't look happy.

At 8:00 P.M., the jurors were brought in. Judge Hill told them that court was in recess for the night, they would be sequestered, and they absolutely could not continue deliberations, even as they ate dinner.

She then ordered everyone to be back in court at 8 A.M., Saturday.

CHAPTER 30

The streets of downtown Houston were empty on the morning of Saturday September 22. Parking places that were usually hard fought for and expensive were available for free on every street, even directly across from the courthouse, even where the TV vans were usually parked. One lone TV cameraman staked out the courthouse's glass front doors.

At 7:50 A.M., the Kennedy family walked through the doors. Rusty Yates already sat inside the lobby. A few reporters stood inside, too. No one was allowed on the courtroom floor just yet.

George Parnham entered, hefting three books, two by Hemingway, one by Stephen Ambrose, his anticipated reading while the jury deliberated. He joked about his habit of starting one book just before finishing the last.

At 8:05 A.M., the jurors, toting their overnight bags, stepped off a Harris County Sheriff's van and, led by a deputy, walked into the courthouse, strode onto an elevator, and disappeared.

Just as they vanished, cameramen appeared everywhere, like city pigeons on a sidewalk. They shot Rusty Yates and the Kennedy family through the windows, taunting the security guards that they weren't setting foot in the courthouse, just as the judge had ordered.

Rusty rose, eased away from the window, and said he wouldn't talk to the *Houston Chronicle* because he didn't want to taint the Houston jury pool. He'd talk to the national media though, he said, because he wanted to get the issues out there—as if Houstonians didn't read and watch national news reports.

He said he was worried about the interview he'd done with *60 Minutes*, that he'd go to jail for contempt. But then a *60 Minutes* producer had phoned him and told him he wouldn't be going to jail—Harris County District Attorney Chuck Rosenthal had broken the gag order and spoken to them, too. Rusty Yates grinned.

Wendell Odom entered and walked toward the elevator.

Rusty Yates quoted the elevator's capacity in pounds. He noticed the details in numbers, and quoting those made him smile.

Yates talked about how he and Andrea used to watch ballgames together, he watched the plays while she watched the uniforms. He smiled again.

His reflections turned serious as he thought back to his wife's hospitalizations. In 1999, he said, we made some mistakes, but in 2001, we did everything right. That was contrary, he said disgustedly, to what *The Dallas Morning News* had reported.

Finally, everyone was allowed up to the fifth floor. Rusty Yates stepped onto an elevator. His mom wasn't with him this day, and he seemed desperately alone, so much so that even a reporter could be a friend.

On this day of only reporters and family—most spectators having given up on hearing the verdict in person—Dianne Clements from Justice for All still sat alone in the courtroom, which was as cold as a coroner's locker.

At 10:02 A.M., the bailiff knocked on the jury room door. A note was slipped to him, and the door was shut. He stood between the jury door and a door marked "Private," read the note, then walked through the "Private" door.

Judge Hill walked out another door and said, "Ms. Williford, can I see you, please?"

"Okay—"

Molly Odom, who had worked with her brother on the case, walked into the courtroom, where George Parnham was talking with reporters, and pulled him away.

The bailiff returned and walked toward the jury room, carrying a coffeemaker and cream and sugar. It appeared that it was going to be a very long Saturday.

Lisa Teachey, from the *Houston Chronicle*, talked about her trip to the smoldering, stench-filled Ground Zero of the World Trade Center. She'd returned the day of Andrea Yates' jury selection—five dead babies to 5,000 dead Americans, and back again.

Williford was standing in the spectator gallery, and whispering with Dianne Clements from Justice for All.

At 11:32 A.M., the bailiff walked over to the jury room door. It opened, the one male juror stood there, and handed the bailiff another slip of paper. Again, the bailiff walked through the door marked "Private."

George Parnham walked into the courtroom with a thumb up and said, "Verdict."

Reporters scrambled to their seats and notepads. Rusty Yates sat on the front row, directly behind where his wife would sit. Mrs. Kennedy sat next to him, then John O'Sullivan, Brian Kennedy, and Andrew Kennedy.

Andrea Yates was brought in.

At 11:40 A.M., the jury took their seats.

"Good morning," Judge Hill said.

The foreman, the female juror who sat the closest to Andrea Yates, read, "We, the jury, find the Defendant, Andrea Pia Yates, mentally competent to stand trial at this time."

Rusty Yates shook his head.

George Parnham patted Andrea Yates' back.

The jurors were polled. They all stated "Competent." Sniffles were heard in the room. And the jurors were excused.

Rusty Yates put his head in his hands, almost as if he were praying. He looked near tears, and his skin began to turn red. Emotion *was* showing.

The attorneys gathered at the bench.

Rusty's head was still in his hands, his elbows were on his knees, and he still shook his head.

Karin Kennedy stared straight forward.

Rusty's body began to quiver.

Judge Hill whispered softly to the attorneys as rowdiness emitted from behind the closed door of the jury room.

Rusty's body began to shake more and more.

Judge Hill called John O'Sullivan to join them at the bench. She announced that any pre-trial hearings and the trial would be set the following week.

Quickly, O'Sullivan returned to the Kennedy family and told them that he needed to talk with them. He motioned them and Rusty Yates to a corner that he hoped was far from the reporters' prying ears. He handed them copies of the gag order. The judge had told him to remind them of it.

Rusty Yates walked away, leaned slightly against the first pew, and stared blankly.

"All things work for good," a bystander said to him.

He continued staring blankly.

"For those who love the Lord."

He still stared blankly.

"And try to do His will."

Yates still stared blankly.

"But sometimes that's hard to believe." And the bystander walked away.

Parnham eased over to the gallery railing as the media rushed toward him. "The good sign is that she will be with people who can care for her medically and care for her with their hearts," he said.

And with that, most of the press ran downstairs and out the courtroom doors to query family, attorneys, and jurors as they exited. A few reporters stayed in the courtroom until the bailiff ordered them out, telling them they couldn't interview the jurors.

Outside, Rusty Yates stood near the curb, holding his umbrella, as George Parnham again made a brief, innocuous statement for the cameras and tape recorders. When attention turned to Yates, he was asked what he was going to do next. He replied, "I'm gonna go home and pay bills."

Then the media waited for the jurors . . . and waited . . . and waited.

Finally, the tattooed bailiff exited the courthouse and announced to the sidewalk media pool—in an almost "Hear ye, hear ye" style—that they couldn't interview the jurors: it was in the judge's orders that they couldn't, and he'd been sent down there by the judge to tell them such.

"It's not legal," yelled Cynthia Hunt, a reporter for KTRK, the local ABC affiliate. "She removed that part from the order."

"I can't argue with it," the bailiff sternly bellowed back. "It's not my problem."

"It's not legal. She removed that part from the order!"

The bailiff left, but soon returned, the media order in hand, and, like the town crier, he read it out boldly.

"Anybody gonna cross the line?" said one reporter.

"We'll watch," came the chorus.

"Do you want video for the big trial?" said a cameraman. He advised his counterparts to pick their battles, and this wasn't the time to pick a battle, he said.

"This is still illegal," Hunt loudly argued. "I'm calling my attorney Monday morning!"

At 12:50 P.M., more than an hour after the jurors rendered their verdict, four jurors exited the courtroom, an escorting deputy waving away the cameras. Slowly, in small groups, the jurors exited. And the reporters, fuming at the continued secrets of the Andrea Yates case, plotted their phone calls to their companies' attorneys.

That same day, Judge Hill granted the State's motion for Andrea Yates to undergo a psychological examination by a psychiatric expert "designated by the State subject to Court approval." The exam would be conducted without the presence of attorneys and would be videotaped, with a copy made available to the defense.

If Yates refused the exam, the Court ordered "any psychiatric expert(s) at trial *vis-à-vis* the Defendant's notice to assert an insanity defense which is based upon an examination of the Defendant be excluded, and that any psychiatric testimony from the Defendant's psychiatric expert(s) be limited to testimony solely derived from hypothetical questions."

The following evening, the men of Clear Lake Church of Christ surrounded Rusty Yates with a group hug and prayed for him.

Monday, September 24, Rusty's aunt, the Reverend Fairy Caroland, a Presbyterian minister in Georgia, learned that Harris County District Attorney Chuck Rosenthal, a man who wore a "what would Jesus do?" bracelet, was using the Old Testament, New Testament, Jesus' name and teachings, and even, ironically, the prophet Noah to back his death penalty stance against Andrea Yates.

". . . I begin with the premise that the Bible teaches that Jesus is God," Rosenthal stated in letters to death penalty protesters. He then noted the book of John in the New Testament, Noah in Genesis 9:6, Exodus 20:12, Matthew 5:17 and 5:20, and the 13th chapter of the book of Romans.

He said he had an obligation to uphold the law. And he had "an obligation to the five victims whose lives were snuffed out by Andrea Yates. I have an obligation to try to keep others from taking the lives of children when they become burdensome or when some need in the murderer's life is not being met."

Then he claimed that it offended his religious beliefs to force his beliefs on others.

Reverend Caroland sent Rosenthal an email.

"Having never studied Biblical languages yourself," she wrote, "I guess you're able to conveniently miss the fact that God and Jesus deal equally with mercy in their justice."

She noted that the DA "tossed out" the concept of mental illness. "No one in the family of these children . . . wants Andrea put to death. Every family member misses the children AND knows Andrea is seriously mentally ill." She pointed out that Andrea's memories would always be psychotic memories, never normal memories.

"If you believe that murder is wrong, you could not support murder by the state either. I DO believe your focus is your office, maintaining your position, and protecting your own backside. You may as well play an instrument in your office's 'Death by Injection' garage band—the mentality is all yours—truly tasteless."

Rosenthal responded, asking who had said that Yates was going to get the death penalty and stating that mental illness does not absolve criminal responsibility. "If you do not believe that God and Jesus are one being and that God cannot contradict himself, I doubt your Biblical scholarship," he told the Reverend. Then he said he'd never played in a garage band or any other kind of band. "I do my job without considering political consequences," he wrote. And he stated that the "foregoing" led him to believe that Reverend Caroland had jumped "to conclusions without sufficient evidence."

Rusty Yates was working out at Bally Total Fitness when he glanced at the machine next to him and saw Dr. Mohammad Saeed.

Saeed then looked up and saw Yates. "Oh," he said, stunned and startled, "how are you doing?"

Yates glared at him. "Not that good." He wanted to pick Saeed up and toss him over the nearby railing. *How can he even show his face in public?*

Saeed quickly stepped off his exercise machine and left the building.

On October 2, attorneys for the *Houston Chronicle* filed a motion in Judge Hill's court, asking her to modify her September 18, 2001, order precluding the media from talking to the Yates competency hearing jurors. Her order, the attorneys argued, "unconstitutionally prohibits the Houston Chronicle and its reporters from engaging in constitutionally protected activity . . ." That constitutionally protected activity, the attorneys made clear, was newsgathering.

A copy of the motion was sent to Chuck Rosenthal.

Almost two months later, ten days before Mary Yates would have celebrated her first birthday, Judge Belinda Hill handed down her decision barring the media from contacting any jurors from Yates' competency hearing. She upheld that ruling, but she omitted a section banning the media from publishing information about the jurors. She also claimed she'd previously told the jurors that they could contact the media, the media just could not contact them.

The media did not have the Constitutional right and freedom to ask the questions.

CHAPTER 31

Tuesday, October 30, 2001, George Parnham and Wendell Odom filed thirty-four pre-trial motions in Judge Belinda Hill's 230th District Court of Harris County, Texas. Several motions involved prosecutorial behavior and concern that Owmby and Williford would try to inflame the jurors with their arguments and photographs of the victims and the crime scene. One motion asked to see those crime scene photos.

Other motions requested disclosure of juror data, including their arrest records, and the D.A.'s selection process. One motion asked the Court to declare unconstitutional the section of the *Texas Code of Criminal Procedure* that disallowed jurors from learning that a not guilty by reason of insanity verdict did not set the defendant free and immediately return them to society.

Another motion asked that the Texas standard for insanity be declared unconstitutional because it "ignores the nature of mental illness . . ." Others asked that the indictment be set aside and the death penalty be excluded as a possible punishment.

The defense attorneys also asked that Yates' confession be thrown out. "At the time of the custodial interrogations (both at home and at the station house) the Defendant lacked the prerequisite mental capacity in order to knowingly, intelligently, and voluntarily waive her Constitutional rights much less understand them," they argued.

Both the defense and the prosecutors filed motions asking for the other's list of expert witnesses. The defense was expected to call Dr. Lucy Puryear, a Baylor College of Medicine professor of psychiatry who had been quoted in the *Houston Chronicle* about Andrea Yates, and Dr. Phillip Resnick, the professor of psychiatry at Case Western Reserve University who had appeared on *Nightline* the day after the murders.

The State would be calling forensic psychiatrist Park Dietz, who had testified against child-killer Susan Smith and serial killer Jeffrey Dahmer. Dahmer had unsuccessfully pled insanity—in part, because of Dietz. In a 1994 issue of *Johns Hopkins Magazine*, Dietz was quoted as saying, "I spend my time trying to understand sex and violence. What could be better than trying to understand such interesting things?"

After all that had happened, the woman from Starbucks, the woman who'd known Rusty and Andrea Yates since before they'd wed, finally wanted to reveal the secret she'd held inside since June 20, 2001.

Not long after she'd met the Yateses, the woman recalled, she stood outdoors talking with Rusty. He mentioned that he'd heard she was a registered nurse and asked at what hospital she worked. When she told him the name of the hospital, which was a psychiatric hospital, and explained that she was a psychiatric nurse, he replied, "I don't believe in mental illness."

"You don't believe in it?" she responded incredulously.

"No, I don't believe in it," Yates replied. "I believe everybody has choices in life, and that's a cop-out."

Her anger grew. The woman had simply seen and dealt with too many psychotic and schizophrenic patients to believe it was anything but real.

But Rusty Yates continued on, saying that psychiatric illnesses were a bunch of malarkey, that a person could control his or her brain if he or she wanted to, and a person could change if he or she wanted to.

Furious, the woman left Rusty Yates' side and walked back to her house, ranting at her husband and thinking to Rusty, *You never know when it's going to be at your back door.*

Not only was Rusty Yates' wife pleading not guilty by reason of insanity, but twice every three weeks he was seeing a therapist—the NASA psychologist who had arrived at his door the day his wife told police, "I killed my kids."

One month to the day after jury selection began in Andrea Yates' competency hearing, Rusty Yates heard the doorbell ring at his Beachcomber home, turned off the alarm system, and, by key, unlocked the front door from the inside.

It was the kind of fall evening when drivers rode with their windows down, music flowing from one car to the next. It was the kind of day when neighbors opened up their windows for a breeze of fresh air. Rusty Yates opened the door, then locked it after he closed it back, and reset the alarm.

The house, even with the lights on, felt dimly lighted. A couple of drooping potted plants stood by the window that faced the driveway. Water stains beneath the pots speckled the brown tile floor with white.

A long, narrow table replaced the few chairs that had once been scattered across the den. The table was stacked high with the mail Yates had received since June 20. He somewhat apologetically walked around the table, into the kitchen, and opened the cabinets to show off how he'd perfectly cleaned and organized them.

Gone was the china from before. In its stead was plastic. Rusty Yates explained that he'd spent some of his time cleaning the house. In part, he'd done it to clear away messiness. In part, he'd done it to prepare for Andrea's return home.

He had talked that day with his wife's jailhouse psychiatrist. They'd discussed how Andrea's return to that particular home would affect her mental health. Rusty still planned on his wife coming home to be with him. The psychiatrist suggested that that house might not be good for her—too many bad memories. Andrea Yates, her husband reported, was the lowest he'd ever seen her. She was being prepared for what she'd hear at the trial—that she'd methodically drowned her children—and the realization of what she'd done was destroying her. Sometimes, she remembered the thoughts she had on June 20, but she couldn't figure out or understand why in the world she'd had those thoughts.

He'd visited Andrea two days earlier, then came home and wrote her a note. "I can't imagine what you're going through," he penned—the loss of her children, the separation from her husband, the hearing of what she'd done . . . and living with that.

Rusty Yates was cleaning the house to clear away her bad memories, or perhaps to sell the house so Andrea wouldn't have to return to the death site. Although Rusty Yates occasionally mentioned that his wife might be convicted and might not be paroled for forty years—if she didn't get the death penalty—most times he seemed to deny that he wouldn't ever have her in his home again.

The kitchen sink held an unwashed skillet. Rusty had cooked spaghetti the night before.

He smiled as he described how Noah used to climb up on the cabinets and, all by himself, fix his brothers peanut butter sandwiches when Andrea was in the hospital. Noah and Andrea were such great friends, Yates continually remarked.

He walked into the dining room, which was his office. There, facing what used to be the children's schoolroom, was his computer and scanner, the place where he read emails from supporters and haters, the place where he worked on yateskids.org. He saved the kind emails and letters. The angry ones he deleted or shredded, he said.

He spoke of his debate over whether to buy a new computer or just upgrade the one he had. He wanted the ability to make DVD videos of the kids and give them out as Christmas presents.

Rusty Yates moved into the schoolroom, his pace somewhat lethargic, as if he wasn't sure he actually wanted to walk into the space where Andrea had once taught his children. Gone were the four desks that had filled the room. Gone were most of the home school supplies. He'd given them away, along with nearly all of the kids' toys, the stuffed animals left on the lawn in memory of the kids, the bunkbeds he'd made for the kids. He and a friend named Ron had loaded up their vehicles and taken the goods to Ron's house. Yates remarked, with what appeared to be a bit of pride, about how many home school supplies there had been.

He glanced at the dry eraser board covering a wall, neatly filled with his to-do list. "Don't look at that," he said, and released the tiny white gate that separated the schoolroom from the entryway.

In the entry hall, he opened a closet, clean and organized to engineer neat. It was Andrea's crafts closet, he said, and it used to barely close because of Andrea's jumbled mess of crafts. He indicated that it was now ready for her to come home and do the crafts that she loved so much.

Rusty walked back into the den and turned to his left to go down the hallway that led to *the* bathroom. He motioned toward the family photographs lining the hallway and mentioned that one of them had once hung in the den, over the love seat.

It was the love seat where Andrea had sat after she told the police she'd killed her kids. It was where she'd sat as the police questioned her and as Rusty stood outside, peering through the windows, banging on the walls, screaming, "How could you do this?"

He walked straight into the bathroom, tiny and narrow, barely space enough for an adult between the toilet and the tub. He stood and stared into the tub. He hadn't yet been able to take a shower in it, he said, but maybe someday. He noted that his brother, Randy, had taken a shower in it right away. It didn't seem to bother Randy. But they moved to the Extended StayAmerica and resided there for a week after the deaths.

Whereas Rusty Yates had seemed hesitant to enter the schoolroom, in the bathroom he seemed almost like he didn't want to leave, as if he were spending time with the children—the place where his children's spirits had soared to Jesus.

Eventually, though, he walked back into the hallway and turned to the children's bedroom. It was completely empty. The only reminders of children were the dirty carpet and dirty walls from plenty of play . . . and tiny red hearts pasted on the walls. Noah had made the hearts all by himself and tacked them all around the house, on the bedroom walls, on the walls in the den, scattered wherever he thought they'd look pretty. As often as Yates mentioned what good friends Andrea and Noah were, he mentioned how Noah loved crafts and would go off by himself to make something.

Rusty explained the bunkbeds he'd made for the boys and how the children had helped. They'd gone with him to buy the wood, helped him select the lumber, then worked as a team to help him load it into their blue Suburban.

Andrea had made the valance over the mini-blinds in the room.

Rusty Yates didn't seem in a rush to leave the room, but he crossed the hall to what was now his room, a good-sized bedroom with brown tile flooring, just like in the den. He said the room previously had been used for storage. He just couldn't sleep in the master bedroom, nor on the mattress where Andrea had laid to rest all the children but Noah. He'd cleaned out the "storage" room, bought a new bed, and moved in there.

Scattered about the room were a few memories from his youth—a trophy he'd won at his Tennessee Nazarene church, a trophy for a physical fitness event in elementary school, a gift of a ceramic football player wearing Rusty Yates' number from someone who remembered his days at DuPont High.

He walked out the door and stopped at a few photos hanging just outside the master bedroom. One photo was of Andrea on their wedding day, looking beautiful with her mother, father, brother Andrew, and sister Michele.

He laughed a bit as he spoke of how Andrea had hated her hair that day and didn't like change. She'd gone to the hairdresser for a special wedding hairdo. The hairdresser had created a French twist, which Andrea didn't like at all. She came home, and Randy's girlfriend at the time, who was thankfully a hairstylist, redid Andrea's hair. It hung down long and curled a bit, still not to Andrea's liking, but definitely better than the fancy French twist.

Yates walked into the master bedroom he'd once shared with his wife. The mattress that had rested on the floor was gone, given away. Andrea's clothes, stuffed into bags, leaned against a wall, beneath the sheer valance with pink flowers that she'd sewn. To the right of the clothes were the children's possessions—the crowns Andrea had made for their medieval costumes, clothes, toys, and stuffed animals, a few kept from those left outside by mourners, a pink one Andrea would have liked. Also on the floor was a clown suit, which had been Rusty's father's. Rusty didn't know why he had it or how he'd gotten it. But it was tucked close to his children's favorite possessions.

He moved back down the hallway with the dirty carpet and into the den, where a tour of the bus was mentioned. Yates seemed to turn white in the face, went silent, thought, then answered that he couldn't. He'd been renovating the bus, and it was a mess and a danger with hot wires.

He smiled as he began reminiscing about the boys helping him with the renovation. He'd give them a hammer to bang away at and rip down the walls. Then the children would get bored and want to run off to play. So, starting with the youngest boy first, he'd dismiss them one by one to play, but with each child working a bit longer than the last.

Yates dug through the stack of junk on the long narrow table and found a photo of a bull moose. It was Paul's favorite photo, he said, and had once been framed. But the frame had been broken, and Rusty Yates said he wanted to get it reframed and hung.

The phone rang. "That's probably Andrea."

She called frequently. Sometimes she asked about their dog Blackie, he later said. She took care of that dog like it was a child. Part of Rusty wanted to give Blackie away. He required too much attention; the dog wanted to lay its head in Rusty's lap when Yates wanted to lie down or work on his computer. And Blackie had torn up the yard. But if Andrea came home . . . she even talked to the jail psychiatrist about the dog. And the psychiatrist had asked Rusty about Blackie.

Luke grew up with Blackie, Yates fondly recalled. The dog would run over Luke, but tiny Luke was fearless and would pop right back up.

The father chuckled thinking more on his son's fearlessness. At the Kennedy house, Yates said, Luke would go to the back fence, stand twelve inches from it, drop his arms to his sides, and stare at the full-grown rottweiler glaring six inches on the other side, as if the three-foot-tall Luke were "staring down" the dog.

"Luke was sort of intimidating," Yates said, using the same word he once used to describe his father. Whereas Rusty always felt like the dad with the other boys—stronger, the leader, guiding them—with Luke, he said, he felt like, *Okay, Luke, I'll get out of your way.*

Luke, he emphasized, always felt like an adult. He was "a powerful, pure soul," with eyes so deep and blue that it "looked like a galaxy in his eyes."

Yates had dreamed about the boys, and that Luke had survived June 20. "The reality," he said, "is worse than the nightmare."

The phone caller wasn't Andrea. It was Ron, the friend who'd helped move the children's possessions, just doing his regular check on Rusty's well-being.

Yates hung up the phone.

He reached his arm about eighteen inches above his head and explained that his grief had been about there, then it subsided, and he moved his hand down to show how much. Then September 11 happened—and Rusty Yates raised his arm to its original height—and his grief returned, so high that it just went over his head.

CNN's Greta van Sustern had been in Houston, staying at the Four Seasons, and she'd sent a car for him, he further explained. On the way home, the car hit a cat. "At least it wasn't a dog," Yates recounted saying. Normally he would have wanted to stop and take care of the cat, he said. But now, he was too numbed to death. No one in New York City, he said, had suffered a loss like he had—five dead children and a wife charged with capital murder.

He eventually walked over to the alarm system, reset it, unlocked the front door, walked out, locked the door, and headed for the Colosseum Italian Restaurant.

The Colosseum was an inexpensive pizza spot just a few blocks from his home, a place where the staff had told him that if he ever needed a place to hide, he could come there. Yates glanced across the street to a shopping center that housed a Mr. Gatti's pizza. "Andrea liked to go to Mr. Gatti's."

In the cool darkness of the autumn night, he walked into the Colosseum—cafeteria-style in the daytime, restaurant style at night.

On that Thursday evening, there were a few tables of customers in the non-smoking section; there was one table of customers in the smoking section. Yates was led to the smoking section, where he sat in a booth and ordered iced tea, a salad, and a small pizza.

He talked about how he'd never dated much, despite the

fact that since third grade his mother had pushed him to have a girlfriend. Then, in high school, he dated some. And every single girlfriend he'd ever had, he said, had gotten in touch with him since the deaths.

He mentioned that he and Andrea had lived together for a year before they were married, that he'd been intimate before, but she hadn't, despite the fact that she'd dated one other man before him. Although she wanted, was ready, for intimacy, he said, she wasn't comfortable with her body. She wore denim dresses two sizes too large. She dressed in a closet. He'd tell her she was beautiful. She'd either look down at the ground or make a joke.

He said he had hoped she'd be happier with intimacy after they married. But he didn't feel that she was.

Sometimes the values of one's grandparents are more attractive than the values of one's parents, Rusty Yates softly mentioned. His grandparents had had many children. And he often wondered why having a large family with a stay-at-home wife and working father was considered so bad in today's times, when forty or fifty years ago it was considered just fine.

He thought of the TV shows that emphasized large families—*The Partridge Family*, *The Brady Bunch*, *Eight is Enough*. But those shows had all been in prime time decades ago. Nothing today indicated that large families and stay-at-home moms were okay, he pointed out.

Andrea's family and friends didn't approve of her having so many kids, home schooling the children, and worshipping at home, he said, but he and Andrea were just more traditional in their thinking.

In January of 2000, he said, he and Andrea had discussed the possibility of Andrea going back to work. He'd work half-time, he explained, and she could work half-time. She'd do the home schooling, and he would help in other ways with the kids' care. Andrea said no, he reported, she wanted to stay home with the kids. "I'm a mom, now. That's what I do," he quoted her.

They discussed getting a babysitter, too. But who could they trust? they wondered. Besides, Rusty said, who would want to babysit five children?

When Andrea got sick again, after her father died, Rusty Yates phoned Dr. Starbranch's office seeking help. He trusted Dr. Starbranch. But Rusty got a recorded message that said it cost $60 just to talk to Starbranch over the phone. He forked over the bucks. Then, for various reasons, he was forced to try other hospitals. They were either full or didn't have psychiatric facilities.

Finally, Devereux Texas Treatment Network was recommended. He phoned the facility. It could take Andrea immediately. He and Andrea's brother Brian each took Andrea by an arm and walked her over to the Suburban. She stiffened her legs and refused to get in. The two big men eventually overpowered the thin young mother and forced her into the truck and drove her to Devereux.

"Brain disease," Rusty Yates said. He didn't think of Andrea's illness as mental illness; it was brain disease. And he talked about how Andrea told him that Dr. Saeed would just poke his head through the door and say hello. Dr. Starbranch, Rusty said wistfully, always spent at least twenty minutes with Andrea.

Rusty Yates had three goals: (1) stop Andrea's trial from happening, (2) have Andrea found innocent, and (3) maintain the integrity of his family. He added a fourth goal to his mission list—make sure Dr. Saeed never practiced medicine again.

The customers had all walked out of the Colosseum. The waitress brought out her vacuum cleaner. And Rusty Yates got up to go home. By then, he'd polished off a piece of warmed pecan pie topped with a scoop of melting vanilla ice cream.

*   *   *

Yates scooted the long table filled with mail out of the way and stuck a videotape into his VCR; it was the same home video of the children he'd provided *60 Minutes*. He stretched out on his sofa and watched, remembering, reminiscing, and sniffing back occasional tears.

He bragged as Noah appeared with a cuckoo clock he'd made by himself, turning the clock by hand, announcing the time, then slipping the cuckoo bird attached to a Popsicle stick through the door, and cuckooing.

Paul came on the screen. "Paul always said 'Cheese' when he saw a camera."

The boys marched through the den with homemade musical instruments, seemingly their own version of *The Music Man*, but Andrea was the bandleader, making the instruments, teaching the boys about percussion and wind instruments, quizzing them about their instruments, encouraging them to play and learn.

The video panned into the master bedroom, revealing their mattress on the floor. Yates explained that he and Andrea had kept their mattress on the floor rather than in a frame so that they could play and wrestle with the kids and there would be less distance to fall from the bed.

Noah appeared on the TV, with spindly legs shining out from a homemade Indian costume constructed out of paper bags. It was December, just after Mary's birth. Andrea held the camera while she asked Noah about Indians. He explained how they used buffalo. He pointed to an intricately detailed Indian village he'd made, complete with teepee and fire. He seemed like a boy knowledgeable beyond his years. He seemed like a boy with a teacher who cared.

Andrea's voice was deep and strong as she continued to question him about the Indian culture. Occasionally there was a bit of off-screen laughter and giggles from Andrea's friend Debbie Holmes.

Rusty was asked about the diary that had been mentioned in the press months earlier.

"I don't know anything about that," he said, and then

suggested that perhaps Marlene Burda Wark, Andrea's friend from high school, had one.

But the diary was written by Debbie Holmes and detailed the weeks before the drownings, Andrea's mental decline, and Rusty's actions. The diary was considered "top secret" with *almost everyone* denying its existence.

Andrea, Rusty pointed out, had some friends, in fact, more friends than he did. He didn't need any, he continued, because he had the boys—they were his friends. But Rusty Yates quickly expressed his gratitude and surprise that his friends from his NASA co-op days had come to his aid and support.

The video returned to the kids playing in the bedroom, two weeks before the birth of Mary. Andrea aimed the camera at a mirror she stood before, and filmed her big, pregnant belly. She did not film her face.

The video cut to the hospital. Mary had been born and lay sleeping in Noah's lap. Rusty, holding the camera, asked Noah what he thought about having a girl in the family. "I can't believe it," Noah responded, with a big bump on his forehead as if he had tripped face-first on that brown tile floor at home.

Andrea sat upright in her bed and said, with a bit of a smile, that she was in pain, as always. She then fed Luke from her own hospital food.

Throughout the remainder of the tape, Noah was often photographed holding Mary.

One week after Mary's birth, Andrea appeared happy in the video, in fact, very happy.

"Mary was a good roller," Rusty said. Noah, Paul, Luke, they all walked early, he continued. John, though, was more laid back. In fact, he had them a bit worried about walking. Rusty made Andrea a one-dollar bet that John would be walking by a certain date. Walking, Rusty explained, was taking six steps. Andrea had to pay him the dollar.

He watched the TV as John's last birthday came on screen. Balloons stretched across the den. A hot-air-balloon birthday cake sat on the dining table. "Noah and Andrea made that."

John bounced perfectly and agilely on a giant ball, which was his birthday present. Noah got on the ball, bounced, and kept falling off of it. "Noah would get jealous of John," Rusty said.

And Rusty Yates began describing each of his children. Noah liked electronic things. Paul was good with a hammer.

John bounced across the screen again.

"He never got tired of it," Rusty remarked. John had to be disciplined more than the other boys, unlike Noah and Paul, who seemed to be quick learners as to what they were and weren't allowed to do. Isolating John seemed to work well with him. But sometimes, Rusty said, John seemed to need a "reassuring" paddling.

Rusty Yates talked about his desire to "train" his children. He would give them an instruction a time or two, but if they didn't quickly follow it, he said, he didn't see any reason to keep telling them—he'd simply get the paddle.

Paddling, he explained, was love and teaching. Hitting, he said, was anger and jealousy. "You can't explain diplomatic relations to a two-year-old."

He continued describing his boys. Noah preferred picking daisies to playing T-ball. He could read, spell, and was good at math. But John had better handwriting than Noah. Noah constantly made Andrea cards.

Rusty Yates reached for a plastic box of his children's drawings. His hands shook as he rapidly flipped through the pictures. Admittedly, if the drawing was good and unsigned, Yates attributed it to Noah. He was the son he missed the most, he said. He got up to get a plastic cup of water.

Noah was good with space and time and perception and he could see ahead and think ahead. He knew exactly how old he'd be when he finished his state quarter book. "He was anxious to be an adult."

When Noah was six, he heard the phrase "quarter of a million" mentioned on TV. "That's two hundred and fifty thousand," Noah responded. He was a seven-year-old who could count backwards from one million. He could add long columns of numbers in his head and would get angry when Rusty made him do it "the long way."

Five-year-old John could solve "less than, greater than" problems, Rusty went on. John was like Rusty in that he liked to get a "rise" out of people. He would latch on to a word he'd heard—like "dude"—and say it over and over again, just to irritate Andrea. "Dude, dude, dude, dude," Rusty quoted, with a grin.

John and Luke were alike. Noah and Paul were alike. Noah was like Rusty and Andrea. Andrea worked crafts quickly, like Noah did. But Noah was more sophisticated in his thinking. Andrea's thinking was simpler, Rusty said. Noah looked more like Andrea with his brown eyes and skinniness. And the proud father went on and on.

Slowly, though, the conversation returned to Andrea and her "brain disease." The first time he saw her in jail, Rusty said, she looked so different. "The police say they have a seventeen-minute statement from her. That's more words than Andrea spoke since the day her father died." He shook his head and quoted from First Samuel in the Old Testament, explaining that man looks outward, while God looks at the heart. So, Rusty continued, if Andrea's mind is bad, but her heart is good . . .

He spoke of Nebuchadnezzar, the king of Babylon who conquered Israel.

And his conversation eased around to his faith.

He'd always felt that church was more about business than anything else. And as a young boy, and then a young teen, he wondered what made those folks sitting in the pews only for the sake of doing business any better than him. "Grace," he constantly heard in church. Still, he didn't understand it. He continued questioning why churchgoers were any better than he.

He remembered the preacher who had sold them their bus; Rusty was "disappointed" with the vehicle. As he

ripped out walls to renovate it, Rusty found burn marks. He
wrote the preacher and told him that the bus "was less than
it was advertised," he said. Rusty Yates felt trampled on.

But, he pointed out, you can learn something from anyone.

Andrea, he said, met the preacher, liked him, too, and
corresponded with him.

Yates confessed that he was reluctant to talk about the
preacher because, over the years, the man had become
"more confrontational and zealous." Yates called him "fire
and brimstone. And I don't agree with that."

Watchman Nee, though, was the man Rusty Yates
claimed had a great influence on him. His teaching attracted
Rusty's analytical side. Rusty Yates, by his own admission,
was very analytical. According to Yates, Nee taught that
salvation was a matter of faith, which was the exact same
way Yates thought. Once you're His child, he said, you're
His child—and that's by faith.

Andrea, growing up Catholic, Yates continued to explain,
was more "works and shame" oriented. People want to earn
their salvation through works, he said, but salvation is a free
gift from God. Andrea, he said, found it difficult to believe
that God had already done the work for her.

Rusty sounded like a man talking about grace, the very
word he objected to as a child. He smiled a bit and said he
now liked the word *grace*, just not all the "gobble-de-gook"
he heard as a kid. And that's why he liked Byron Fike, he
said. Fike didn't talk about gobble-de-gook; he talked about
the character of men and women.

Yates' own Bible studies with Andrea and his kids, he
said, were "cute" Bible studies. And it wasn't done every
night, he said. Sometimes, it was preempted by a run to the
store and returning so late that it was past the kids' bedtime.
When they did do it, Rusty said a prayer, then Andrea,

Noah, John, Paul, and Luke said a prayer. Luke closed with "Ba-bay," and they'd pray for Mary.

Andrea, Yates said, took the Bible very seriously. And despite telling the doctors that she was concerned about her salvation, Yates said they didn't talk about it much.

His conversation turned to Andrea's mental illness. In the months before June 20, he explained, she went through the motions at home—ironing, giving the kids their baths, reading to them. If she was asked a question, she'd answer, but it was only a one- or two-word answer. Sometimes, she'd just stare.

If someone is quiet, he explained, you simply see them the same as always. Rusty Yates had no way of hearing the voices she heard or seeing the visions she saw—she never told him about them.

After Andrea was arrested, she was out of it, he said. Then her mind started clearing some, but she still wasn't saying much. Then she said some things; then she only cried. Eventually, her mood became very elevated. Then, he said, her mood came back down. Over time, she had appropriate highs and lows.

One day, Rusty cried while talking to Andrea, and she didn't cry with him. That was very unusual, he pointed out, because normally she was the emotional one and he wasn't. But since the competency hearing, with the preparation for the trial, he said, as he had earlier in the evening, that she was more down than he'd ever seen her before. It was something Rusty Yates couldn't get off his mind.

He dwelled on it—she remembered things and realized the extent of what she'd done, but dealing with those memories and not being able to make sense of what she was thinking at the time was frustrating. She could remember some of her thoughts, but she couldn't figure out why she had thought them.

"Her soul is tormented," he said. "Nobody is suffering like Andrea is suffering now." She was so honest that she

always returned the change when given too much, unlike
Rusty, who gave it back only when he thought someone
might get fired. She was loving, caring, gentle, kind, smart,
respectful, a model person, he said. "She doesn't deserve
what she's getting."

CHAPTER 32

On a warm December 3, 2001, Rusty Yates walked into the Harris County Courthouse, his attorney Edward Mallett by his side and photographers trailing them both. Yates, in a short-sleeved plaid shirt, jeans, and his silent black shoes, carried a folder full of notes and a book for reading. He would be forced to sit on a bench outside Judge Belinda Hill's courtroom as pre-trial motions were heard.

Inside a tiny courtroom with only three rows of seats, his wife wore a white sweater over her orange jail-issued jump-suit. Judge Hill quickly granted most of the defense's motions. However, testimony had to be heard on the defense challenges to the gag order, the death penalty, jury selection process, insanity defense, and the admissibility of Andrea Yates' statement to the police.

David Knapp, the first officer to arrive at 942 Beach-comber on June 20, 2001, stated that when Andrea Yates opened the door at 9:55 AM and said, "I killed my kids," he replied, "What?" And she repeated, "I killed my kids." He was then led to the bedroom where he found four of the children, their heads on pillows, and their bodies covered as though they'd been tucked in for the night.

He testified that Yates was calm and emotionless that day and maintained eye contact with him, much like, he said, she is right now.

Andrea Yates sat in the courtroom quietly swallowing back tears.

Officer Frank Stumpo stepped into the witness box. "I observed a small little head through the shadow and thought it was a doll," he stated, of a child on the bed. "I looked down on it and realized it was a human being." He found the fifth youngster, he said, facedown, in a bathtub half-full of water, while Knapp sat with Yates.

As he testified, Yates lowered her head and wrung her hands, her lips quivering.

"She was stoic and extremely calm," Stumpo continued. Later, he looked for a set of keys to open a locked back door, and Yates told him where they were. "It was unsolicited response to a nonquestion," he stated.

Homicide detective Eric Mehl took the stand and said that when he looked at the dead children, six-month-old Mary was resting on the shoulder of her five-year-old brother John. He said he asked Yates if she'd drowned her children because they were bad. She answered no. He said he asked her how long she'd been thinking about hurting them. " 'Probably since I realized I wasn't a good mother to them,' " he quoted her.

He then asked her why she didn't think she was a good mother, and she replied it was because the children weren't developing correctly. Yates' demeanor never changed in the 17 minutes he spoke to her, he said; she was "very focused and attentive." And she told him she wanted to be punished.

"She mentioned that she was prepared to go to Hell for what she had done?" George Parnham asked.

Yes, Mehl answered.

"The fact that she wanted to be punished and the way to achieve that was by drowning the children—did that strike you as a bizarre statement?" Parnham said.

"No," the detective responded. "A lot of people die for a lot of reasons, some less than that."

Kennedy family attorney John O'Sullivan testified for the defense that he tried to talk to Yates before the police interviewed her, but he was not allowed the visit.

Dr. Mohammad Saeed was sworn in and questioned

about his last appointment with Yates, two days before the murders. "I did not see any evidence of psychosis," he stated. He was not forthcoming in his testimony.

The day ended with arguments from Rusty Yates' attorney, Edward Mallett, trying to convince Judge Hill to release his client from the gag order. Mallett noted that the D.A. sought the death penalty to give the jury a full range of punishment. But his motion asserted, "There is no 'full range' less than life; only death is added when the District Attorney 'seeks the death penalty.' "

He explained that in Texas life meant 40 years before there was any chance of parole. In 40 years, the motion said, "Andrea Yates will be seventy-seven years old, if she is still alive."

Mallett also claimed that Rusty Yates was issued a witness subpoena only "to keep him from speaking and from attending his wife's court proceedings," when the State had no intention of calling him.

Whispers floated through the courtroom that the NASA engineer's *60 Minutes* interview was scheduled to air six days later, and if Mallett wasn't successful in his argument, Yates might be held in contempt.

Prosecutor Kaylynn Williford denounced the motion as an attempt to violate the gag order—its very contents violated it, she declared. She pleaded with the judge to seal the motion and prevent its publication, as reporters already had copies.

Judge Hill refused to bar the motion's contents from publication, apparently trying to ease media criticism—reporters had to go through her to even see the Yates file, which was public. But, appeasing the prosecution, Hill denied Mallett's motion in full and ordered it sealed. Rusty Yates was still under the gag order.

At 9:10 A.M. on Tuesday, December 4, another unusually hot winter day in Houston, Rusty Yates stepped into the witness box. He wanted to help his wife.

Around June 4, he said, she was tapered off her antipsychotic Haldol, which took three days. By June 18, when they last saw Saeed, she was "really sick." And on June 20, he said, she was psychotic.

"She would stand still, hold the baby and stare blankly ahead," he stated. "She would speak only when spoken to and when she did speak it was in one- or two-word answers."

The night before his children's drownings, he testified, they stood outside and shot baskets. Andrea shot 10 or 12 times from the same spot, then turned and walked away.

Three days prior, he said, he told Andrea that she needed to begin "weaning" herself from her dependency on Dora Yates.

And he claimed that he wasn't allowed to help his wife before she confessed to police.

"Never out there did you yell through that door, 'Andrea, do you want a lawyer?'" prosecutor Joe Owmby hotly crossed.

All Yates could do was yell to his wife, "How could you do this?"

Andrea Yates blinked back tears.

Spectators rumbled that Owmby did not seem to understand that at the time, every single one of Rusty Yates' children had just died.

The prosecutor asked Rusty Yates what Andrea Yates was doing on June 20 that made him think she wasn't functioning normally.

She was nervous and didn't put down Mary, he answered, carrying the infant on her hip. "She ate some Sugar Corn Pops out of a box, which was really uncharacteristic for her."

Owmby asked Yates about some notes.

Rusty Yates said he didn't have them with him.

Owmby demanded the notes, carped about the notes, yelled about the notes.

Some spectators thought the prosecutor was acting like a

petulant child. Others feared he might be having a meltdown in front of the judge, the defense, and the press.

He screamed again for Rusty Yates' notes, and Edward Mallett went to get them. Owmby snapped them out of his hand and argued that the State wanted a copy.

Wendell Odom disputed that they were protected by attorney–client confidentiality.

Owmby yelled for the Court to secure the notes before Rusty Yates destroyed them.

The defense once again cited attorney–client privilege.

Judge Hill didn't buy it.

Rusty Yates was riled. But at the demand of Owmby, he read from his police statement. "I can't look at her. She took our babies away."

Judge Hill denied the motion to suppress Andrea Yates' confession. She also denied the defense challenges to the death penalty, jury selection process, and insanity defense.

Andrea Yates would be judged by a jury that wouldn't know she could *not* walk free even if she were found not guilty by reason of insanity. She would be judged by a "death qualified" jury in Houston, Texas—the death penalty capital of the nation.

Epilogue

"The whole world is watching! Moratorium now! The whole world is watching! Moratorium now!" two hundred marchers against the death penalty yelled on Saturday, October 27, 2001, in Austin, Texas, the day the sky was crystal azure. "The whole world is watching! Moratorium now!" Rhythmic, pounding drums beat their way through the autumn air and filled the ears of the state troopers guarding the capitol building steps from the marchers.

"Moratorium now!" It was the second annual march for a moratorium against the death penalty in Texas, sponsored in part by the Texas Moratorium Network, the ACLU, Amnesty International, and the Andrea Pia Yates Support Coalition. The protestors had gathered at the state capitol that George W. Bush had once run, and across the street from his former home—the governor's mansion.

But there was no mention of Andrea Yates' belief that Governor Bush, although he was President Bush at the time she heard the voices, was going to put her to death. In fact, there was no mention at all of the woman sitting in an orange jumpsuit in a county jail, three hours away.

Jeanette Pop, an attractive, conservative, middle-class blonde, stepped up to the microphone. Her daughter, Nancy DePriest, had been murdered in an Austin Pizza Hut. An Austin jury had convicted the wrong men for the crime. They served time as the true killer confessed, and his confession was ignored. That crime—convicting the wrong men—turned Pop into a moratorium supporter.

"The whole world is watching! Moratorium now!"

And no one noticed as Rusty Yates eased into the crowd, wearing his blue jeans, plaid shirt, and black shoes.

"How can we make more victims than the victims we already have?" Pop asked the crowd.

"Exactly," Rusty Yates said softly.

"That closure never comes."

"Exactly," he echoed.

"Although I cannot forgive [the killer's] act, I can forgive the person."

Rusty Yates applauded. Just a week earlier, he had said he wasn't really, completely against the death penalty. But on October 27, he turned and said, "The death penalty should be unconstitutional." It was, he explained, "cruel and unusual punishment."

He spoke of his aunt's email to Harris County District Attorney Chuck Rosenthal and Rosenthal's Biblical response. Rusty Yates had forwarded the Rosenthal email to George Parnham, who wrote back, "So much for separation of church and state."

A man slipped up to Yates and asked, "Are you Rusty?"

Yates responded affirmatively.

The man asked him if he'd like to say a few words to the crowd.

Yates declined.

Another man handed Yates a flier promoting an "Act Now to Stop War and End Racism!" rally in Houston. The black-and-white flyer read, "Stop the U.S. War Against Afghanistan! We condemn the horrific attack of September 11, and we grieve for the victims and their families. But the war against Afghanistan and possible attacks on other peoples in the region are not the answer. The hatred which led to the recent tragedy is rooted in U.S. exploitation and war policies. More of the same will not end terrorism."

Yates read.

"We must end the genocidal sanctions against the Iraqi

people and support an independent Palestinian state. We must end U.S. support for Israel and the oppressive Arab kingdoms," the flier said.

Yates looked up from his reading, waved the flier in his hand, and said, "This could only be written by someone who's suffered loss." Loss, he explained, made one more compassionate. Since June 20, he said, he'd become more compassionate and he'd learned the importance of freedom.

He walked over to a table and signed up for the moratorium's newsletter, then followed the crowd over to the Governor's Mansion, talking as he had a week earlier about Nebuchadnezzar, how his story is found in the book of Daniel, and laughing about how hard it is to spell Nebuchadnezzar. He spoke of Job and all of his trials and how Job never questioned God.

Then Yates stepped in line with the protestors and marched with them twice around the mansion, yellow crime-scene tape marking their path. When someone mentioned how wonderful it'd be to die and go to heaven, Yates quickly disagreed. Life on earth, he said, was pretty good. "Look at this day."

The sky was that crystal azure.

A young blond woman drummed in front of him, her bottom twitching with the rhythm, and Yates returned to the importance of freedom, the freedom, he said, to live one's life the way one wants as long as it's not hurting anyone else. He pointed to the Saudi Arabians. The way they lived has worked for them for thousands of years, he said, so what right do we have to tell them how to live?

And he walked around the young woman whose hips twitched like those of a belly dancer draped behind her veil.